S0-GYE-632

Cuban Festivals

#44461854

Cuban Festivals

A Century of Afro-Cuban Culture

Edited by

Judith Bettelheim

mc 10/15/01

GT
4825
A2
C83
2001

Ian Randle Publishers, Kingston

Markus Wiener Publishers, Princeton

OHIO UNIVERSITY
LIBRARY
WITHDRAWN

Copyright © Judith Bettelheim 2001

This edition first published 2001 in Jamaica by
Ian Randle Publishers Ltd.
11 Cunningham Avenue
Kingston 6

ISBN 976-637-001-X paperback

A catalogue record for this book is available from the
National Library of Jamaica.

All rights reserved. No part of this publication may be reproduced, stored in a retrieval system, or transmitted in any form, or by any means electronic, photocopying, recording or otherwise without the prior permission of the author and publisher.

Published in the United States of America 2001 by
Markus Wiener Publishers Inc.
231 Nassau Street, Princeton, NJ 08542

Library of Congress Cataloging-in-Publication Data

Cuban festivals/ Judith Bettelheim, editor; with contributions by Fernando Ortiz . . . [et al.]; translations by Jean Stubbs.—
New or rev., updated/expanded.
p. cm.
Includes bibliographical references and index.
ISBN 1-55876-244-2 (pbk.: alk paper)
1. Festivals—Cuba. 2. Cuba—Social life and customs.
I. Bettelheim, Judith, 1944- II. Ortiz, Fernando, 1881-1969.

GT4825.A2 C83 2000
394.2697291—dc21 00-043443

Book and cover design by
Prodesign Ltd, Red Gal Ring, Jamaica, W.I.

Printed in the United States of America
on acid free paper

Cover: The Duchess of the Court, Joaquima Caballero, performing with the Cabildo Carabalí Isuama during Carnival 1989, Santiago de Cuba. © J.B.

Contents

Illustrations

Editor's Preface

Ever since I began my doctoral work at Yale University I have pursued the study of festival arts. In preparation for the anthology and exhibition *Caribbean Festival Arts* (1988), I visited Cuba in 1985 and obtained official permission from the Agencia Literaria Latinoamericana in Havana to translate and publish Fernando Ortiz's *La Fiesta Afrocubana del Día de Reyes*.

In 1985 I also attended the annual meeting of the Association of Caribbean Historians held in Havana, where I met Dr. Jean Stubbs. In 1986 I attended the Festival of Caribbean Culture, sponsored by the Casa del Caribe in Santiago de Cuba and met the researchers Rafael Brea and José Millet. During a subsequent trip to Santiago we discussed their ongoing research on popular festivals, and I asked permission to translate and publish their manuscript. Thus an anthology took shape. I conferred with the scholar David H. Brown, who is acutely aware of the importance of a culturally specific understanding of Afro-Cuban vocabulary. Brown agreed to establish a glossary to accompany this first English language translation of Ortiz's text. The glossary is a *tour de force* of scholarship, simultaneously explicating and expanding/updating the original Ortiz. I chose Santiago de Cuba as a base for my research, considering the historical breadth and aesthetic force of its festival traditions. On my many trips to Cuba I would meet with Jean Stubbs and Pedro Sarduy. I so enjoyed Sarduy's incisive commentary on his own culture, his particular perspective as a Black Cuban, and his unique sense of humor. He was actually delighted at the idea of writing a personal account of Carnival, as it had been a force in his own life. This anthology is now balanced, beginning with an intellectual account from the 1920s and ending with a personal perspective from the 1990s.

So much transpired in Cuba during the decade of the 1990s that an update on cultural circumstances is absolutely necessary. 1990 marked the beginning of the 'special period.' (This is the official name used to designate the austerity measures that have resulted from Cuba's recent economic crisis.) Between 1991 and 1993 the effect of the withdrawal of Soviet funds was felt in all aspects of Cuban life. In 1993 the United States dollar was legalized. The reverberations in all aspects of Cuban society have been intense.

In addition, publications on Cuban history and culture have exploded during this same period. The Biennial of Havana has been held since 1984; the Third was held in 1989 and the Seventh Biennial in November-December 2000. Art exhibitions of Cuban artists of the generation of the 1990s are common on the international circuit: from Arizona State University's *Contemporary Art from Cuba: Irony and Survival on the Utopian Island,' to 'Utopian Territories: New Art from Cuba,* the Morris and Helen Belkin Art Gallery at the University of British Columbia, to *While Cuba Waits: Art from the Nineties,* Track 16 Gallery, Santa Monica. Important European exhibitions include 'Kuuban Nouri Taide/Young Cuban Art,' Pori, Finland, and 'Contemporary Art from Havana,' Riverside Studios, London. Cuban musicians also play internationally to sold-out audiences, and the phenomenon of the Buena Vista Social Club, whose CD sold millions of copies in North America alone, continues. In academic circles more books about Cuban history, and specifically Afro-Cuban history, are being published. There will be a conference celebrating the work of Fernando Ortiz in New York in Spring 2000 and another honoring the work of both Ortiz and Lydia Cabrera at Florida International University in fall 2000, and the story continues.

I am delighted that the contributors to this volume also have continued their publications on Cuba. *Afro-Cuban Voices* by Pérez Sarduy and Stubbs was published in 2000 and David Brown's *Thrones of the Orichas* appeared in 1993. Raphael Brea and José Millet's book-length study of Carnaval appeared in Cuba in 1997, and Millet has continued his research on Vodú and Espiritismo in eastern Cuba. My own work continued throughout the 1990s. If the academic work of the 1990s is any measure, Cuban studies is extraordinarily strong and increased communication and exchange will continue in 2000 and beyond (despite the USA blockade!).

Judith Bettelheim
Oakland, California
Spring 2000

Translator's Preface

Fernando Ortiz (1881-1969), one of Cuba's most erudite and prolific scholars, is little known in the English-speaking world, beyond *Cuban Counterpoint: Tobacco and Sugar* (Doubleday, New York, 1947). And yet, his pathfinding work in seeking to explore facets of the Cuban national culture and identity made him for 60 years a major intellectual influence in Cuban thinking, and a scholar of international repute. He started out as a lawyer, and ran for political office on the Liberal platform. In the 1920s, he joined the Minority Group of progressive intellectuals against the Machado dictatorship, revitalised the Society of Friends of the Country, and founded the Hispanic-Cuban Cultural Institution and the Afro-Cuban Studies Association. In the 1940s, he organised the Cuban Alliance for a Free World and chaired the Cuban-Soviet Cultural Institute. He was editor of the *Revista Bimestre Cubana, Archivos del Folklore Cubano*, and *Estudios Afrocubanos*, and he published his own books and those of other Cuban writers. When he died at the age of 88, he was preparing new editions of his work. Ortiz lived the better part of his childhood and adolescence in Spain and studied law at the Universities of Havana, Barcelona, and Madrid. He was profoundly influenced by the anthropological positivism in the legalistic approach of Italian Cesare Lombroso. It was the linking of criminality with atavistic retentions of primitive man that led him to become self-taught in anthropology, ethnology, sociology, history, archaeology, philology, and musicology. Ortiz is most attributed with lifting the veil on 'the other side 'of Cuba's history: that of the Cuban population of African origin. His research into what he early called the Afro-Cuban underworld stemmed directly from his work as a lawyer in the Cuban prison system, and his criminalistic approach of the time was not devoid of the biotypic determinism common to contemporary European criminalistic work. Ironically, he discovered Abakuá, the secret *ñáñigo* society brought to Cuba by Africans, in a Madrid museum: drums, costumes and attributes of the *íreme*, or *diablito*, on display by courtesy of the Spanish colonial authorities.

Afro-Cuban culture was subsequently to become a major part of his life's work. The early *Hampa Afrocubana: Los Negros Brujos* (Afro-Cuban Underworld: The Black Obeah, Havana, 1906) was a first attempt to study the various nations of origin of the black people in Cuba. Its sequel *Hampa Afrocubana: Los Negros Esclavos* (Afro-Cuban Underworld: The Black Slaves, Havana, 1916) was one of the most complete studies on slavery and its negative consequences for Cuban society. From the twenties on, his views changed. Painstaking and thorough in his knowledge, positivist in his outlook and methodology, he developed an encompassing humanist view of humankind and pioneered modern sociology and anthropology in Latin America.

Ortiz was compelled to create his own terms to explain the phenomena he was studying, to denote new concepts and new scales of values that revitalized social anthropology and the cultural processes characteristic of emergent continents. In this vein, 'Afro-Cuban 'and 'transculturation' symbolize the symbiosis of cultures. He rejected 'acculturation' as a one-way process whereby a newcomer culture adapts to that already existing, in favor of a two-way process of transculturation whereby each culture becomes influenced by the other, thereby creating a dynamic new culture.

This view led Ortiz to affirm that the innumerable forms of miscegenation ruled out any static notion of a pure race, and he postulated a similar miscegenation of ideas in the intermingling of world cultures. He was the first in Cuba to attempt to explain from a historical and sociological point of view the religious practices of the Africans and their Cuban descendants and its close relationship with the religious practices brought by the white Europeans.

The Afro-Cuban Festival 'Day of the Kings' is a reflection of this. It was a classic in its time, and remains so today. There have been several versions of this piece published over the years, and this translation is from the most recent (1960) edition. However, it differs little from the earlier versions. Some lengthy passages of references to other countries have been omitted, and the opening two paragraphs were slightly changed, as were a few instances of terminology: the more offensive 'wild' became 'black 'Africa in the opening line of paragraph three.

In itself, the article was not easy to translate. Ortiz used many culturally specific words which I have left in the original, and these are annotated in David Brown's glossary. Following Ortiz's tradition, this glossary serves the double function of explaining and updating text. There is also a double noting system: the translation of Ortiz's own footnotes (1-105) and the translator's (a-f). Ortiz was somewhat erratic in his footnoting. Where source material was available for checking, references have been completed and errors corrected; otherwise, the footnotes have been left as in the 1960 version.

Part I of the article includes some highly charged contemporary accounts of the 'Day of the Kings' festival that denote social attitudes of the time. As far as possible, translation has tried to be true to their original flavor, while using modern English. Parts II and III draw on other anthropologists' work to refer to analogous festivals around the world, in Africa as well as in Europe, Asia and the rest of the Americas. Original English-language quotes are reproduced verbatim. Part IV attempts to bring together disparate elements to establish the sociohistorical significance of what was in its time *the* carnival of blacks in Havana.

The last recorded 'Day of the Kings' in Cuba appears to have been in 1884. In terms of music and dance forms and costume, however, elements from nineteenth century Día de Reyes celebrations, like costumed *íremes*, were to be found in carnival and festivals in towns and cities throughout the twentieth century; and they are still integral to carnival today.

It was decided in the early years after the 1959 Revolution to move carnival to July. A major reason for this was to make a festive time at the end of the sugar harvest. It thus become more akin to cropover in other Caribbean islands. It was also a time to celebrate the anniversary of the July 26, 1953, attack on the Moncada Garrison in the eastern city of Santiago de Cuba, which symbolized the start of the 1950s insurrection.

Post-1959 Cuba has seen the flourishing of folklore groups and institutions the length and breadth of the island, in what could well be described as a post-revolutionary cultural revival in the best Ortiz tradition. The best known is the National Folklore Group in Havana, whose founder and key adviser still today is Rogelio Martínez Furé, who himself studied under Ortiz. Both in the 1960s before Ortiz's death, and since in tribute to him, ethnologists and historians, creative writers and filmmakers – such as Miguel Barnet, Nancy Morejón and Tomás Gutiérrez Alea – have all built on Ortiz's life work. Others have added new dimensions to it: Ortiz himself was very steeped in western Cuba, and Casa del Caribe in eastern Santiago de Cuba is just one institution that has broadened the scope of research. The 1980s saw the posthumous publication in Havana of much of his writing.

The 1990s witnessed a veritable Ortiz revival in the United States. It began among the Cuban American academic community, with the publication of Gustavo Pérez-Firmat's *The Cuban Condition: Translation and Identity in Cuban Literature* (Cambridge University Press, Cambridge, New York, & Melbourne, 1989) and Antonio Benítez-Rojo's *The Repeating Island: The Caribbean and the Postmodern Perspective* (Duke University Press, Durham & London, 1992 [1990]). Both drew heavily on, and engaged with, the work of Fernando Ortiz, and postmodernism. Their analyses were linguistic and literary, but in historical and anthropological context. Pérez-

Firmat argued that Cuban national identity is translational not foundational. He was particularly interested in how key Cuban works emerged from exogenous models and forms, creating a vernacular literary language, a Cuban 'nation language', a Cuban voice, a *criollismo*. Ortiz, he reminded us, was heralded as Cuba's 'Third Discoverer' (after Columbus and Humboldt) by Juan Marinello, his contemporary. This was primarily for his understanding of transculturation, which was far broader than a history of African customs or of race relations in Cuba. Yet his insularity made him relatively unknown outside Cuba. Pérez-Firmat highlighted how the metaphor of the *ajiaco*, a stew of Amerindian origin, the culinary emblem of Cuba, was not so much *fusión* (a melting pot fusion) but *cocción* (an incessant simmering concoction). It is not difficult to see how powerful a current of thinking this might be for Cuba *emigrés*, exiles from their homeland, legitimising, so to speak, their *cubanidad*. In Pérez-Firmat, Ortiz transculturates into Mr. Cuba.

Benítez-Rojo borrowed from Chaos theory, whereby in nature order and disorder are not the antithesis of each other but rather mutually generative phenomena, to argue that, within the socio-cultural fluidity, the apparent disorder, of the Caribbean, there emerges an 'island' of order. This repeats itself, in the paradoxical sense it appears in the discourse of Chaos, whereby every repetition entails the unpredictable flux of transformative change, transition and return. He characterised the Caribbean above all as a region of performance, whose coherence is that of rhythm and polyrhythm, improvisation and difference, *mestizaje* – understood as both cultural and race mixing – not as a synthesis but a 'concentration of differences', 'generalised promiscuity', a 'tangle of dynamics', the 'impossibility of a stable identity'.

A gender dimension was added to the debate with the publication of Vera Kutzinski's *Sugar's Secrets: Race and the Erotics of Cuban Nationalism* (University Press of Virginia, Charlottesville and London, 1993). Kutzinski, describing herself as a white African-Americanist who is also a European, found compelling the notion of crossing socio-cultural boundaries of difference and otherness, which makes identity an open question, always compromised, to be negotiated and renegotiated on an almost daily basis. She applied cultural and feminist theories in attempting to understand the interplay of race, gender, sexuality and class in *mestizaje* and the cross-cultural imagination that came to be seen as the defining element of Cuba's national identity. If *cubanía* or *cubanidad* is, to all intents and purposes, synonymous with *mestizaje*, this was encoded in the iconic, and licentious, form of the *mulata*. Her concern was to explore the historical settings of stereotypical representations of the erotics of race and nationalism, ranging from 'ethnic lynching' to the 'promised utopia'.

That same year saw Pedro Pérez Sarduy and Jean Stubbs' (eds.) *Afrocuba: An Anthology of Cuban Writing on Race, Politics and Culture* (Ocean Press/ Latin America Bureau, Melbourne, New York, London, 1993). The introduction took its title 'The Rite of Social Communion' from Ortiz' introspective 1942 address 'For a Cuban Integration of Whites and Blacks', which was included as the opening text of the anthology. Several of the contributors, ethnographer, singer and composer Rogelio Martínez Furé, ethnographer and writer Miguel Barnet and writer and literary critic Nancy Morejón in particular, were nurtured on Ortiz' ideas. The extract from Martínez Furé's *Diálogos Imaginarios* (Editorial Arte y Literatura, Havana, 1979) is his own imaginary dialogue with folklore and begins, as does the book from which it is taken: 'To my maestro Don Fernando, Science, Concience, Patience' – Ortiz' own motto. The extract from Nancy Morejón's *Nación y Mestizaje en Nicolás Guillén* (UNEAC, Havana, 1982) engages directly with the Ortiz concept of transculturation applying it to the work of Guillén, as would Pérez-Firmat and Benítez-Rojo almost a decade later. Little translated, the work of Martínez Furé and Morejón suffers from the same insularity as has that of Ortiz.

The stage was set for a new English-language edition of Fernando Ortiz' *Cuban Counterpoint: Tobacco and Sugar* (Duke University Press, Durham & London, 1995 [1940]), his only major work translated into English, aside from John Turpin III and B.E. Martínez's *The Batá in Cuba: Selected Writings of Fernando Ortiz* (Institute for the Study of Ancient African Traditions, Oakland, Ca., 1980). *Contrapunteo*, as it is most often referred to, was the work in which Ortiz developed his major concept of transculturation. The preface by Fernando Coronil, a US-based Venezuelan anthropologist who has lived and worked in Cuba, took the debate to a new plane, heralding Ortiz as a thinker ahead of his times, in tune with the fluidity of the contemporary world, fashioning binary opposites as metaphors, or tropes, for events, ideas and interpretations that were far from static, but rather in constant flux. Coronil applied the postmodernist maxim that each reading of the book opens up a different book, a perspective Ortiz would have welcomed, 'recognizing the contrapuntal play of text against text and of reader against author.' The Coronil text paid tribute to Ortiz 'by engaging in this transcultural exchange, as Ortiz's book does, in counterpoint with the historical conditions of its own making.' Coronil argues that the Ortizian text has particular relevance in a contemporary world where divides between capitalist and socialist, center and periphery, no longer have the same meaning, nor are those worlds seen as inexorably moving in linear fashion to achieve modernity.

That same year, the Fundación Fernando Ortiz was set up in Havana, headed by Miguel Barnet. The following year saw the publication in Cuba of

Araceli García-Carranza, Norma Suárez Suárez, and Alberto Quesada Morales, eds. *Cronología Fernando Ortiz* (Fundación Fernando Ortiz, Havana, 1996). This was subsequently translated and included in the trilingual (English, French and Spanish) *Miscelanea II of studies dedicated to/de estudios dedicados a/des études dédiées a Fernando Ortiz, 1991-1969* (INTERAMERICAS Society of Arts and Letters of the Americas/Sociedad de Artes y Letras de las Américas, New York, 1998). Among its important contributions is a reprint of three tributes to Ortiz by Concha Romero James (1943), Jean Price-Mars (1956) and Andrés Iduarte (1956). Most moving of all, perhaps, is the tribute by Price-Mars, who proposed Ortiz for the 1951 Nobel Peace Prize: 'Few men have given over such a long period of their life to serve an ideal of human solidarity and fraternity as has Fernando Ortiz. Few writers have dedicated such a major part of their existence to develop, defend and illustrate a body of ideas as has Fernando Ortiz. Few citizens like Fernando Ortiz have had the courage and the will to brave prejudice, antipathy and the rigidity of social conformism to rise against the injustice dealt an important segment of their community.'

In her introduction to the volume, INTERAMERICAS Director Jane Gregory Rubin narrates the process of embarking on the joint venture with the Fundación Fernando Ortiz to make more known Ortiz' voluminous published work, unpublished manuscripts, and documents. Fundación President Miguel Barnet, in his foreword titled '*La Casa-Templo*', which was his 1996 speech at the inauguration of Ortiz' former home Villa Isis as home to the Foundation, describes it as a 'temple alive with men and women who will know how to honor it 'a laboratory for the meeting and creation of ideas [where] a formula for *cubanidad* was developed, not by magic but rather in the wake of a profound scrutiny of cultural roots and a clearing in the dense tangle of the Cuban ideological forest'. (*Miscelanea*, p.8) Both Rubin and Barnet end with what are now the watchwords of the Foundation: *Ciencia, Conciencia, Paciencia.*

The original Spanish-language edition of Benítez-Rojo's work was dedicated 'To Fernando Ortiz, the distant master, on the half-century of his *Contrapunteo*'. The year 2000 marks the 60th anniversary of the first publication of *Contrapunteo* in Spanish, to be celebrated at a Symposium in New York in March, bringing together scholars residing on and off the island, and again at a conference in Miami in October. Whatever else transpires, they are bound to be true to his memory, in that the very fluidity of *cubanidad* will be much in evidence. One interesting dimension of the revival is the extent to which Ortiz is interpreted as giving primacy to harmony over conflict (or vice-versa), especially that of the races, a highly charged notion in Cuba's crisis 1990s. This is much in evidence in the sequel volume Pedro Pérez

Sarduy and Jean Stubbs' (eds.) *Afro-Cuban Voices: On Race and Identity in Contemporary Cuba* (University Press of Florida, Gainesville, 2000), which includes interviews with both Martinez Furé and Morejón, among others. The message is a sobering one, wherein what emerges uppermost is a less harmonious, more conflictual and contended terrain of racial paradigms facing Cuba (and the world) as we enter the new millenium.

And yet, while interpretations of his work vary widely, both on and off the island, Ortiz' utopian vision remains as a beacon to many, as does his understanding of transculturation. This renders all the more timely a reprint of his early classic: "*The Afro-Cuban Festival 'Day of the Kings'*."

Jean Stubbs
London 2000

The Afro-Cuban Festival 'Day of the Kings'

Fernando Ortiz

Annotated and Translated by
Jean Stubbs*

I

Up until the law of abolition of slavery, that is, until 1880,[a] there was one day, January 6 of each year, when both the free and the slave Afro-Cuban negroes[b] celebrated their festival; in the Catholic Church it was Epiphany, the Adoration of the Three Magi, commonly called Día de Reyes, 'Day of the Kings.'

The 'Day of the Kings' was a free day for the Africans in Cuba, and the creole negroes were equally enthusiastic in joining the clamor of celebrations. It was undoubtedly one of the most picturesque scenes of colonial life to be captured by the artist's brush and the writer's pen in those times. It is not difficult, therefore, for us to identify external attributes, turning to contemporary accounts for the flavor of the period.

That day, black Africa, its people, its costumes, its music, its tongues, its song and dance, its ceremonies, its religions and political institutions, were brought across the Atlantic to Cuba, especially Havana. The tyranny and might of slavery that coldly separated parents and children, husbands and wives, brothers and sisters, compatriots, was for one day mitigated as the negroes came together in the streets, with their own, with those of their tribe, their caravels, proud in the ceremonial attire of their land, venting their rousing monotonous African chant, charging the air with the noise of their drums and their bells and other primitive instruments, enjoying above all an illusion of freedom, in an orgy of ritual, dance, music, song and cane spirit.

Figure 1. Día de Reyes as celebrated in the Plaza de San Francisco, Havana, 1830s. Painted by Pierre Toussaint Frédéric Mialhe, b. 1810 in France and a Professor at the Academy of Painting, Havana, 1831–1834 and 1857–1861. Published in the *Album Pintoresco de la Isla de Cuba*. Berlin: Sturch and Kramer, 1838.

Meticulous engravings of the festival have been handed down to us from artists of the time. (Figure 1)[1] Landaluze, the Andalucian-born Cuban *costumbrista*, made various attempts on the same theme in his painting. Figure 2 is a reproduction of one of his paintings, and others can be found in Fernando Ortiz, *El Baile y el Teatro de los Negros en el Folklore de Cuba* (Havana, 1952).[c]

Cuban scholar Ramón Meza has left us this full description of the 'Day of the Kings.'[2]

> From daybreak, all over can be heard the monotonous beat of those big drums made out of hollowed tree trunk and covered on one end by a patch of ox-hide tempered by fire. The house servants would leave very early in the morning. The plantation slaves would come in from the nearby estates: some jammed into rear railroad wagons, others crammed onto carts that carried the enormous barrels of sugar, and not a few came on foot. All were hurrying to join their respective *cabildos*[3] whose chief was generally the elder of the tribe or *nation* to which they belonged.
>
> All around, circles would be formed. The enormous drums would be placed to one side as the battery; astraddle, the drummers, tire-

Figure 2. The celebration of Día de Reyes as depicted by Victor Patricio Landaluze, probably in the late 1870s. Oil on cloth, 51 x 61 cm. Landaluze arrived from Spain in 1862 and published this painting in *Tipos y costumbres de la Isla de Cuba*, Havana: Miguel de Villa, 1881. Courtesy Museo Nacional de Bellas Artes, Havana.

lessly beating the taut ox-hide with their callused hands, to which were attached hollow metal or wooden spheres, filled with small stones and decorated with feathers, shaking their shoulders, grinding their teeth, their eyes half-closed, as if possessed with ineffable fulfilment. Two or three couples would dance in the middle, going into the most extravagant contortions, jumping and whirling, their steps in tune to the wild drum beat. The joy and agitation bordered on frenzy. The captain, that poor broken-down bundle of flesh, bone and nerves, surely relived the days of his youth; for he not only shouted till he was hoarse but often delighted in joining the group of dancers. The one bearing the banderole would blaze it over the group. The profusion of peacock feathers on the heads of dancers, quivering from their agile movements, shone with metallic iridescence in the glaring sunlight that bore heavily down on that motley crew. The tiny mirrors on the hats, the sequins and the lamé of the costumes, the large earrings of polished gold dangling from ebony ears, the collection boxes passed around for the *aguinaldo*, the cutlasses, they all glinted, as dazzling to the sight as the noise was deafening to the ear. Looks sparkled on those faces of pure African[d] race; red mouths and pointed white teeth opened to let out wild shouts and laughs. Bells, drums, horns, *rayos*, triangles and huge gourd rattles accompanied the voices to a deafening pitch.

At midday, the merriment was at its height. On Mercaderes, Obispo and O'Reilly Streets, there was a continuous procession of *diablitos*, all making their way to the Plaza de Armas. The place was soon crowded and it was hardly possible to pass by Government Palace. Onlookers packed the balconies and the sidewalks and climbed the bases of columns, windows and stone balconies surrounding the square. The rows of laurel trees with their spreading dark-green foliage, the variegated and flowering shrubs of the square, the slender palms cutting an elegant panache silhouette against the purest blue sky, the sailors of all nations coming down in groups to watch half-bewildered such an exotic sight, the soldiers guarding the nearby buildings, the many flags flying in the wind and the thousand and one colors adorning the negroes' attire, in all truth, painted a picturesque spectacle. In turn, *cabildos* would come into the Palace courtyard. There the vaults resounded for many hours with the thunderous drumbeat, wild chant and enthusiastic cheers of the Africans. And while below the dancers demonstrated the best of their skills, the captain of each *cabildo*, pointed hat tucked under his arm, sack across his chest; the standard-bearer, his standard resting against his shoulder; and the teller with his tin box all went up the Palace stairs in the most orderly fashion and, vociferously professing their loyalty, received at least half an ounce in gold for the collection. That day the Palace was demonstrably generous. From the windows rained cigars and coin pieces of varying value, onto which hundreds of hands avidly hurled themselves in dispute. The old negro women, the most expressive or the most nervous, were the ones who most shook on high their hollow gourd rattles covered in netting, delirious almost in asking God to watch over and preserve for many years the health of His Excellency the Governor General.

Then they would leave the Palace to make room for the others to file in, in perfect order: the *Congo* and *Lucumí*, with their great feathered hats, blue-striped shirts and red percale pants; the *Arará*, with their cheeks lacerated from cuts and branding iron, covered in shells, crocodile and dog teeth, threaded bone and glass beads, the dancers from the waist down in a voluminous vegetable-fiber hooped skirt; the *Mandingo*, very fancy in their wide pants, short jackets and blue or pink silk turbans, embroidered with marabou; and the many others with the difficult names and whimsical costumes that were not entirely in the style of those of Africa but changed and modified by civilized industry.

But not all the negroes joined the *cabildos*, which the creoles and certain of those belonging to the nation thought the less of. Rather than attire themselves in the outlandish dress that made up the costumes of their countrymen, they would dress as Paris dandies. Elegance consisted in the exaggeration of fashion, which is why the weaker sex showed a preference for ribbons, baubles, tassles, large earrings, fancy shawls, a profusion of rings, bracelets, and contrasting bright colors. In the stronger sex this preference found marked form in wide collars, frilled shirtfronts, large cravats and a choice of the most brightly colored jacket and pantaloons. Others would be dressed as sailors, carrying a small, constantly moving boat on a piece of crumpled canvas, painted green and white, representing the sea spray and waves, asking for their *aguinaldo* at more or less acceptable intervals. Others were on their own, dressed as minstrels, getting their money through clowning. A good many carried glass-cased Virgins of Regla or Brown Virgins of El Cobre, [e] replete with ribbons and offerings, using them to personally profit on the candid devotion of others.

In the more distant parts of the city and on the less crowded streets, *ñáñigos* did as they pleased, their rough cloaks somewhat reminiscent of the gown of Holy Office, but so big and bulky that arms and legs were like simple side appendages. All the gross and barbaric imagination of the African tribes was carried to an extreme with the *ñáñingo*. The institutions, the symbols and dress were all highly repugnant. It was a sight to see the wild mass following from among the lowest class of people, regardless of age, sex and race, for that ridiculous feathered symbolic figurehead to each of those fierce groupings gorged on cane spirit and cock's blood, who, according to public hearsay, could swear a mortal wound on any human breast. The other tribes drew attention for their picturesque, exotic song, costume and dance: everything about the *ñáñigos* was wild, somber, and nauseous. Replete with daggers and knives, they marched slowly, not in formation but grouped behind the dancers, who were incessant in their offensive convulsions, shaking the many bells tied around their waists. And when two, on the whole enemy groupings of this nature met, for they would always be declaring war on one another, the war would be on and in the fighting there would ensue ferociously cruel wounds and killings.

At 2:00 in the afternoon, the police, represented by the legendary *celador* and *salvaguardia*, had their hands full throwing the great mob out beyond the old walled part of the city.

Other pens have written on the 'Day of the Kings'[4] in Cuba, but always in a descriptive vein. I shall include some of the expressive paragraphs here:

> On the Day of the Kings, all individuals of color, the name we give to all those who are non-white, are empowered to ask for an *aguinaldo*, either on their own, in groups of four or six, or in bigger bands called tangos, with their *tamboriles*, horns and diabolical shouts that have undoubtedly given rise to those who use them to their particular end being called *diablitos*.
>
> The *pardo* and *moreno* slaves, and some free coloreds, of greater prosopopoeia, dock or gang overseers or hired laborers, dress in long coat and fur top hat, breast pin, gold cuff links, watch and even walking cane and cotton gloves, carrying a ballad sheet which would have cost them one or two *pesetas*, greeting the gentlemen in their path, both known and unknown, as they pass by, and the ladies, who generally confine themselves to escape impertinence, only to be seen in windows and on balconies to entertain themselves with the leaping, dancing and running of the masquerading figures.
>
> In small groups or parties, elegant negro and mulatto women pass through the city, four or six at the most, with rattles, maracas or bells, or simply chanting, in an exasperating monotone, a shrill tune that penetrates the innermost room. Their costumes are curious on close examination: almost all are made of satin, tulle or muslin, with silk ribbons, stockings and shoes (this year they will probably be flaunting their *malaçoes*, headdresses, quilling, petticoats and all), their best jewels, fan, kerchief, sashes, flowers and crown, some with their parasols to guard against the tiresome rays of the sun; by midday the heat and fatigue tend to undo their painstaking toilette, and some can no longer stand their shoes, seeking to kick them off.
>
> These parties with their tailored dress, and their special songs and dances, in which no member of the other sex intrudes, go down better and with more positive results, being allowed to enter into many homes to dance for some ten minutes in dining room or courtyard for a *peseta* or *real* that they then share out or spend, preferably at some candy or confectionery street vendor's cart where they get more for their money.
>
> The *tangos* or *cuadrillas* are the most fearsome, for their thundering noise, for the leaps and assaults of the *diablitos* at their head, and

Figure 2A. A '*diablito ñáñigo*' drawn by Victor Patricio Landaluze, probably in the 1870s. In Cuba today, the term *ñáñigo*, which had pejorative connotations, has been replaced by the term *íreme* , referring to the masquerades of the Afro-Cuban Abakuá brotherhood.

> because they take up the street from one side to the other, obstructing traffic and stopping passersby from walking even on the sidewalk, taking it up with their retinue, *tamboriles* and escorts. These *tangos* are generally made up of the stronger sex without much care taken over elegance of dress, for they are generally jugglers and gymnasts amusing themselves with evolutions, sprints, contortions, grotesque movements, dancing in large circles, and performing on stilts and in other such ways. Some dress as Indians with feathers, bells, and necklaces of nuts or buttons; others paint their face, arms, chest and legs, going barefoot for great agility; yet others dress up in ribbons, flowers, flat caps, short troubadour capes, pants trimmed with gold braid, patent leather and silk low-cut shoes.
>
> The retinue, in addition to the horns, *tamboriles*, scrapers, *botijas* and other rustic instruments, carry the flags and the banners, and the stewards collecting the money wear sashes over the long coat and pantaloons distinctive of their rank.
>
> It is easy to see, just by looking, the state the bodies of these individuals are in after 12 hours of continuous exercise so strenuous that many cannot continue into the afternoon. And yet they all get something out of it and enjoy themselves in their own way, even if only one day of the year.

Another writer, P. Riesgo,[5] expressed the following:

> Numerous groups of negro men and women cross this big city in all directions, to the beat of the bass drum. They are ludicrously dressed, with a profusion of ribbons, glass beads, mirrors, old feathers and multicolored strips of cloth. In the middle of each of these groups, there is one of colossal stature whose face is covered with a kerchief, or painted white and flesh-color, making it laughable and ridiculous in the extreme. This man has from his waist a burlap-covered hoop-shape, adorned with ribbons, forming a kind of skirt down to his knees, which moves violently each time he dances in front of the windows or balconies of his masters or the masters of his friends and retainers. When the dances finish, an old negro man requests the usual *aguinaldo* and the boys and girls who have enjoyed the African dance and laughed at the leaps and grimaces of their slaves, drop the requested offering into the negro's hat.
>
> In the midst of all this tumult, this letting loose, there is not for one second any disturbance of the public peace, there is not one mishap, none is forgetful of his respective duty. As the darkness of night begins to fall over the land, the large groups of negroes begin to disperse quietly, returning to their masters' homes, to rest after such

agitation, to tell their fellows of the day's events, of the happenings at their great festival celebrations.

The following paragraphs are from Pérez Zamora:[6]

Countless groups of *comparsas* of African negroes go through the streets of the capital; the crowd is huge; its aspect horrific . . . the noise of the drums, horns and whistles is everywhere deafening to the ear of the passerby; here is to be seen a mock *Lucumí* king amidst his negro phalanx, there a *Gangá* or *Carabalí*; all kings for a day, they chant in disagreeable monotone, in African language, the memories of their peoples; and hundreds of voices, some shrill, some hoarse, all wild, respond in chorus to the African[d] king, forming a diabolical concert that is difficult to describe. In addition to the groups mentioned so far, there are others no less rabble-rousing, whose individuals dance like ghosts in the night or the shadows of hell, screeching, gesticulating, moving to the noise of the drums and the whistles around a negress they have proclaimed queen. They are all the children of Africa's ardor in their frenzied January 6 celebrations in the capital of Cuba; they all commemorate the tradition of their homeland; and, as they commemorate them every year, each slave is free . . . but for a single day!

The costume of the negro kings is a lambskin complete with tail. Their faces are painted with bright colors that make them fearful-looking. Some brandish a large stick in their hands; others rise like giants on stilts, going through the streets of the city with their cohorts, and there are those who let out dreadful shouts akin to the bark of great mastiffs or the roar of lions in the forest.

All half-naked, kings and subjects, in their different groups, form the most repugnant sight possible to the eyes of civilized man. Some play the discordant instruments already mentioned above, that are damaging to the hearing, while other wretches dance feverishly, contorting their bodies in such a way as to be offensive to the sight.

The negroes in Cuba have no greater joy at any other time of the year than on the Day of the Holy Kings. They spill out in all directions like a black cloud over the city: from the morning hours, it is as if the slave servants were spirited away from the house of their masters; those who have achieved their freedom also partake of the enthusiasm and general frenzy; all, in short, snatch these moments of madness from the heavy yoke that is their fate. Because man in all countries, under all conditions of life, in all states, of all ages, needs a certain palliative to strengthen the spirit so as to bear the bitterness of existence; it is vain pretence to stifle for ever the pleasures and enjoyments of the soul, because that would be to bury alive the poor human heart.

On the 'Day of the Kings' in Havana, dear readers, your pockets must be continually open. Do you know why? To give . . . should you go to a café, should you sit down to rest on the bench of some public promenade, should you enter the home of a friend or one who is not of your acquaintance, you will be accosted by negroes, adults and children of both sexes, coming up to you, insistent and importune in asking for the popular gift: '*El aquinaldo! El aguinaldo!*' That is the term which will sound incessantly in your ear; that is the sacrosanct word you will always be hearing, whether in the seclusion of a study or in the squares and streets.

The clamor of a lively, free, expansive crowd fills the spaces like a cloud . . . joy and madness flow in torrents, fed by the wine and cane spirit and liquor. While the slaves in the city take their open-air pleasures, their great masters take flight to the country like swallows, to spend a quiet, tranquil, completely calm day away on their estates with their families, or in the company of friends.

The negroes have their *cabildos* or congregations in Havana, and all the individuals that belong to the same tribe proclaim one of their *nation* as a mother superior, giving her the name *maestra*. The *maestra* plays an important role, and all the members of each of the respective congregations give her a monthly contribution, in the form of a *medio sencillo*, a coin the value of a real, for the funds of this, a kind of society.

The *maestras* are the queens who come out triumphally on January 6, surrounded by a retinue from their respective tribes. The savage look on all those faces, the skins many use for clothing, the varied color of the parasols and the dresses of the more civilized negro women, set the tone; they are what most stand out and momentarily catch the eye of the traveler and all who spend a first 'Day of the Kings' in Havana.

The negroes are truly delirious about dancing, and so the men and women of this unfortunate race dance incessantly on the day, as they would in their native land.

The journalist A. de García wrote in the January 6, 1842, issue of the Havana *El Faro Industrial*:

. . . this is a day not only to admire the extraordinary gathering; the *tangos de diablitos* have to be seen to be believed as they parade through the city during the day, after their *aguinaldo*, highly original types mentioned to readers before, for words can hardly express the extravagance they exude.

> Readers of my spirit, who read this copy, I deceive you not: you who contemplate those multicolored sea-and salt-swept faces, those hyperbolic gestures, those costumes, more extravagant than the most exaggerated idea of the greatest extravagance, and those unparalleled instruments, listen to them, and to that unharmonic howling of voices, to the echo of which they execute their singular dances, and at the same time marvel at the ludicrous gravity with which the *cabildos* practice their ceremonies, bearing their blessed standards up front, the veneer of religious solemnity they give to these profane acts and the sumptuousness of the negro women of the *nation*, alongside the outlandish attire of their retainers and *diablitos*.

A year later the same Havana journal was to publish the following penned by Escolástico Gallardo, referring to an engraving:

> . . . and what about the foolish negro *Canga Cafú* in the right foreground? Do you not fancy you are watching him dance *o'-ñaña-'o*? His supple, half-frenzied contortions turn the heads of a huge crowd of other negroes in tatters, who mimic and sway to his movements and provide the chorus to his wild monotonous chant. And what about the monstrous Brichi, in his grotesque *diablito* trappings, in the middle of the engraving, right fist raised, hands on hips, his posture imposing, his face indescribable, looking a thin black woman up and down.

Naturally, this Afro-Cuban Epiphany festival drew the attention of travelers, like Wurdemann, Beauvallet and Marmier, who referred to it in their writing. Beauvallet gives us a description of the king of a *cabildo*, on the 1856 'Day of the Kings' in Havana:

> [One had] a genuine costume of a King of the Middle Ages, a very proper red, close velvet vest, and a magnificent gilt paper crown. This negro, who was enormously tall, and had a tolerably good-looking head, gave his hands gravely to a sort of feminine blackamoor who represented some queen or other. He walked with a deliberate majestic step, never laughed, and seemed to be reflecting deeply on the grandeur of his mission to this world.[7]

Marmier wrote in his *Lettres sur l'Amérique*, quoted in a valuable study by Luciano de Acevedo:

> There are negroes who wear a headdress of feathers or a forest of artificial flowers. There are those whose face and neck are covered by a thick mask, behind which can be seen darting bright eyes; there are others who have taken great pains to give their faces the appearance of a bird of prey or wild animal. Many are naked from the waist up,

their cheeks, shoulders and chest tattooed or painted, some with yellow, others with white stripes. Some who do not consider themselves black enough have smeared their bodies with bitumen. The women wear brightly colored costume, have a flower in their hair and a cigar in their mouth, and their faces are painted red, green or white.

A description in verse goes as follows: [8]

If today were to be the first
Day a foreigner could study
The good people of this country,

In the judgment formulated,
Of what he hath contemplated,
He'd be bound to make a mistake.
For today African people
The City of Havana all over
Run shouting with such great pleasure.

And their chanting is so savage,
So wild their laugh and their visage,
Incessant in their day's passage.

Their faces all covered in flour,
With ribbons, burlap and paper,
They are so laughably adorned;

A negro tall and corpulent
Dances looking with great content
At all those that are around him.

Negro men and negro women,
Whirling in his vicinity,
Laugh and strut in their vanity.

Very showy in their own costume,
Every kind of contortion
They perform to pounding drumbeat.

When the dancing comes to an end,
The slave population doth wend
Its way through the city shouting;
And they start up again dancing
If where their masters are living
Through these same streets they chance to pass.

Then with an infernal thunder
Come back the chanting and clamour
In the general street tumult.
In their movements they are frenzied
In sweat is bathed the whole forehead
Of these would-be evil spirits.

The *diablito* decorated
On his stilts is elevated,
A masked figurehead so grotesque.

Like a lion agitated
Wildly roaring and excited
For him any street is too small.

Then on their way they go marching
And at the foot of each railing
Their dance when allowed they repeat.

Great is their joy and merriment,
The same picture they represent
At every hour of the day.

Such descriptions give a general idea of what a Havana 'Day of the Kings' must have been like. But we must concur on their lack of careful, methodical, analytic observation: they do not distinguish, for example, between the costume, dancing, and song of one *nation* and another. The whole is a motley assortment of nebulous features. Today, naturally, distance makes its profile that much more confused.

The 'Day of the Kings' was celebrated in all the large cities of Cuba, although naturally not on such a scale as in the capital. One Anglo-Saxon writer in 1844 referred to the 'Day of the Kings' in Güines [Havana province] as follows:

> Almost unlimited liberty was given to the negroes. Each tribe, after having elected its king and queen, paraded the streets with a flag, having its name and the words Viva Isabella! [9] with the arms of Spain painted on it. Their majesties were dressed in the extreme of fashion, and were very ceremoniously waited on by the ladies and gentlemen of the court, one of the ladies holding an umbrella over the head of the queen . . .. Three of the tribes paraded at Güines, and an athletic negro in fantastic dress accompanied the procession performing a wild dance and all sorts of contortions.[10]

Three *nations* were involved in the parade in Güines which would seem to have been led by an athletic negro in fancy costume, executing a wild dance and all kinds of contortions, that is, the *diablito*.

Figure 3. According to Fernando Ortiz, this 'colored captain' of a *cabildo* marched in honor of Our Lady of Regla, whose procession occurred on September 8. The town of Regla lies across the harbor of Havana, and the Virgin guards the waters.

There were the same celebrations in Matanzas, as the reader can see from 'Memorias de Lola María,'[11] and in other cities.

The 'Day of the Kings' was not the only occasion for street festivities of the *cabildos*, although during the latter years of such festivities they were limited to that day.

During the 18th and early 19th centuries, on September 8, the *cabildos* would go to the Monserrate Hermitage, today a parish church. In an 1881 article, Rosainz wrote:

> The colored class also protected this hermitage. *Cabildos* of the *Arará*, *Lucumí* and *Congo* marched there with their flags on Our Lady of Regla Day, most of the negroes in formal dress, the captains or heads of *cabildo* with wide satin sashes and batons, some costly, made with solid wood of India, others with a silver knob. African[d] ladies dressed with finery and elegance, with large sunshades and costly parasols. Their masters would loan them their costumes. (see Figure 3)

A notable likeness to the Afro-Cuban saturnalia can be found in Texier's description of the Haitian carnival.[12]

From their associations or *cabildos*, it can be seen that the negroes tried to relive in Cuba that which was most important in their land and which it was impossible for their child psyche to forget. The Afro-Cuban *cabildos* were integrally tied up with the 'Day of the Kings,' as are the carnival *comparsas* that still go through the streets of poor areas of Havana today; but their study must be left for elsewhere.[13]

Even today, when many years have transpired since the 'Day of the Kings' was given to a negro bacchanalia, I have seen an old negro woman's face light up like a child's talking about the 'Day of the Kings,' as she even tried out a few steps of the *tango* or dance of her *nation*, moved at my having evoked the few joyous days of the past for which she had happy memories, chanting:

Queen of the *cabildo!*
Ueleléa!

II

What was the origin of the 'Day of the Kings?'

Generally speaking, the 'Day of the Kings' is one of the most widely observed, traditional folklore days of the year. Among Christians, it is devoted to the Three Wise Men or Magi who traveled to Bethlehem to worship the recently born Messiah, whom legend has it were of royal lineage, were therefore called the Three Kings, and were depicted in crowns and royal cloaks of velvet and ermine. In some countries, it is called Twelfth Day, because it marks the end of the time-honored twelve festive days after Christmas or the birth of the Lord, that is, the winter solstice, which is December 25.[14]

In Cuba, such a solemn universal date could hardly go unobserved, and yet Cuban folklorists and historians have still not related it to the traditions of other peoples to explain its origin and significance.

In an article published in *El Museo* (January 7, 1883), it is said that the festival of the Kings came about because the *cabildos* had their chosen king and queen, which would seem to me to be facile.

I have been told that the negroes celebrate King Melchior, the one of the Three Holy Kings they had adopted as their heavenly patron, given his likeness to their race. This opinion could be founded to a certain extent, bearing in mind that there are in Cuba today various negro associations with the name of that Holy King, as for example the *Congos Reales del Santo Rey Melchor*. And yet, this is no solid supposition, aside from which there is no proof of the number or names of the mythological Three Magi. The Gospel of St. Matthew, the only one to refer to the Magi, has nothing to say on this. In the so-called Christian countries, there is much confusion. In some, the black king is Melchior; in others, Balthazar or Caspar. The black king is, moreover, a historically unfounded, purely folkloric innovation. The black king only begins to appear in history in the images of the 15th century, when black Africans were reintroduced in large numbers into Christian societies as slaves, as a direct consequence of the discoveries and injustices of European Christians regarding African negroes, large numbers of whom they subjected to servitude.

The three 'races' of the Three Magi were to symbolize the white, yellow and African races of the world.

Along similar lines their ages changed: one was old, with a white beard; another was in the prime of his manhood, with a black beard; and another was young and beardless. The same happened in Cuban folklore with 'the three Johns' of the legendary canoe of sailors to whom the Brown Virgin appeared: one was old and white, another was young and Indian, and a third was black and just a lad.

Bachiller y Morales[15] confesses to having been unable to ascertain the origin of the festival in question. He supposed that the negroes simply mimicked seeing the troops ask for their *aguinaldo* with whistles, drums and bugles, on the 'Day of the Kings.' But what kind of mimicry was this whereby the authorities tolerated it so that in Havana it became a deeply rooted annual festivity? Certain deductions can be made from what Bachiller y Morales himself wrote:

> From time immemorial, the days of the Holy Kings were occasion, in the colonies of Spain in the Indies, for respects to be paid to the Spanish viceroys and chiefs for the Majesty they represented in the Indies.[16]

He himself referred to the specific day the troops asked for their *aguinaldo*, the gift customarily given to children, said to have been brought by the Kings. The same author in another article[17] wrote, 'The King's slaves, [18] who were many throughout the Americas, would come to ask their master's representative for the *aguinaldo*.' This quote would suffice to explain the origin of the festival. Over time, other slaves would go, perhaps at the request of the governors themselves who found this a way of propagating a popular festivity and winning the sympathies of the slaves in general, of whose support they could never be too sure, according to what has been said. Proof of the origin of the festival is the later prohibition on negroes who were not of the *nation*, that is, of Africa, to form *cabildos* and go to the Palace for the *aguinaldo*. But free negroes who were of the *nation* would also go the Palace with their *cabildos*, because these were their organized social representation, like their kings or captains or, expressed otherwise, from that point of view, their consuls. A better understanding of this can be ascertained from reading our study on the *cabildos*.

The slaves of other countries of the Americas also celebrated their festival the day their masters gave their customary gift. Thus, according to Bachiller y Morales, in the British colonies, the negro bacchanalia took place at Christmas time[19] and the New Year. Similarly, in Santiago, Chile,Torquemada wrote:

> In 1609, there was tumult and rumor of an uprising of negroes; it was said that on the night of the Kings many of them had gathered and elected a king . . . in all truth, it turned out to be an affair of the negroes . . . and there was nothing to it; I do not care to refer to the great folly that is said to have taken place among them that night.[20]

In the Anglophone island of St. Kitts, the negroes dance every day in the street from Christmas Eve to New Year, in grotesque masks and costume. Some bear horns, others are dressed like Indians, etc. There are men dressed as women, and others on stilts, as was the custom in Cuba and can be seen from Figure 1. 'The whole negro population seemed to be bitten by the tarantula,' says one author. 'The performances are called 'moka jumbic' [sic] dances, and probably have their remote origin in the forests of Africa . . .' [21]

In Bermuda, the negroes celebrate their Gombay festival[22] on Christmas Eve. From 11:00 o'clock at night well into the early hours of the morning, the negroes are masked, bearing the heads and horns of animals or imitations of houses and ships lighted with candles. In their merrymaking, they sing and dance, and claim small gratuities before passing along.[23]

The Jamaican negroes also hold processions with kings and queens at the head:

> In the towns, the processions were headed by a tall, athletic man with a hideous headdress, surmounted by a pair of oxhorns and boar tusks . . . [who] carried a large wooden sword and danced violently.[24]

Peytraud found parades and processions of the negroes in Martinique in the mid-18th century; some, 'dressed in very rich garments, represented the king, the queen and all the royal family, up to the grand officers of the crown.'[25]

Referring to the Afro-Caribbean festival of St. Kitts, W. W. Newell[26] wrote that for the New Year such spectacles were up until recently common in many American towns and cities. The custom of these masks, he says, has spread in parts of the United States to typically American festivities such as Thanksgiving Day.

In the United States, the negroes also elect a king for their festivities who is adorned with all the insignia of his rank.[27] In some states, such as Massachussetts, Rhode Island, and New Hampshire, instead of a king he is called a governor.[28]

The eve of the 'Day of the Kings' in Bahia, writes Mello Morales,[29] was the occasion for the *bacumbys* of the negroes 'in feather dress, singing African chants and making a barbarous noise with their equally barbarous instruments.' Nina Rodríguez describes the *reisados* or *ranchos de Reis* at Epiphany in Brazil, especially the symbolic figures of animals and certain totemic survivals of Africa: 'The *cucumbys* of the kings in Bahia are truly American festivities.'[30]

In Peru, by the 16th century, African dances were already being celebrated on public occasions and fraternities of African negroes would go to bull fights, along with the bands of fools and jesters.[31]

This having been said, there are other factors of diverse origin and nature that helped shape this raucous Cuban 'Day of the Kings' festivity. Aimes, the American sociologist who so successfully studied Afro-Cuban slavery, is of the opinion that the negro processions, parades and masquerades, including the Havana 'Day of the Kings,' come directly from Africa, brought by the Africans, who in their own land 'had elective kings or chiefs . . .'[32]

It should first be said that analogous popular festivities are to be found in Africa.

Binger[33] writes of the masquerading *dús*, dressed like Havana *diablitos*, who go around the villages and fields terrifying the timid, becoming intoxicated on the drinks people offer them . . . . Through the night until dawn, men follow the *dús* chanting loudly. Their turnout is rare and Binger ventures to affirm that it is mostly at the onset of winter, to scare away the evil spirits and to bring on the rain. The same traveler said that he had found similar customs among the Bambara and Malinke people of Upper Senegal, and the Kasonke, but that these masked figures were only for fun, an opinion that might well come of not knowing the original cause for the masquerade. Analogous to the latter is the *mokho missi ku*, a black masquerader quoted by the same author.[34]

The masqueraders known as Egungun also turn up in the villages each year.[35] And still on an afternoon the Yoruba in Cuba dance Egungún. Also, in the Congo, there are masked dances for religious offerings.[36]

The description of certain Bambara religious festivals evoke an imaginary 'Day of the Kings' in Africa.[37] In the old Musée du Trocadero in Paris can be seen Bambara devils very similar to the *ñáñigo* devils or *diablitos*, in feather and sackcloth costume, with a large pointed headpiece, also of feathers and sackcloth.

We are told of frequent festivals in Nigeria, especially religious ones, like the annual devil-driving or expulsion of the devil. References in 1844 to such a festivity suppose the whole people to be in a state of intoxication and frenzy. The fetish man walked in front, sprinkling water on the people, some of whom were firing muskets, others beating drums or blowing horns; many were covered in the skin of beasts or wore caps of the most fantastic shapes and all appeared to be anxious to make the greatest possible noise. . . . Concerning the 'custom' made by the natives on the finishing of the harvest, and the beginning of their new year . . . the first day was dedicated to a king . . .[38]

Then there was dancing, masquerading, music, shouting, intoxication . . .[39]

In Benin, this ritual ceremony is the 'grand devils' festival.[40] Fawckner wrote of these grand devils:

> Eight men were dressed in a most curious manner, having a dress made of bamboo about their bodies, and a cap on the head of various colors, and ornamented with red feathers taken from the parrot's tail; [41] round the legs were twisted strings of shells, which made a clattering noise as they walked, and the face and hands of each individual were covered with a net. These strange beings go around . . . driving the evil spirits from the town. They go around to all the chief's houses, and, in addition to the noise they make, perform some extraordinary feats in tumbling and gymnastics, for which they receive a few cowries.[42]

Among primitive peoples, the expulsion of evil is a very common festivity, and it is not occasional but periodic.

Frazer, the celebrated British anthropologist, has dealt extensively with these rights, which are very marked in West Africa.[43] 'The negroes of Guinea annually banish the devil from all their towns with much ceremony and a time set apart for the purpose.' At Axim, on the Gold Coast, this procession is preceded by a feast of eight days, during which mirth and jollity, skipping, dancing and singing prevail, and 'a perfect lampooning liberty is allowed, and scandal so highly exalted, that they may freely sing of all the faults, villainies and frauds of their superiors as well as inferiors, without punishment, or so much as the least interruption . . . On the eighth day in the morning they hunt out the Devil with a dismal cry, running after him and pelting him with sticks, stones, and whatever comes to hand. In this way, he is expelled in more than a hundred towns at the same time.'[44]

Another writer,[45] referring to the Gold Coast, added 'there are stated occasions when the people turn out en masse (generally at night) with clubs and torches to drive away the evil spirits from their towns. At the given signal, the whole community start up, commence a most hideous howling, beat about every nook and corner of their dwellings, then rush into the streets with their torches and clubs, like so many frantic maniacs, beat the air and scream at the top of their lungs until someone announces the departure of the spirits through some gate of the town, where they are pursued several miles into the woods and warned not to come back.'

In Old Calabar, which sent many shiploads of slaves to Cuba, the same festival can be found. There the evil spirits are personified in effigies and cast into the river after thunderous attempts to terrorize them.[46]

The ritual would also seem to have been observed in Dahomey every year before the rains.[47]

The evil spirits are driven away not only symbolically by threatening shouts, blows in the air, fires and firecrackers. The devil is often corporal in form. In Niger, a human scapegoat would be sacrificed for the community, as bearer of all the sins of the Lucumí.[48]

An Ashanti priest told an English anthropologist[49] how still today his people celebrate an annual festival which consists of a day of liberty and licence for all, men and women, freemen and slaves; when all can say what comes to mind out of spontaneous joy or premeditated revenge and aired injury. This African philosopher explained the psychological foundation and need for such a custom, for spiritual well-being, a derivation of concentrated hate, a penal substitute, as the Italian criminologist Ferri would say. Rattray is of the opinion that analogous beliefs played their part in Mediterranean saturnalia.

Other highly similar festivities can be observed in various countries of West Africa.[50]

In all, masked figures play a predominant role. Suffice it to open any work of general reference on African ethnography to find ritual masks plus descriptions, illustrations and photographs of the religious symbolism of devils.

It is scarcely necessary to refer to the monumental work of Leo Frobenius,[51] exclusively given over to this theme, which we will deal with on a future occasion.

It might well be said that there is not one African people that does not have such festivals with the full moon, or at the end of harvest, or on the solstice or New Year, etc. The list would be long and unnecessary. All were gradually fused in Cuba in the only one that remained licit, the 'Day of the Kings.'

Should not the most direct cause of the negro festival of the 'Day of the Kings' in Cuba be sought in these festivals, the dances and pantomime, especially the masked figures, which, while not priests, serve a priestly function in festivals held at the start of the winter and are so similar to the *diablitos*. The explanation for the date of the festival in Cuba, January 6, could be attributed to the tradition of giving the troops and the king's slaves their *aguinaldo* that day, aside from other analogous European folk festivals which we will discuss later. Also, shortly after the onset of winter, on Christmas Eve, there are other carnival festivities in Gorée and St. Louis (Senegambia) that have survived in Cuba.

The African precedents mentioned here, and many others narrated by travelers to West Africa, all helped shape the 'Day of the Kings' festival in Cuba. Initially, each *cabildo* must have revived the most important festivals of its country; later, all must have gradually fused to the point of the confusion and disorder of latter years.

When did the 'Day of the Kings' festival start in Cuba? No one knows and possibly no one ever will, because it did not come about by ordinance but through the collective spontaneity of the Africans, around the annual *aguinaldo* that was the custom of the whites in Cuba, as in their countries of ethnic origin – particularly when the negroes always participated in public ceremonies and popular festivities along with the whites.

In 1573, the Havana City Council or *Cabildo*, as it was then called, ordered all emancipated negroes to aid in the Corpus Christi procession with their 'inventions and games,' as tailors, carpenters, cobblers, blacksmiths and caulkers.[52]

But there is no exact date for the first 'Day of the Kings' held in Cuba.

III

Why was this festival called the festival of devils or *diablitos*? Almost certainly because, on looking for a name, the whites found in the motley costumes of the Africans, in their leaps and capers, their horns and masks, certain analogy with the devil masks accompanying the old Catholic procession of Corpus Christi in Cuba, as in Spain and other countries.

Diablitos or *diablillos* appeared in the Corpus Christi procession in the metropolis. In 'Mojiganga del Alma,'[53] this religious festival of the late 18th century is described as follows:

> There is a great procession that
> Marks the festival opening
> Then the devils come in running
> To drive away in so doing
> All those that are in the same spot
> The whole place thereby emptying.[54]

In verse, the objective the *diablitos* is explained: to open the way for the procession with their devilry.

In Puerto Rico, there were certain devils in religious processions called *vejigantes*, 'in devil's masks.'[55] A Puerto Rican writer expressed in verse:

And there go the *vejigantes*
That were once devils on the loose.[56]

One such devil or *vejigante* appears in the cart or wain of the Cortes of Death in Don Quixote.[57] And they still accompany religious processions in Spain, much to the amusement of the children. Rodríguez Marín refers to this in a note to his edition of Don Quixote: [58]

> In Cervantes' time, the *moharraches* or *mamarrachos*, masquerading figures, would accompany the Corpus Christi procession in Seville, opening the way through the crowd, making people laugh. 'First, to the great entertainment and merriment of the crowd,' it is said in the *Memorias de la Real Academia Española*, Vol. XI, P.404, 'is the *tarasca*, a wooden figure in the form of a huge reptile, drawn on four wheels by many men . . . accompanied by wild figures dressed in painted linen jerkins and puffed cow's bladders to scatter the crowd . . .'

This kind of costumed figure continues in our popular customs. In Baza and Guadix (Granada), it is called the *Cascamorras*, from *cascar*, to beat, and *morra*, head, because of the blows it delivers on children. This was how it was depicted by my late friend Don José Domínguez, church canon and preacher in that lovely little novel entitled *Nieve y Cierno*, award-winner of the Seville Atheneum and published in Barcelona (1902):

> 'The *Cascamorras*,' he said, 'a scurrilous knave or jester who appears in the clumps of furze (on the afternoon of Santa Rosa de Lima, August 30), amidst firecrackers and drumbeats. He wears doublets and breeches, half red, half yellow, with various streaks of lizard green, darting here and there, without rhyme or reason, and bears a whip with a cloth and hide ball on the end of a string, to scare off the children and youth who follow in pursuit in jest, to vex it.'

By the 17th century, negroes were dancing in processions in Andalusia: hence the verse of 'Entremes del Platillo,' by Simón de Aguedo (1602):

Mulattoes around
Go dancing on
The day of God
And that of St. John.[59]

The 'Mojiganga de la Gitanada' and the 'Mojiganga del Alma,' with negro dances, were done for Corpus Christi.[60]

It can be seen, then, that not all the Cuban *diablitos* came from Guinea, and that the negroes had white *diablitos* here to mimic and pardon their no less pardonable extravagances.

Figure 4. A *diablito* performing during Día de Reyes. Formerly *diablito* referred to all masquerade performers costumed in an 'African' manner.

The black *ñáñigos* and *brujos* or *obeah* men must have contributed in large measure to the vitality of the *diablitos.* (Figures 2, 2a, 4, and 5) Undoubtedly, the Afro-Cuban *ñáñigos* added their exoticism to the 'Day of the Kings' festival. This was not only because their *cabildos,* sets or powers took part, accompanied by their *diablitos,* but also because among African customs, in which Cuban *ñáñiguismo* was rooted, there was an equivalent annual ceremony.

As of 1836, the year in which, according to one writer, the first group of *ñáñigos* was set up in Havana, they have taken part in the 'Day of the Kings,' to request their *aguinaldo,* divided, according to Enrique Fernández Carrillo, in bands, later sets, with the Illamba or the Isué at the head and the Macombo, or Supreme Being, bearing the flag in a picturesque costume called *amirifimo.*

As a result of the frequent bloody clashes among the sets of *ñáñigos,* since they also waited for that day to seek vengeance, the authorities started restricting them more and more, until finally they were prohibited to come out on the 'Day of the Kings.'[61]

Ñáñiguismo can still be found in Cuba and it is to this that is to be attributed the retention of the *diablito,* who can be seen in public in *comparsas* and burials. In the presidium of the Republic even, prisoners tell of *ñáñigo* dancing, complete with *diablito* and all.

Figure 5. A *diablito* performing during Día de Reyes.

The Afro-Cuban religious retention of *brujería* or *obeah* also contributed picturesque elements to the 'Day of the Kings.'

The Lucumí or Yoruba kept their overseas religion alive in the cult of Egungun, the spirit of the dead, who was made to reappear on earth personified as masked *diablitos*, covered from top to toe. This cult has its annual ceremonies when the Egunguns come out dancing extravagantly, first before the mock king and then for the population, receiving gifts and very much at the center of the crowd. Moreover, as we had occasion to write some years ago: [62]

> The characteristic figures of the old festival of the 'Day of the Kings' give an idea of what the adornments and wild taste in costume of the *obeah* men were and still are like in good part today. While there is no proof, it can be ventured to say that the greater part of the picturesque African dress, which time back was brought out annually on January 6, was that of the fetish men of the *cabildos*, aside from some that could be of a warrior or hierarchical nature. The hypotheses is founded, bearing in mind the partially religious nature of the *cabildos*, which was initially demonstrated overtly, to the point that they carried the idols of the *cabildo* in their bacchanalia. It is logical to assume that the fetish man would not waste the opportunity to don the sacred attributes of his high position, to display them before his

compatriots and celebrate the ceremonies of his cult. In effect, among those that most drew the attention of Havana people on the 'Day of the Kings' were the *diablitos*. They were, according to Pichardo, those 'negroes ridiculously dressed as a masquerading or harlequin figure that, on the 'Day of the Kings,' paraded through the streets with their *cabildo*, jumping and pirouetting, sometimes with a doll effigy of the same figure and name.'

Another *diablito* of the *Lucumí* cult was the personification of the deity Ologboijeun, masked and threatening with a sword. There are also *diablitos* that personify trees, or *ígis*, generally with horned figures.

La Culona[f] was the farcical name Havana people gave to the *diablito* that danced in a wide-hooped vegetable fiber skirt. We originally thought[63] that the Havana name came from the form of dress, although we did find it strange that the word is the feminine form when the *diablito* was eminently masculine. (Figures 6 and 7)

Today we believe that *culona* was none other than the Malinke and Mindingo word *kulona* or *lonna*, an adjective meaning 'wise' or 'educated'[64] that was used to describe the priest fetishists. In Cuba, this African word must have become Castilian in form, taking on the feminine article given its feminine ending.[65]

Figure 6. The *diablito* named 'La Culona,' a name identified by Fernando Ortiz as Malinke in origin, meaning 'wise or educated person.' In colloquial Cuban, the term can also mean 'big-assed woman.'

Figure 7. La Culona followed by Queens of *cabildos*. Drawn by Victor Patricio Landaluze, probably in the 1870s.

A performer with Conga Los Hoyos, during Carnival 1987, Santiago de Cuba, wearing a costume inspired by an illustration from Fernando Ortiz' *Día de Reyes* article. © J.B.

The horns or horn adornments common to Afro-Cuban diablitos come from the *kijinga* or horned crown of the kings or *soba* of Angola and other regions of what was the Congo.[66]

There are antecedents to the fiber costume in various parts of Africa, but it is particularly like the ones used in the Congo by those initiated into the rites of *kindembo*,[67] a term that is still used in Cuban folklore.[68]

Diablitos was the name given to these mystic masked figures in Cuba, as seen in Pérez de Luna,[69] and also perhaps to African masqueraders in their atavistic processions.

In the hinterland of Brazil, Africans and their descendants still hold these civic-religious festivities in the Catholic churches, with their grotesque *cabildo* kings, and all the *congado*, as they say there, in masquerading dress, chanting to the accompaniment of tambourines and drums, the old rhythms of their race.[70]

Some of these *diablitos* were the African fetishers or priests in their strange and wild dress. They were the *babalaos*, as we would say today, or black *obeah* men; the *uangas*, as they are still called in some parts of the Caribbean and Louisiana; the *nganga*, in the Congo; or the *mohinganga* or *mojiganga* that made such an impression on the discoverers and governors of the coasts of Guinea, whose name was carried over into Iberian theater in the 16th and 17th centuries.[71]

Of no other public festival can it be more rightly said that it was a true *mojiganga* than of the African festival of the 'Day of the Kings' in Cuba.

IV

It would be worth our while to elaborate somewhat further on the sociological significance of this Afro-Cuban festival. We have rightly said that it was the carnival of the negroes, and this should be taken in its true meaning. The blacks did not copy or imitate the carnival of the whites. Rather, both blacks and whites, as all peoples, have their own carnival, their loud orgy of festivity, firmly rooted in the popular mind, as rank religious ritual withstands the action of time. And carnival is also a retention of profound religious significance.

After the intensive studies by Frazer in England and Manhardt in Germany, the sociological theory of carnival has been firmly if not definitively outlined. Here we will make but brief reference to this, referring the reader to the work of these scholars.[72]

In all primitive peoples, the phenomena of the successive seasons of the year have given rise to various rites, which can go so far as the real or symbolic ritual of the death of gods, kings and priests, on whom natural phenomena, especially those of the plant world, are thought to depend. Were these figures not to die, animal and vegetable life tied to their existence in a magical relationship would not follow its natural course. In Africa, the Americas and Europe, such rites are still to be observed today in all their primitive splendor and meaning or in nebulous vestiges that have been handed down. Burying the sardine, carrying out carnival, handing the strawman called Judas, Old Woman Sunday, etc., are, for example, age-old rites of spring. Lent and the death of Christ are also part of universal religious beliefs, of all places and all time.

The meaning of these rites is sometimes very clear: the spirit of the dead winter vegetation is killed and buried.

Sometimes such rites are later in the year, to celebrate the revival of vegetation, of nature awakening from its winter, and they are celebrated with symbols of magical meaning and strength propitious to the arrival of spring, germination and the abundance of fruit.[73]

These festivals are held at the start of the year, on what we know as Christmas Eve, at New Year, on the 'Day of the Kings,' etc., when people mark the beginning of the year with the winter solstice; or in March in the sowing season, the spring equinox, when certain people mark the start of their year; that is why different peoples hold their carnivals in these two periods of the year, in essence to be interpreted only as the religious solemnity of the new year. These rituals correspond to the periodic expulsion of devils or evil spirits or sin from a social grouping. They are, as Frazer says, [74] a deliberate moral cleansing, coinciding as they do with a change of season, generally the beginning of winter, and being preceded by a period of extraordinary licence, involving a human divinity or animal as a scapegoat or redeemer of all sins.

Such quasi-religious retentions are interpreted by Manhardt as a metamorphosis of ancient rites to drive the evil spirits from the vegetation, those of sterility, and also to help germination, ward off the rain, etc.

The Chinese and the Koreans have an identical annual custom of driving out evil spirits with the 'firing of guns and popping of crackers' on the last day of the year, to terrify and scare away the devils.[75] This custom is observed today in Cuba. In Havana, just as in any capital of China, the noise of Chinese crackers and other deafening products of popular pyrotechnics symbolizes the arrival of a new year.

This peculiar rite of driving out the evil spirits each year is almost universal; it takes on various forms in the various countries and has produced some very curious customs. In the Tyrol, witches are driven out in the month of May, with much thunder and ringing of cowbells. Analogous customs were observed up until recently in Bavaria and among the Germans in Bohemia, around Lake Lucerne and other parts of Switzerland, and in the south of France. And from the Shetland Isles in the north of Europe to southern Italy, the most propitious period of the year for such mysterious ceremonies was that of the Twelve Days between Christmas and Epiphany, the most folkloric days of the year in all countries.

In ancient Rome, there were festivities introduced by Tarquinius Prisius called *compitalia*, in the month of January, noisily celebrated by the slaves and servants when plowing was finished. Some folklorists are of the opinion that not a few European customs have been handed down from these pagan festivals, among them Plough Monday in England, which is what farmers used to call the day after Twelfth Day, that is, January 7. In some regions, right into the 19th century, masquerades and dancing processions were held and a collection taken.[76]

Bonilla y San Martín, in his brilliant studies of the origins of Spanish theater, [77] recalls certain old Spanish customs that could well be the equivalent of the Havana 'Day of the Kings,' and forms of agrarian rites that are universal in nature. He quotes Alcalde del Rio[78] relating two Paleolithic drawings of persons with the heads of birds, probably masks, discovered in the prehistoric cave of Altamira, in the province of Santander, with an old Santander custom:

> On the last days of the year, a festival is held in several villages called *cijanera* or *ciejanera*, which consists of certain dances we might well call wild. At daylight, those with an active part in the festival, who are largely the graziers, take to the streets covered from top to toe in

> animal skins and with countless brass bells strung from their waist.[79] Masquerading in so original and wild a disguise, they run, leap and whirl about as if possessed by a mad rage, making an unbearable noise as they go by. . .

They end up fighting the youth of the neighboring village. The same custom, adds Bonilla, exists today in Becerreá, Galicia.[80] But there the old year is represented by a stuffed doll. He also mentions the old Catalan custom of masquerading as deer and other animals on the first day of January. [81]

There is a special preference in Europe for Epiphany as the time to drive out malignant powers. *Befana* is a custom of the Tuscan Romagna, Abruzzi, Sicily, etc., that still exists today[82] and, according to Grimm and Frazer, comes down from driving out evil, in this case personified by an old hag.[83]

The whites in Cuba carried over their old European religious carnival tradition, to celebrate their mystic festival around the spring equinox; the negroes, reflecting their carnival rites of the winter solstice, chose Christmas Eve and Epiphany for their festivities. The Roman saturnalia were held in December or March, depending on whether the solar year began at one or the other time, according to astronomy. This does not mean that Epiphany, such a ceremonial occasion for the Afro-Cubans, did not also have folkloric importance and meaning from remote times. The Christmas of the winter solstice is the first of the Twelve Days, as Frazer says, that as of old, from the Aryans, has been considered an augurial period for the coming twelve months. Thus also Epiphany is the last of that symbolic year of twelve days. The one and the other have been marked by custom, superstition and agrarian rites among many peoples, some of which still survive: the *aguinaldo*, Santa Claus, the Three Kings, the *cabañuelas*, etc., along with other practices still to be found among European peoples such as sawing the old woman, carrying out death, burying carnival, the *mi-carème*, etc. Some of them take place on January 6, and some have been fused in carnival and Lent and Christian readaptations of age-old solar and agrarian rites.

They are universal traditions, born spontaneously of the interpretations of primitive man to satisfy his mental curiosity and try to harness unknown forces, related to the seasons of the year and their close connection with the vegetable kingdom.

The ritual superstitions surrounding rural ceremonies of a magical nature, so brilliantly studied by Frazer, are basically those of all peoples of the world, whether they be held on the winter solstice (Christmas, birth of the sun, the year according to astronomy, the year of the Lord) or around New Year, Epiphany (the last of the Twelve Days), Shrovetide, Lent, Easter (the spring equinox), the May-tree and the summer solstice, or St. John's Day.

And so, similar practices, ceremonies, figures and creeds are to be found on the same or similar dates of traditional significance in agrarian ritual over time, from ancient Egypt to the present day, over continents and races, in Asia as in Europe, in Africa as in the Americas.

In our no longer observed 'Day of the Kings,' there are precise details that reveal to us its ancestral origin and the survival in Cuba of rites analogous to those mentioned as part of ancient custom on the Old Continent. Hence, on the Havana 'Day of the Kings,' as in the saturnalia of ancient Rome, during the festivities the slaves had complete freedom, the only authority being that of their own burlesque kings, which, it can be read in the Latin classics, were chosen by them.

Those Roman festivals most certainly were in the vein of agrarian rites, and nothing would have seemed to strike the ancient Romans themselves more than the temporary licence granted to slaves at this time to rail at their masters, become intoxicated like their betters, sit down at table with them, etc. According to Horatius, Macrobius, Justinius, Plutarch, Lucianus and Porfirius, the slaves could with impunity do during the saturnalia what in normal times would be punishable with the whip, imprisonment and death.

There is an analogous festival on the coast of Guinea to drive out the evil spirits, during which invectives of slaves and the poorer classes of the population against their kings and superiors are perfectly permissible. They might rail against the wrongdoings and villainy of their chiefs without even a word of reproof or punishment. They had complete licence.[84] The same applies to the Zulus, for example, who were quite distant from Guinea. They celebrate their new year with a festival that is like a saturnalia, with great merrymaking and dancing. Those who take part are not held responsible for what they say or do. Even the king himself, dressed in grass costume, performs several dances·[85] The annual festivities of the negroes are even more outlandish.[86] During these, all the tribe is given over to orgy, drink and incessant scandal: the king temporarily renounces his authority and all can do what they want, including crimes against person, property and sex, without any order being imposed. Even the chief is insulted with impunity when this would be punishable by immediate death.

Among the Ashantis, during the annual festival of the New Yams, which is a saturnalia, neither theft nor deception nor aggression are punished: during the solemnities, gross freedom prevails and there is complete abandon to sexual licence.[87] Another explorer tells that all laws were suspended; that each could do whatever he saw fit, even look at the king's wives; and that Carnival ended in a great orgy.[88]

The annual Ibo festival is Ekuensen Day, which is held to frighten the devil, and the people can satisfy all manner of excess without restriction. The festival of old would end in fighting and bloodshed; today colonization has put an end to the crimes, although it has not been able to wipe out the scenes of those times.[89]

These warrior dances refer to the agrarian battles of winter and summer in carnival ritual of primitive peoples.[90] (Figure 8)

Such ceremonial battle or warrior dances can be found also on islands of the British West Indies. St. Kitts still has its *moko jumby*, a dance of David and Goliath, both armed with scimitars.[91] Similar battle and warrior pantomime is to be seen in the African *cucumbys* in the north of Brazil.[92]

In Jamaica, rival black figures by the names of John Canoe and John Crayfish roam the streets at New Year. They are masquerading figures bearing on their head a cardboard boat full of effigies of sailors, soldiers or plantation slaves. The negroes were given three days of festivities at Christmas and New Year's Day, which was for them the most important. That day, John Canoe had to be present, accompanied by a long procession with his band of musicians and red flags.[93] The population divided into two bands, scarlet and blue, as is still the style in rural festivities in Cuba, with their king and queen sumptuously adorned and with carnival floats in artistic competition at Christmas time, with lots of rockets and firecrackers in the old parts of Salvador and Carmen in the Cuban township of Remedios.[94]

Little wonder, when that township was once prey to hundreds of thousands of demons, and its mayors had to show great valor in triumphing over evil. (See Fernando Ortiz. *Historia de Una Pelea Cubana Contra los Demonios*, Havana, 1959). Today, they are still scaring off the devils.

Figure 8. Identified by Fernando Ortiz as a 'warrior dance of the Congos [people].' Ortiz suggested that such ritual combat was related to worldwide carnival celebrations honoring seasonal festivities.

Even the choosing of a king by the *cabildos* would seem to have had its equivalent among the whites, given that Frazer refers to the same festivities[95] having a widespread European custom of choosing a king of the bean and having a festival of fools on Epiphany. In France, Belgium, Germany and England, this popular custom is still observed. The kings of France even contributed to the age-old practice of mimicking royalty.

In England, Twelfth Day was occasion for 18th century masquerading, in London even, and certain rural districts still observe the king and queen's banquets, as in the north of France and in Germany.

The custom of kings for Epiphany was also common in Spain, during the early centuries of the settlement of the Indies. Tirso, in *La Eleccíon por la Virtud*, records this song of kings.

Long live Felix
of kings most felicitous
now that Christmas hath passed
and Easter is upon us.
The highlanders have

chosen their king
God make him in reality
what he just should be.
. . . .
Those who merrymaking
would come to see him
offer their obedience with praise.[96]

An 18th-century writer was of the opinion that the old custom of choosing a king and queen at dinner on the night of Epiphany came from the Romans, to whom it was handed down by the Greeks, who threw dice to designate the *rex convivii* or, as Horatius said, the *arbiter bibendi*.

Anaquillé was the name given to the puppet figures on the streets of Havana on the 'Day of the Kings.' It was the idol or figure on the end of a stick held by dancers in certain religious or ceremonial dances of African ritual.[97] (Figure 9)

It is possible to see the origin of the *anaquillé* in Africa in the effigies of Old Calabar in the biennial festival to drive out the devils, where the figures or images are called *nabikém*. In Dahomey, such fetishes are taken to analogous festivities, like the Saints in Catholic processions, with great pomp and loud chants. A host of ugly figures are taken by night by canoe to the center of the lake and there thrown into the deep. According to some, these images represent death, which is thereby warded off from Porto Novo; according to others, they are demons and evil spirits that are driven off Dahomey soil.

Figure 9. According to Fernando Ortiz, a '*negra curra,*' or a black woman of the flamboyant street subculture of nineteenth century Havana, carrying an *anaquillé*, or small puppet/effigy figure related to the *nabikém* figures used in rituals in Old Calabar. [Nigeria]

Today still in Cuba, in certain of the ritual Lucumí dances, small idols are held that might well have come down from the old *anaquillé*. (Figure 10)

Another typical scene on the 'Day of the Kings' was that of killing the snake. This was a dance of the mob, according to Pichardo; it might well be said to have been a pantomime or symbolic ritual dance. Some negroes would go leaping, dancing and singing through the streets of Havana bearing an enormous artificial snake several meters long, stopping in front of houses to take a collection. The scene enacted represented the death of the snake whose features were extolled:

> Look at its eyes like fire
> Look at its pointed teeth.

The snake would be laid out on the ground and the dancing and chanting would start around it, ending thus:

> The snake is dead, dead . . .
> *Calabasón, són, són . . .*

According to Bachiller y Morales, [98] the chant ended as follows:

> The snake is dead, dead . . .
> *Sángala, muleque . . .*[99]

Figure 10. A figure representing the *oricha* Changó, identified by Fernando Ortiz as 'an *anaquillé*, or small effigy figure, of contemporary Cuban *brujos*.' This one was used in Lucumí [Cuban Yoruba] dances. Ortiz dates this statue to c.1900.

Another *son* of the snake dance was that sung by a negro girl and the *diablito*:

> *Negro girl*: Mama, mama, come, come,
> I'm being swallowed by the snake, come, come.
> *Diablito*: No, no, my black one, come, come.
> It's a game in my country, come, come.

On the 'Day of the Kings,' this very popular pantomime was performed all over Havana and then put on in the courtyard of the Palace of the Captains-General, before the Captain-General himself. And this ophiolatric scene is characteristic of many carnivals of Africa, India and other continents.

The already mentioned *ranchos de Reis* in Bahia, consisting essentially of a pantomime struggle between animal or object; the *rancho* totem, and the dancers, can be related to this dance. Here, the animal is represented by a figure of huge proportions in the form of the chosen animal.[100]

Restricting ourselves to the more exact African antecedents, an analogous festival is to be found among the negroes of the Spanish island of Fernando Po. There, every year, with great ceremony, a huge reptile would be killed and the skin hung from a branch of the highest tree in the public square.[101] Frazer,[102] after referring to many examples of ritual animal deaths, concludes that the sacred animal is slain once a year with great solemnity. Before or immediately after its death, it is taken from door to door, for adulators to receive the divine powers emanating from the dead or dying body.

Animal worship and animal deaths are frequent among primitive peoples, and Frazer affirms that in prehistoric times these processions must have been held in Europe, judging from the many retentions of the same.

Killing the snake can also be considered a collective cleansing rite of the devil-driving kind that has been here related to the 'Day of the Kings.'[103]

The snake, monster dragon or *tarasca*, is still used in the procession of Corpus Christi in many Catholic countries of Europe, as in the old cities of Cuba and all the West Indies.[104] The death of the snake or dragon, that is, the sacred animal, is a ritual in the carnivals of many white peoples, according to Reinach.[105] Doutté, like Frazer, sees in the widespread, old primitive form of pantomime, in the death of the sacred animal or agrarian deity, the origin of the dramatic arts.

It might well be said, then, that the Afro-Cubans, on killing the snake, were subconsciously carrying out an ancestral rite, deeply rooted in almost all peoples and continents. The fact of its being, on top of all this, extremely raucous—as in primitive carnival ritual to drive away the spirits of the dead—only adds to the Afro-Cuban 'Day of the Kings' being but an amalgam, a fusing in Cuba of a host of African, and it might be said universal, scenes and rites of almost unknown, forgotten meaning, that contemporary sociology attempts to explain today. It was, in short, the carnival of the negroes in the mystical sense that any authoritative, scientific interpretation can attribute to the expression.

Translator's Notes

a. The law was passed in 1880, although abolition was not complete until 1886. The last recorded 'Day of the Kings' appears to have been in 1884.

b. We have chosen to translate the Spanish word *negro* for negro and not black, given its common usage in English at the time this article was written. There is only the one word for both in Spanish.

c. Cuban historians warn of elements of fantasy and realism in 19th-century engravings. This includes the work of Spanish-born Victor Patricio Landaluze, who was much influenced by romanticism and some of whose images are claimed to be faked.

d. The Spanish word is 'Etíope,' literally translated as Ethiopian, but which was used synonymously for African.

e. The town of Regla lies to the east of Havana, across the harbor, and has an imposing statue of the Virgin overlooking the water. El Cobre is a copper mining town outside Santiago de Cuba, in eastern Cuba, in whose church is to be found the statue of the Brown Virgin. Legend has it that it was discovered in the sea by three fishermen, as referred to in Part II of this article.

f. La Culona could be vulgarly translated as a 'big-assed woman,' deriving from the word 'culo,' which means 'ass,' 'bottom,' 'behind.'

Notes

1. Taken from Pierre Toussaint Frédéric Mialhe. *Album Pintoresco de la Isla de Cuba*. Berlin: Storch & Kramer, 1838. (b. France, April 14, 1810. Professor at the Academy of Painting in Havana, 1831–34 and 1857–61.) This is a color version which differs from the original black and white in that the backdrop of San Francisco Square is from a different angle. The figures, however, are the same.
2. Ramón Meza. 'Día de Reyes,' *La Habana Elegante*, Havana, Year V, No. 2, and *El Hogar*, Havana, January 11, 1891.
3. The *cabildos* were organizations of Afro-Cuban negroes, comprising mainly free blacks that tended to maintain the social cohesion of Africans from the same nation and to practice mutual self-help and collective forms of enjoyment. See Fernando Ortiz, 'Los Cabildos Afrocubanos,' *Revista Bimestre Cubana*, Havana, 1920.
4. Antonio Lorcas. 'Los Diablitos o el Día Infernal en La Habana,' *Prensa de la Habana*, January 6, 1859.
5. P. Riesgo. 'Día de los Santos Reyes en La Habana,' *La Prensa*, Havana, January 6, 1843.
6. Aurelio Pérez Zamora. 'El Día de los Reyes en La Habana,' *El Abolicionista Español*, Madrid, Year 2, No. 7, January 15, 1866.
7. Leon Beauvallet. *Rachel in the New World*. New York, 1856, p. 363, quoted in Hubert S. Aimes. 'African Institutions in America,' *Journal of American Folklore*, Vol. XVIII, 1905, p. 16ff.
8. Vincente. *El Faro Industrial de La Habana*, January 6, 1842.
9. 'Long Live Isabella,' referring to Queen Isabella of Spain at the time.
10. John George F. Wurdemann. *Notes on Cuba, An Account of its Discovery and Early History*. Boston: James Munroe and Company, 1844c., reprint 1971, p. 83, quoted in Hubert S. Aimes. 'African Institutions in America. A History of Slavery in Cuba,' *Journal of American Folk-Lore*, 1967, op. cit.
11. Dolores Ma. Ximeno De Cruz. 'Aquellos Tiempos . . . Memorias de Lola María,' *Revista Bimestre Cubana*, Havana, 1924.
12. C. Texier. *Au pays de géneraux*. Paris, 1891.
13. Ortiz. *Los Cabildos . . .*, op. cit.
    Just as the *comparsas* of the Havana carnival were handed down from the Day of the Kings, so are the Afro-Brazilians' *cumbys* and the *ranchos de Reis* that appear in Rio de Janeiro at Shrovetide, according to Nina Rodríguez.
14. See William S. Walsh. *Curiosities of Popular Customs, Rights, Ceremonies, Observances, and Miscellaneous Antiques*. Philadelphia and London: J. B. Lippincott Company,1897c, Rev. 1925 by Katharine Walsh, p. 396ff.
15. Bachiller y Morales. *Los Negros*, Barcelona, p. 114.
16. Ibid., p. 113.
17. Bachiller y Morales. *En Tipos y Costumbres*, p. 31.
18. There were slave quarters for the King's negroes next to San Isidro in Havana, in what was known as *el palenque de los negros del rey*, as of 1765.
19. The *Congo* in Sagua la Grande (Cuba) celebrated their own festival at Christmas, according to informants of their *cabildo*.
20. Torquemada. *Monarquía Indiana*, Vol. 1, Book 5, Chapter 76.
21. Alfred M. Williams. 'A Miracle Play in the West Indies,' *Journal of American Folklore*, Vol. IX, 1896, p. 117ff.
22. Phonetically similar to the old Spanish African dance form *cumbé*. See Fernando Ortiz. *Glosario de Afronegrismos*, Habana, 1924, p. 154.
23. H. C. Bolton. 'Gombay, a Festival Rite of Bermudian Negroes,' *Journal of American Folklore*, Vol. III, July-Sept, 1890, p. 225.
24. James Marshall Philippo. *Jamaica: Its Past and Present State*. London, 1843, p. 242, reprint 1970. Negro University Press, Westport, Connecticut, quoted in Aimes. 'African Institutions . . .,' op. cit.

25. L. Peytraud. *L'Esclavage aux Antilles Françaises avant 1789*. Paris, 1897, p. 182.
26. W. W. Newell. 'The Saint Kitts Miracle Play,' *Journal of American Folklore*, Vol. X, 1897, p. 81.
27. James Fowler. History of Durham, p. 161, quoted in Aimes. 'African Institutions . . . ,' op. cit.
28. Hubert S. Aimes. *A History of Slavery in Cuba*. New York, 1907, p. l8.
29. Mello Morales. *Festas e Tradiçoes Populares no Brasil*, Rio de Janeiro.
30. Nina Rodríguez. 'A Raça Negra na America Portuguesa,' *Revista de Brasil*, July 1822, p. 203ff.
31. Ramón Palma. *Mis Ultimas Tradiciones Peruanas*, Barcelona, pp. 48 and 327.
32. Aimes. 'African Institutions . . . ,' op. cit. fn. 7.
33. Gustave Binger. *Du Niger au Golfe de Guinée par le Pays de Kong et la Mossi*. Paris, 1892, Vol. I, p. 378. These are the negroes that in Cuba are called *Gangá*.
34. Ibid., p. 106.
35. A. B. Ellis. *The Land of Fetish*. London, 1883, p. 168.
36. *Expediçao Portuguesa a Muatianwa*, p. 235.
37. Abbé Jos Henri. *Les Bambaras*. Münster, 1910, pp. 122–3.
38. A. J. N. Tremearne (author, John Newman). *The Tailed Head-Hunters of Nigeria*. London, 1912.
39. See the many *diablitos* or masked negroes in the rites and festivities of the Lucumí or Yoruba, according to Luis Desplagues. *Le Plateau Nigérien*. Paris, 1907, p. 304ff.
40. Narrative of *Captain James Fawckner's Travels on the Coast of Benin, West Africa*. London, 1837, p. 102.
41. In Cuba, parrot feathers still have symbolic meaning among the usual adornments of Afro-Cuban *obeah* men. See Fernando Ortiz, *Los Negros Brujos*. Madrid, 1906, p. 182. See also the references there to Guiral, Monnier and Ratzel, showing that a similar custom is to be found in various countries with negro populations.
42. *Narrative of . . .* , op. cit., p. 102ff.
43. James George Frazer. *The Scapegoat*. London, 1920, pp. 128 and 131.
44. William Bosman. 'Description of the Coast of Guinea,' *Voyages And Travels*. London, 1814, Vol. XVI, p. 402; and also as quoted in Frazer, *A New and Accurate Description of the Coast of Guinea*. New York: Barnes & Noble, 1967.
    Pierre Bouch. *La Côte des Esclaves*. Paris, 1885, p. 325.
45. John Leighton Wilson. *Western Africa*. London, 1856, p. 217, reprint 1969.
46. Thomas J. Hutchinson, Esq. *Impressions of Western Africa*. London, 1858c, p. 162, reprint 1970.
    H. Goldie. *Calabar and its Mission*. London, 1890, p. 49ff.
    A. G. Seward. *The Lower Niger and its Tribes*. London, 1906, pp. 449 and 451.
    Mary H. Kingsley. *Travels in West Africa*. London, 1897, p. 495.
47. F. Terrien. *Annales de la Propagation de la Foi*. Paris, 1881, p. 375.
48. This mystic idea of a scapegoat figure, whose sacrifice redeems the sins of others, is very widespread among primitive peoples and still exists as a contemporary religious practice.
49. R. S. Rattray. *Ashanti*, Oxford, 1923, p. 153.
50. E. Noirot, op. cit., p. 51.
51. Leo Frobenius. *Die Masken und Geheimbünde Afrikas*. Halle, 1898.
52. José M. de la Torre. *Lo que Fuimos y lo que Somos*, 1913, p. 162.
53. E. Cotarelo. *Collección de Entremeses*, I, p. CCCI.
54. The verses follow:

    After,
    with their pennants go the tailors
    and hot on their tails the dancers
    their own day's fate they are dancing

come help and we'll dance together.
When the music comes following,
It's a sonnet they are singing . . .

Satan comes out
and with his tempestuous look
shoots off a mighty firecracker
making the crowd all excited.

And yet
I was forgetting what was best.
Which is?
The wonderful giants
that their strength and powers
do flout.

There was, then, no lack of models for African negroes to mimic. The negroes might well believe that these Catholic festivals had the same social significance as the primitive meaning of their own festivals, as if they were African festivals transposed into Spanish.

55. A. Malaret. *Diccionario de Provincialismos de Puerto Rico*. San Juan, p. 147.
56. Alejandro Tapia, quoted in Malaret, ibid.
57. M. de Cervantes, *Don Quixote*, Part II, Chapter XI.
58. Francisco Rodríguez Marin. *Edición Crítica de El Ingenioso Hidalgo Don Quijote de la Mancha*. Madrid, 1916, Vol.IV, p. 236.
59. E. Cotarelo. *Colección de Entremeses*, Vol.I, p. 230.
60. Ibid., p. CCCI.
61. Emilio Roig de Leuschenring. 'La Fiesta del Día de Reyes o de Diablitos,' *Social*, Havana, January 1923.
62. Ortiz. *Los Negros Brujos*. op. cit., p. 184.
63. Ibid.
64. E. Hopkinson. *A Vocabulary of the Mandingo Language*. London, p. 46. Un missionaire de la congregation du Saint-Espirit. *Dictionnaire Français-Malinke et Malinke-Français*. Conakry, 1906, p. 138.
65. See Fernando Ortiz. 'Personajes del Folklore Afrocubano,' *Archivos del Folklore Cubano*, Vol. I, No. 1, p. 70, and *Glosario de Afronegrismos*, Havana, 1924, p. 152.
66. Heli Chatelain. *Folk-Tales of Angola*. Boston, 1894.
67. H. Johnston. *George Grenfell and the Congo*. London. Vol. II, p. 669.
68. F. Ortiz. *Glosario de Afronegrismos*, op. cit.
69. Rafael Félix Pérez Luna. *Historia de Sancti Spíritus*. Sancti Spíritus, Cuba, 1888, p. 411. Pérez Luna refers to the cost of the giants, the *tarasca*, the *moctezumas*, and *diablitos* in the procession up until 1786.

    "For the Catholic Church, even the Day of the Kings was a day of festivity and religious licence. In many festivities of Catholic rejoicing and, of course, on Epiphany, there has been singing in the vernacular of diverse songs in the theater, in farce, sung divine . . . such that the *zarambeque* negro dance and *yo soy solo* . . . ballads, the *escaramán* and merry comedy tunes have been sung. (*Papeles de la Inquisición*, Vol. 41, File 11, quoted by Paz y Melía in *Introducción a las Sales Españoleas*)"

    In the Catholic City Cathedral of Menorca during the offertory of Holy Mass, this same author heard over several years late last century the Aragonese tune *Los Tres Ratas de la Gran Via*, played to the accompaniment of castanets and tambourines.
70. Prado Ribeiro. 'Os Congos,' *Revista do Brasil*, Sao Paulo, 1924, p. 88.
71. See Ortiz. *Glosario do Afronegrismos*, op. cit. for the meaning and Congo etymological root of *mojinganga*.
72. Frazer. *The Scapegoat*, op. cit. The whole of this famous work is given over to his most

interesting theory of the scapegoat, which is amazingly well documented. See also Manhardt. *Walk und Feldkultur.*

73. The dogma of Christian resurrection and the ritual of Lent, etc., are ancestral religious ideas that intimately reflect this theory. They are the carnival of Christian religions, as what is today called carnival has been handed down from pagan, pre-Christian carnival, preserved through folklore.
74. Frazer. *The Scapegoat.*, op. cit., p. 224.
75. J. J. M. de Groot. *The Religious System of China*, Vol. VI. p. 944ff and *The Religion of China.* New York, 1910, p. 38. J. H. Gray. China: *A History of the Laws, Manners & Customs of the People.* London, 1875, Vol. 1, p. 252. W. W. Rockhill. 'Notes on Some of the Laws, Customs and Superstitions of Korea,' *The American Anthropologist*, Vol. IV, 1891, p. 185.
76. W. Carew Hazlitt. *Faiths and Folklore of the British Isles.* London, 1905, Vol. II, p. 496. Ref. & Bibliog. Berk. Lib. 1965. See also Walsh. *Curiosities*, op. cit., p. 814.
77. Adolfo Bonilla y San Martín. *Las Bacantes o del Origen del Teatro.* Madrid, 1921, p. 37.
78. Alcalde del Rio. *Las Pinturas y Grabados de las Cavernas Prehistóricas de la Provincia de Santander.* Santander, 1906, p. 22.
79. Like the *ñáñigo diablitos* of Cuba.
80. Alfredo García Ramos. *Arqueología Jurídico-Consuetudinario-Económico de la Región Gallega.* Madrid, 1912, p. 17.
81. M. Mila 'Orígenes del Teatro Catalán,' *Obras Completas*, Vol. VI, p. 205.
82. This custom, extensive to Latin America, is still somewhat observed in Havana as *domingo de la vieja* (Old Woman Sunday). See Fernando Ortiz. *Un Catauro de Cubanismos.* Havana, 1924.
83. Frazer. *The Scapegoat*, op. cit., pp. 166–7.
84. Bosman, quoted in Frazer. *The Golden Bough.* London, Vol.ll, 1914–20, p. 318.
85. J. McDonald. *Light in Africa.* London, p. 216.
86. J. McDonald. *Religion and Myth*, p. 136.
87. T. E. Bowdich. *Mission from Cape Coast Castle to Ashantee.* London, 1833, p. 266ff.
88. H. Ling Roth. *Great Benin: Its Customs, Art and Horrors.* Halifax, London: Routledge and Kegan Paul Ltd., 1903c, p. 76., reprint 1968.
89. G. T. Basden. *Among the Ibos of Nigeria.* London, 1921, p. 220.
90. Frazer. *The Scapegoat*, op. cit. Our carnival battles of streamers, confetti and flour-filled eggs are the last vestiges of this primitive ritual combat.
91. Williams. 'A Miracle Play . . . ,' op. cit. This would appear to be a curious case of Christianization of African religious rites and practices. Other interesting cases can be found in Ortiz, *Los Negros Brujos*, op. cit.
92. Nina Rodríguez. 'A Raça Negra . . . ,' op. cit., p. 205.
93. It hardly needs to be said that those red flags did not symbolize radicalism but were probably reminiscent of Africa. We do not know what the emblems of the *nations* of Africa were then. However, we would recall that the flag of the *Congo cabildos* was red and gilt in Cuba, like that of His Majesty the King of Spain.
94. M. G. Lewis. *Journal of a Residence among the Negroes in the West Indies.* London, 1845, pp. 24 and 26.
95. Frazer. *The Scapegoat*, op. cit., p. 317.
96. Julio Cejador. *La Verdadera Poesía Castellana.* Madrid, 1921, Vol. 3, p. 319.
97. Ortiz. *Glosario de Afronegrismos*, op. cit., p. 25. *Anaquillé* was also once the name of an Afro-Cuban dance.
98. Bachiller y Morales. *Los Negros*, op. cit., p. 117.
99. *Sángala, muleque*, in the tongue of the coastal slave traders, either meant 'cane spirit, boy' (*Sanga lamulé*, which is *ñáñigo*) or, what is more likely, 'dance, boy!' Another variation recorded by E. Roig de Leuchsenring in *Carteles* magazine, Havana, January 11, 1925, goes as follows:

The snake is dead, dead
Calabazún, zum, zum.
I myself killed it.
Look at its eyes like fire
Look at its pointed teeth.

The snake is dead
Sángala, muleque.

100. Nina Rodríguez. 'A Raca Negra . . . ,' op. cit., p. 206.
101. Thomas J. Hutchinson, Esq. *Impressions of Western Africa.* London, 1858c, p. 196, reprint 1970.
102. Frazer, loc. cit. and *Spirits of the Corn and of the Wind.* New York: Macmillan, 1935, Vol. II, p. 174.
103. This annual death of the snake has nothing to do with the Andalusian superstition against using the word *culebra* (snake), substituting for it the word *bicha* (beast). This Andalusian custom is very widespread among primitive peoples concerning all kinds of animals, especially harmful ones. Regarding the snake, its name is taboo in the north of India and the practice was perhaps introduced by the gypsies (W. Crooke. *Popular Religion and Folklore of Northern India*, Vol. II, Westminster, 1896, Vol. II, p. 142). In India it is called the beast, like the Seville *bicha*, probably taken from 16th- and 17th-century Italian galley crews, for whom it was *biccia*, with analogous superstition, as can be seen in Gabriel d'Annunzios' *La fiaccola sotto il moggio.*
    Frazer. *The Golden Bough, Part II, Taboo and the Perils of the Soul*, London, 1922, p. 402ff.
104. Ricardo Palma tells of a cardboard monster in Peru symbolizing the demon Leviathan.
105. Reinach. Vol. I, p. 19. See also Edward Doutté in his book *Magie et Religion dans l'Afrique du Nord.* Algiers, 1919, pp. 498 and 533.

*This article initially appeared in Havana as "La fiesta afrocubana del 'Día de Reyes'" in *Revista Bimestre Cubana*, Vol. XV, January–June 1920, pp5–26; La Reforma Social, Vol. XVII, No.4 August 1920; and *Archivos del Folklore Cubano*, April 1924 and June 1925. Subsequently published in book form, the last revised version was *La antigua fiesta afrocubana del 'Día de Reyes'*, Ministerio de Cultura, Havana, 1960. This is a first English-language translation of the article based on the 1960 version.

The Afro-Cuban Festival 'Day of the Kings' An Annotated Glossary

David H. Brown*

Introduction

As a supplement to "The Afro-Cuban Festival 'Day of the Kings,'" my glossary attempts to define and/or elaborate upon a variety of African, Afro-Cuban, and Spanish terms that were italicized or otherwise marked by Ortiz in the original text as culturally-specific usages or proper names. In many cases, Ortiz did provide brief definitions in the text itself or in footnotes. In other cases, such terms from the Afro-Cuban and popular idioms were left undefined and untranslated for the reader.

Ortiz, a wide-ranging, meticulous scholar and documenter, came to recognize the special problem of vocabulary and cultural translation as it related to his lifelong study of Afro-Cuban history, society, and culture. Given his deep etymological and philological interests, established from the outset of his career as integral to his scholarly method, he had intended in the early 1920s to present a single chapter of specialized vocabulary in a larger sociological work (*Los Negros Horros* – 'The Free Blacks'; never published as such). Yet, he soon found that it had 'grown to reach unforeseen proportions, coming to comprise material for three volumes.' In short, he explains, 'we would perceive that the terms that the Africans had incrusted in our speech were more numerous than had been noted' (Ortiz 1924:xii–xiv). From this vast material emerged *Un Catauro de Cubanismos* (1923, from 1921/1922 installments in the journal *Revista Bimestre Cubana*) and *Glosario de Afronegrismos* (1924), the former a rich, but much less systematic, treatment than the latter—a massive, detailed work of 558 pages, evincing extraordinary resources and linguistic facility on Ortiz's part. The alphabetical entries comprising these publications were, in Ortiz's words, 'analyses to determine the respective influences of the different African languages: Mandinga, Yolofe, Hausa, Yoruba, Calabar, Congo, Angola, etc; their spheres of germination: zoologic, botanical, toponymic [place-names], musical, vernacular etc.; and other characteristics' (Ortiz 1924:xv). And, of course, the terms were glossed in their Cuban vernacular context. With access to old as well as up-to-date texts from as late as 1924, Ortiz drew data from international sources published in German, English, French, Italian, Spanish, and Portuguese, including histories, travel narratives and proto-ethnographies on Africa, South America, and the Caribbean, as well as numerous dictionaries and linguistic studies of Yoruba, Ibo, Kongo, 'Mandingo,' various Amerindian tongues, and Spanish from the Old and New Worlds.

My path in working out a glossary of terms for the 'Day of the Kings' translation was, then, already consummately charted out by the master himself. Clearly, his glossaries were intended as supplements—'secondary works' in his terms—to his 'principal' sociological and ethnographic projects (Ortiz 1924:xiii). Lexicons that he had encountered in the course of more than two decades of research—including some of those present in 'The Day of the Kings'—fill the pages of his *Glosario de Afronegrismos,* to which later readers of Spanish could always turn in order to more fully comprehend the various italicized terms in his more than 115 books and articles on Afro-Cuban subjects (see León and León 1986). Thus, where possible, I began with, or cited, at least, Ortiz's own definitions and etymologies as found in the *Glosario* and in a 1983 revised edition of the 1923 *Catauro de Cubanismos* entitled *Nuevo Catauro de Cubanismos* (Ortiz 1983b). Such references, moreover, provide a degree of historical consistency, indexing some of the terms in question from a 1920 piece with Ortiz's own definitions compiled during the same period. Simultaneously, the very absence of, or the paucity of data for, certain terms also suggests, historically, the gaps in his work during the 1920s, which Ortiz himself, his students, and other scholars would begin to fill with the surge in 'New World Negro' research in the 1930s and 1940s in the Caribbean, South America, and the United States (see Herskovits 1958[1941], 1966). In some cases, interesting developments in Ortiz's own thinking and research discoveries are uncovered in comparisons of his earlier and later discussions of terms, such as *brujo* and *mojiganga.*

In many cases, it is the work of Cuban scholars who built upon Ortiz's prodigious foundations that I have turned to in order to more fully elaborate upon terms found in 'The Day of the Kings,' especially as regards religious traditions: Lydia Cabrera, Argeliers León, Rómulo Lachatañeré, Rafael L. López Valdés, and Enrique Sosa Rodríguez, as well as the Americans

William Bascom and Robert Farris Thompson. Cabrera's three vocabularies (*Anagó: Vocabulario Lucumí*, 1986a; *Vocabulario Congo*, 1984; and *La Lengua Sagrada de Los Ñañigos,* 1988), and such African language dictionaries as Abraham 1946, for example, are indispensable to any elaboration on Ortiz's terminology. However, few scholars inside or outside of Cuba have written, in great depth, on the subject of Carnival in Havana; here the published work of, and considerable consultation with, Judith Bettelheim, has been important to more than several of the carnival entries, such as *gombay*, *mojiganga*, *moka jumbia*, and *tango*.

While I sought to treat each term with respectable attention, my own particular interests in Afro-Cuban society, religion, and material culture, as well as my African Diaspora–wide and trans-Atlantic perspective, led me to elaborate considerably on certain terms. For example, if one is to fully understand Cuban carnival, or any carnival for that matter, one must investigate not only the expressive cultural practices enacted in the 'carnival moment,' but also the historical, social, and institutional foundations of groups of participants in space and time. Therefore, like Roger Bastide, Sidney Mintz and Richard Price, (Bastide 1978; Mintz and Price 1992[1976]), I am particularly interested here in the terms of institutional structure and ethnic identity: *nación*, *tierra*, *juego*, *cabildo*, *carabela*, and the names of particular nations. Nineteenth-century Cuban carnival placed the African 'nations' and their *cabildos* at center stage. If carnival substituted its 'disorder' or 'antistructure' to the 'order' or 'structure' of everyday life, if it 'carnivalized' or 'inverted' social hierarchy, it also counterposed an alternative, counter-hegemonic set of structures, rules, and practices—preserved, newly-established, and transmitted by the African nations (see Alonso 1990, Bakhtin 1984). Thus, ideally, one would want to see a translation of Fernando Ortiz's seminal 1921 article, 'Los Cabildos Afrocubanos,' as the companion piece to the 'Day of the Kings.' It should be considered essential background, if not a kind of conceptual prerequisite, to the 'Day of the Kings.'

Ortiz projected his scholarly enterprise—'our principal . . . work,' as he saw it in 1924, as comprising five major volumes: 1) *The Afro Cuban Underworld: The Black Slaves (Hampa Afrocubana: Los Negros Esclavos)*, 'already completed, which intended to explain the origins of the blacks, the nature of the slave trade, and slavery in Cuba'; 2) *The Free Blacks (Los Negros Horros)*, 'the uppermost characters of the population of color during the slavery period'; 3) *The Black Sorcerers (Los Negros Brujos)*, which was actually published first (1906), but was in the process of a third revision, which 'encompassed the study of Afro-Cuban religion, magic, and superstition'; 4) *Los Negros Curros*, translatable literally as 'the showy blacks,' might best be rendered as the 'Black Signifiers' (see Brown 1989:34–39). Described by

Ortiz as a study of 'the history of delinquency' in Cuba, it was, in fact, an extraordinary work of cultural history and sociolinguistics, exploring the expressive style of an urban free black street subculture in the first half of the nineteenth century in Havana (Ortiz 1986 [1927]); 5) *The Black Ñáñigos* (*Los Negros Ñáñigos*), 'which refers to that African secret society that even exists fully in the Twentieth Century in various Cuban cities' (Ortiz 1924:xiii). Only *Los Negros Esclavos* and *Los Negros Brujos* were published in the era of their writing in book form. *Los Negros Curros* was serialized in *Archivos del Folklore Cubano* in 1927 and later brought out by Editorial de Ciencias Sociales in 1986 in virtually complete form. Still, just about every conceivable theme, if not every written manuscript (significant numbers of unpublished manuscripts, including treatments of the Abakuá, pepper Havana's Ortiz archives) made it out somewhere in the more than 1500 articles in journals and 84 books that constituted his life's work (León and León 1986, see also InterAmericas 1998). If one were to enumerate other major works by Ortiz closely connected to issues of Carnival's cultural performances, including music, dance, gesture, and costume, one would certainly want to include *La Africanía de la Música Folklórica de Cuba* (1950), *Los Bailes y el Teatro de los Negros en el Folklore de Cuba* (1985 [1951]), and *Los Instrumentos de la Música Afrocubana* (1952–55), a massive, five-volume organology, organized alphabetically within a range of generic musical instrument types.

I hope that the translation of 'The Day of the Kings' and the accompanying pieces act as a catalyst to long overdue further study of Afro-Cuban traditions by scholars in diverse fields, building on the extraordinary path cut by Fernando Ortiz, his Cuban students and followers, and a small number of committed foreign researchers.

* (The author accepts no responsibiity for editorial choices or lacunae that appear in this article. Dr. David H. Brown, January 2001.)

Glossary

Abakuá: (creolized Efik). The Afro-Cuban male brotherhood or 'secret society' of Cross River origin (Ejagham and Efik). The term Abakuá is apparently a Cuban creolized rendering of the Efik term, Abakpa, reported to be an an Ekoi (Ejagham) subgroup of the Cross River Area of West Africa (Sosa Rodríguez 1982:397; see also Thompson 1983:228). The Afro-Cuban Abakuá 'society' (*sociedad*), first founded in 1836 in the Barrio of Belén in Havana (Deschamps Chapeaux 1964:97; see *juegos*), is comprised of numerous lodges (often interchangeably called *tierras*, *potencias*, or *juegos*), each of which is governed by a more or less standard set of 25 offices or *plazas* (see Iyamba, Mokongo, Isué). The society and its members are sworn to protect

An Abakuá procession or *beromo* in Havana, led by a costumed *íreme* in pointed headress. The procession members carry their ceremonial staffs and drums, including the plumed *sese* silent drum.

and honor the 'Divine Voice' of Ekue, a manifestation of God, which is embodied in sacred drums. The voice of Ekue (*uyo*) is sounded during *plantes* (initiatory, funerary [*llanto*], or general ceremonies, which include altar building, sacrifices, drumming, call-and-response singing, and elaborate processions), where marvelous masked figures, called *íreme*—pejoratively referred to as '*diablitos*'—emerge from the secret temple space (*famba*) to dance and perform ritual duties. The Abakuá society is unique to the *barrios* of the port cities of Havana and Matanzas provinces—the City of Havana, a number of Havana municipalities, such as Regla, Guanabacoa, Marianao, and Parraga, and the Cities of Matanzas and nearby Cardenas—and has played a significant role in local social control, including labor hiring on the docks from the late nineteenth to mid-twentieth Century (López Valdés 1985). The Abakuá society has been banned, persecuted, or otherwise put under surveillance on and off since its first formal emergence in the mid-1830s. (See Sosa Rodríguez 1982; Cabrera 1970; Cabrera 1975)

aguardiente: (Spanish). A strong rum made from sugar cane. It translates literally as 'fiery water' (*agua-ardiente*). *Aguardiente* was historically associated with the context of slave life on the plantations, where slaves were treated not to the refined rums marketed internationally, but to the cruder, more unrefined products which were strong and fiery and produced on site. According to Hugh Thomas, small distilleries were often integral to the Cuban sugar mills (*ingenios*). The distilleries 'ma[de] *aguardiente* (a cane brandy, much liked by the slaves)' (Thomas 1971:29). If the drinking of *aguardiente* was ever permitted by masters as a kind of 'steam-valve,' notwithstanding, Cuban scholar Fernando G. Campoamor reports that "the masters knew that the *aguardiente* was the spur that piqued the instinct of rebellion, and thus came the 'prohibition against the slaves drinking *aguardiente* and using firearms.'" (Campoamor 1985:49) Indeed, *aguardiente* has come to have a strong association in the urban setting with rough street types, and, in the Afro-Cuban religions, with 'warrior' deities and spirits. Thus, besides the slave plantation, *aguardiente* is associated with the rustics of the countryside, the working classes, the *ñáñigo* and the 'delinquent,' as well as the *guerreros* ('warriors'), personified in the deities Eleguá, Ogún, Ochosi and several others in the Lucumí tradition, as well as many of the 'fierce' and 'strong' spirits of the Palo Monte/Mayombé (Kongo) tradition. *Aguardiente* is used by the Abakuá, specifically in their opening purification rites, along with 'dry wine,' water, basil, and burning incense, as well as day-long drum-dances, which are carefully monitored by the police for outbreaks of fights. In Lucumí it is called *otí*, *otí bembé*, or *otibó* (Cabrera 1986a:285), from the Yoruba term for 'strong liquor' (*otí*; Abraham 1946:530); in Kongo-Cuban it is *malafo* or *malafo misanga* (Cabrera 1984:17); and in the Abakuá ritual language it is *emboco ocoró* (Campoamor 1985:49) or *ocoro makua* (Cabrera 1988:455). The Palo Monte spirits specifically demand *aguardiente* and strong cigars when they manifest in *misas* (masses), and use the strong liquor as part of difficult cleansings of bad influences (*despojos* and *rompimientos*). *Aguardiente's* association with Africanness and the lower classes finds its metaphor in the rank and color of a certain class of sugars made available to slaves on the plantations: the white refined sugar product (*blanco*) was produced by slave labor and exported to satisfy Europe's sweet tooth while the lowest, darkest leftovers were given to the slaves themselves. The latter – the most coarse and unrefined sugars – called *cucurucho*, *mascabado* or *raspadura*, was 'the sugar of the poor' (Thomas 1971:41). For an in-depth treatment of sugar and social metaphor in Cuba, see Ortiz 1983a[1940]. Clearly, *aguardiente* was part and parcel of the 'license' of Carnival day, but also the potential 'disorder' of its street activities.

aguinaldo: (Spanish, lit. 'tip' or gratuity). *Aguinaldo* was the gift of money demanded and received by pre-Lenten (including Christmas) festival maskers from onlookers along the road and up in urban balconies. While *aguinaldo* was probably collected throughout the city, where it could be petitioned for at every window and gate, the climax of this practice took place in the *solar* of the great Palace of the Captain General of the Island (located on the Plaza de Armas in Old Havana), a courtyard filled with trees, with balconies looming overhead on all four sides. This is how Argeliers León describes the scene that took place annually here: 'The *cabildos* took to the streets on the 'Day of the Kings'. Among them, some remained authorized to show up at the Palace of the Captain General to dance before the authorities who watched them from the interior balconies, and to receive *aguinaldo* that the governor gave them and the donations [*dádivas*] that the gentlemen tossed from up high in order to see them run and throw themselves on the

Aguinaldo is a ritual gift, usually of money, received by festival masqueraders. Detail from Victor Patricio Landulze, *Día de Reyes en La Habana.*

money' (León 1984a:36). In Cuba, and throughout the Caribbean, the collection of money by maskers, often following more or less extended performances, is well documented. One of the most successful maskers in this regard was the stilt-dancer, Moko Jumby, who was able to collect money from elevated balcony observers. In Jamaican Jonkonnu, the collection of money was integral to the performance and represented a significant seasonal source of income for performers. According to Judith Bettelheim, 'processions advanced to centers of patronage or authority in the neighborhood' Following the climax, 'the performers accepted donations before marching on in procession' (Nunley and Bettelheim 1988:44). Roger Abrahams writes that British West Indies mumming dramas played during Christmas and many other 'Christmas Sports' are 'rewarded by spectators throwing coins at performers.' In connection with such other 'sports,' there are 'begging speeches or songs' (Abrahams 1968:192). In this way the members of the troupe 'earn their Christmas money' (Abrahams 1983:16). More importantly, Daniel Crowley suggests, 'the largest number and the finest masques come from the yards of the labouring and artisan classes, financial support is virtually a prerequisite to Carnival participation' (Crowley 1956). At the same time, at least one Jamaican performer explained that this traditionalized practice has had some unjustified stigma attached to it: 'All of these groups are from the poorer classes; they are from run-down areas in the city, and because of this when they go out and perform and ask for money, people get the idea that they are all beggars. But on the whole, they are much better behaved than the ordinary lot in the area. They have a social standing; they are Jonkonnu men' (Nunley and Bettelheim 1988:42). In Trinidad, if Carnival money was 'earned' by various maskers, at least one mask radically redefined the transaction, priding himself in 'robbing' his 'victims,' often following ten-minute terrifying speeches of stylized intimidation. Crowley speculates that these speeches were high among the factors that preserved the robber masks while others had become extinct by 1956; the robbers managed to be 'self-supporting,' bringing in 'larger than average sums' by 'robbing' during the Carnival. Given such pan-Caribbean evidence, one might see *aguinaldo* as a polyvalent concept. It might have connoted a type of 'gift' (Mauss 1967) bestowed by one in power and with wealth to one of a lower status, a client, townsperson, or slave. Yet, if from one point of view *aguinaldo* represented condescension to a socially inferior recipient, it also appears to have played a role in status reversal and an affirmation of personal power on the part of the recipient. Might *aguinaldo* be seen in terms of the power of extraction—the ability to exact tribute on festival day—in the ongoing negotiation between classes that is ritualized during the Carnival moment (see Kinser 1990; Alonso 1990; and see Richard Price's discussion of the polyvalent meanings of gift exchange between Suriname maroons and Dutch colonists in Price 1990:43–46).

amirifimo: (creolized W. African, Cross River). Ortiz uses this term in relation to the colorful suit worn by the standard-bearer of the Abakuá, Mokongo. The term is likely an alternate spelling, or transposed version, of the term *afomiremo*, meaning 'ritual suit of the *iremo* [sic], in the making of which the hand of a woman may not intrude. From *afo*, clothes [*ropa*]'. Within contemporary Abakuá ritual itself, however, Mokongo—the second, or in some cases first, in command—does not formally represent himself in an *íreme* costume; though Mokongo, or any other initiate or officer, may, at an appropriate point, don a *saco de baile* (the *íreme's* hooded masquerade dance costume) in order to dance outside the lodge's secret temple. Yet he is clearly referred to as the *abanderado* ('standard-bearer') of the Abakuá (see Mocombo [sic] below). It may be that Mokongo's 'colorful suit' refers to the embroidered or painted capes customarily worn by Abakuá dignitaries within their *potencias*, or else to some other special carnival wardrobe. Finally (and here we would benefit from knowledgeable etymological analysis), if the *amirifimo* was, in fact, part of the trappings of Mokongo, it is suggestive that the term is similar to 'Efiméremo' and 'Efimeremé,' which appear in Lydia Cabrera's Abakuá vocabulary. Both allude to high official personages such as kings, magistrates, captains and judges (Cabrera 1988:150–151).

anaquillé: refers to 'carved female figure atop pole [that] acted as guardian figures for *cabildo* groups' during public celebrations of saints or at Christmas time and to the dance associated with it (Bettelheim 1988:137) (see illustration of a woman carrying a staff topped by a dressed doll, appearing as figure 9 in the 1960 republication 'La Antigua Fiesta': Ortiz 1960[1920]:22). Ortiz defines *anaquillé* as a 'dance, today no longer in use' (1924:25), and offers a popular song that connects the 'dance' and the figure itself: *al anaquillé como baila el muñeco* (how the doll dances to the *anaquillé*). The doll, Ortiz elaborates, was an 'idol or figure belonging to the African rites, at the end of a stick carried by the blacks in some of their ceremonial or ritual dances.' Ortiz posits three possible origins for the *anaquillé*: the 'fetishes' representing the dead, carried in Dahomean festivals; 'the effigies that the blacks of Old Calabar carry in the biennial festival of the driving out of demons, the doll [figures] of which are called *Nabikém*'; and the dancewands of the Lucumí religion in Cuba (1960[1920]:40–41). Though the origin of the term *anaquillé* remains unclear, Ortiz was, nevertheless, astute in locating this object within the spectrum of transatlantic dancewands and other carved figures, such as the *bocio* sculptures (called 'idols' and 'fetishes' in the eighteenth- and nineteenth-century ethnographic literature) of spiritual power, sorcery, social protection, and transformation, which Suzanne Blier has recently documented for the former Kingdom of Dahomey (Republic of Benin; see Blier 1995; Ortiz 1973b[1906]:26–49,84–85; Verger 1954,1993:*passim*; Drewal et al. 1989:*passim*; Thompson 1983:3–95). In the 'Day of the Kings' illustrations, Ortiz juxtaposes the *anaquillé* to a Cuban Lucumí dancewand (*oshé*) for the thundergod Changó from his own collection (see 1960[1920]). He also astutely hypothesized the figures' possible connection with spirits of the dead. Women dressed in their festive finery—satin and petticoated skirts—still carry such figures in Cuban religious processions, for example, the lavishly-dressed plastic and wood dolls, draped with beadwork, carried in the festival of the Virgin of Regla, Havana, which was reenacted after a long hiatus, on September 7, 1999. These female dolls were said to represent the 'spiritual side of Yemayá.' That is, they are spirits of the deceased (*muertos/eguns*), who, 'in life,' were followers of this Yoruba deity or her Catholic counterpart, the Virgin of Regla.

Arará: (creolized Fongbe [from the Fon of the former Kingdom of Dahomey, now the Republic of Benin]). The term is believed to derive from name of the Dahomean town, Arada or Allada (see Thompson 1983:164), applied as a generic ethonym to the *negros de nación* (African-born slaves) who embarked from that region. In Cuba, numerous Arará subgroups, each with their own distinct brotherhoods and institutional identities, appeared, such as Arará Sabalú (derived presumably from the town of Savalu), Arará Magino (from the Mahi ethnic group), Arará Cuévano, Arará abopá, Arará agicón, Arará cuatros ojos ['four eyes'], Arará nezeve, and Arará Dajomé (see Ortiz 1987[1916]:42–43; Viñueza 1986:23) According to Fernando Ortiz, three notable Arará *cabildos* of Havana—Dajomé, Magino, and Sabalú—'were destroyed in the political persecutions during the government of President Menocal' ([1913–1921]; Ortiz 1952,III:336). However, strong manifestations of Magino traditions are still found on the outskirts of the city of Matanzas, in the towns of Jovellanos, Máximo Gómez, and Perico. Distinct Sabalú and Cuevano manifestations existed historically in Matanzas, but are now said to be extinct (interview with Maximiliano Baró Cespedes [with Francisco Zamora Chirino], 1 August 1989). However, the Arará Dajomé tradition of Jovellanos has been maintained since the nineteenth century by the Baró family in the Cabildo San Manuel, under the direction of Maximiliano Baró Cespedes, grandson of the founder of the Cabildo, Esteban Baró. Magino traditions differ from those of the Dajomé in drum rhythms, pronunciations of ritual words and song lyrics, as well as drum types (see Viñueza 91–152). The basic Arará 'pantheon' of *forduces* (alt. *fodduces*, from the Fongbe, Ewe, Mahi, Aja term *vodun*, see Blier 1995:37–40) is hierarchically patterned like that of the Cuban Yoruba-Lucumí, and the deities possess analogous roles, characteristics, and iconography. The following are the principal *fodduces*, listed in correspondence to the Lucumí *orichas*: Jurajó-Eleguá; Ajuaggún-Ogún; Aggé (Aggué)-Ochosi; Ajosí-Obatalá; Addañó-Oyá; Ferequete-Yemayá; Gebiosó-Changó; Masé-Ochún; Alua-Babalú Ayé (Galzagorry Madan 1983; see also Martínez Furé 1979:79–102; Ortiz 1987 [1916]:42–43; Viñueza 1986:*passim*).

babalao: (Yoruba-Lucumí; also *babalawo*). The term translates as 'Father of the Secret,' and refers to the initiated members of the all-male *regla* (ritual organization) of the diviners of the *Ifá* system of Yoruba provenance (see Bascom 1952). *Babalawos*, priests of the deity Orunmila (alt. Orula), are entitled to use the *tablero de Ifá* and the *ekuelé* divining chain. *Babalawo* is used generally to refer to *Orunmila's* initiated priests, as distinct from *santero*—the priests of the other multifarious *orichas of the pantheon*, on the one hand; yet, within the Ifá hierarchy, the term *babalawo*, strictly speaking, may be considered the lowest rank among initiated priests of Orula. According to some, in this latter sense *babalawo* refers to one who has not previously been initiated into Santeriá, and thus can divine, but cannot 'enter' the 'room' of Santeriá initiation. The *oluo*, on the other hand, according to some, has 'made *ocha*' in Santeriá prior to his initiation into Ifá, and is considered of higher rank. *Oluo* is also used to refer to *babalawos* who have received 'The Knife' ceremony (*guanaldo*), which permits them to initiate others into Ifá (see Bascom 1952; Bascom 1969; Brown 1989:ch.3).

bacumbys: (Central West African, Spanish, and/or Amerindian, see *Gombay*). The term appears to be synonymous with *cucumby*, as found in Brazil. Ortiz's source (Brazilian scholar Raimundo Nina Rodrigues) refers to them as carnival figures 'dressed in feathers. . . .' This may indicate that they were 'Indian' (known as *caboclo*) maskers who, as Crowley notes, were frequent participants in the 'courts' of the *congadas*, that is, among the hierarchy of 'Kings' and 'Queens' represented in the carnival dramas (Crowley 1984:17). See *cucumby*.

Bambara: (also known as Bamana). A major African ethnic group localized on the upper Niger River in Mali, Senegal, and Guinea. The Bambara speak a language of the Mande branch of the Niger-Congo language group. Historically '[t]hey founded two separate empires, with capitals at Kaarta and Segu (Ségou), which controlled large areas in the Western Sudan from the seventeenth to the nineteenth century . . .' (Bascom 1973:31–33). In Cuba during the slave period they were referred to under the generic 'Mandinga' ethnic rubric, as were the 'Iolof' and 'Fula' (see Ortiz 1987 [1916]: 43,48,50,52).

Befana: (Spanish). Ortiz defines the term as a "custom of the Tuscan Romagna, Abruzzi, Sicily, etc. that still exists today and, according to Grimm and Frazer, is a relic of the 'expulsion of evil, personified by an old hag.'" The figure is related to the festival that was practiced in Spain and Cuba, called the 'Domingo de la Vieja' ('sunday of the Old Woman'). It takes place on the second Sunday of Lent (*cuaresma*), and is celebrated with the same ethos of 'burlesque as if it were Carnival.' According to Ortiz, 'Lent is represented with the figure of an old woman [*vieja*] with seven feet, that symbolize its seven weeks [in fact the six Sundays following Ash Wednesday and prior to Easter Sunday]. The old woman contrasts with the youth [*juventud*] of the Three Meat Days before Ash Wednesday [*Carnestolendas*],' and is a 'sign of withdrawal [*recogimiento*] and fasting.' The custom was also, and apparently earlier, also known by the Spanish Peninsular expression, 'dividing the old woman' (*partir la vieja*), and 'meant the halving of Lent,' as the name for the dancing and festivity (I will note, however, that the second Sunday of Lent, 40 days total, is not exactly its 'middle'). The custom remained, however, in Cuban custom as the 'Domingo de la Vieja' (see Ortiz 1983b:225).

botija: (Spanish; literally, a 'clay jug'; alt. *botijo, botijuela, bunga*; see Ortiz 1955:340–362.). In the festival performance context, it refers to a musical instrument, otherwise also used in the traditional Cuban Son musical form. In Cuba, a 'fat' oil jug of barro was optimal. The Cuban equivalent of the instrument used by Southern U.S. African-American 'jugbands,' the *botija* is a clay vessel that, when blown across its opening, produces bass-like tones (*tun, pun, dun*; León 1984:119). The tones can be varied by varying the opening with the palm of the hand. Some *botijas* featured a hole in the side, as well. The jug was later supplanted by the contrabass in the Cuban Son orchestra, according to Argeliers León. Fernando Ortiz believed the instrument was of wide African origin, found in West and Central West Africa, and traced its name, *bunga,* to a string of related Kongo words, such as *mbungu, mvunga, evunga,* and *vunga* ('low sound'), as well as *mbungua* ('cup' or 'goblet'; see Ortiz 1955:352).

Brichi: (Creolized Cross-River; alt. 'Breeche' or 'Briche' in Cuba). It was used during the slave trade to describe one of the numerous ethnic groups categorized in Cuba under the generic 'Carabalí' rubric—the term for Africans believed to have embarked at the Old Calabar slave port (Ortiz 1987 [1916], p. 44; *Carabalí* reverses the 'l' and 'r' of Calabar in the Cuban creolizing idiom). Enrique Sosa categorizes the Brichi specifically as an Ibo subgroup (Sosa Rodríguez 1982:71; see also Cabrera 1988:129). See *Carabalí.*

brujería: (Spanish). Commonly translated as 'witchcraft' or 'sorcery,' it has been used pejoratively by writers and the dominant public to refer to the supposedly malign ritual 'works' (*trabajos*) of Afro-Cuban religious practitioners, works that are often anything but malign, such as obligatory sacrifices (*ebos*). However, it is also used by many practitioners themselves, to indicate the 'strong' defensive, and sometimes, offensive, 'works' they do for other people, and often is used to refer to works effected through the Palo Monte (Kongo-Cuban) religion. A seeming epidemic of *brujería,* as well as *ñáñiguismo* (see below), served as a pretext for a massive more than 20-year campaign of persecution of Afro-Cubans by the government after the foundation of the Republic (1902). *Brujería* was associated with a dangerous, primitive atavism within the new Republic, and (as in the case of European blood libel against the Jews) was believed to be the motive for a string of alleged ritual murders of white children, for which the accused, in fact, innocent black Cubans, were put to death (Helg 1995:80–139; Castellanos 1916; Roche y Monteagudo 1925). See *brujo.*

brujo: (Spanish.; f. *bruja*). It is defined by the Real Academia Española (noun) as 'a [person] who, according to general opinion, has a pact with the devil, through which he/she does extraordinary things' (1984:217). The term has a long history in the Spanish language. According to Ortiz (the following is an excerpted loose translation), it was in common usage in the literature of the Spanish Inquisition, and referred to some characteristics that were found in the Afro-American religions, such as magic, exorcisms, possession, ecstasy, sorcery, conjuring, amulets, maleficia, ritual dances, but also to such aberrations as cannibalism . . . broomriding, orgies with the Devil, witches' sabbaths, deformed demon children, and other wonders of the Catholic theology that were never [in fact] known among blacks. With the transplanting of the religion of the whites to the Americas, individuals outside the Holy Communion were considered 'infidels' (if they had never been baptized, that is, the Indians, Moors, and Jews); 'heretics' or 'apostates' (Christians who had reneged or had accepted other dogmas [Protestants, Huguenots, and members of other sects]); and, finally, *magos* or 'magicians' who were divided into two groups, *brujos* and *hechiceros*—both being seen to have 'direct dealings with demons in order to produce supernatural miracles against the mandates of the church.' 'Given the general ignorance of the issues,' Ortiz continues, 'the term *brujería* prevailed in signifying the magic of the blacks, on the one hand, and the word *hechicería*, for the magic of the whites, on the other hand. In the Antilles, beginning in the sixteenth century, the mysterious rites of the blacks—with their strange liturgies, exotic music, and unintelligible chants—came to be described with the term *brujería* that had been applied in Spain to analogous rites that were persecuted beginning in 1484 when Pope Innocent VIII issued his *Summis desiderantes affectibus*, initiating the Holy Inquisition.' Interestingly, Ortiz points out that, if to the white Catholic, all the cults of the blacks were *brujería*—'abominable things inspired by the demons for the ruin of human being'—it is also the case that one African-based religion has historically used the term against another. For the *babalawo* (Yoruba-Cuban diviner), he says, the practitioner of *mayombé* or *kimbisa* (Kongo-Cuban practices also called 'Palo Monte') is a *brujo*. And at the same time both the Catholic priest and the Yoruba priest used the term *judio* ('jewish' or 'unbaptized') to describe the latter practices. Within the Kongo Cuban practices themeselves, according to Lydia Cabrera, are found two strains, 'Palo Cristiano' and 'Palo Judio' ('unbaptized Palo'), the latter being regarded as less restrained, more dangerous, and possibly more malevolent. I can attest from my own fieldwork that *brujo*/*bruja* is used by practitioners—some of whom are both *santeros* and *paleros*—to refer to certain Congo spirits and to *orichas* in certain 'paths' (for example, Ochún) who are fierce and/or who work with powerful potions and medicines. At the time of his writing (1937), Ortiz notes that the term Santería had replaced the term *brujería*, at least, it seems, to denote the Yoruba-derived practices. A more 'plausible' term, according to Ortiz, "it had early figured in the dictionaries to signify those who practiced a superstitious cult of images, and without doubt was first applied by the same Catholic clerics to the blacks who in their *cabildos* venerated 'La Mersé' (Virgen de las Mercedes as Obatalá), 'La Caridad' (Virgen de la Caridad as Ochún) or Santa Barbara (as Changó), a term that suggested something of contempt toward and divergence from good ritual conduct 'as God commands.'" However, even in its pejorative sense, *Santero* did not have the defamatory content of *brujo*. According to Ortiz, historically, the Church saw the *santero* as one who is in 'error,' yet who worships good celestial entities; the *brujo* is 'perverse,' and worships infernal and malevolent entities. In response to criticism by Rómulo Lachatañeré for use of the term *brujo* (*Los Negros Brujos*, 1906), a volume intended as part of a trilogy entitled *la Hampa Afro-Cubana* ('the Afro-Cuban Underworld' or *mala vida* [the 'bad life' of the 'other half']), Ortiz defended himself, insisting that he "purposely used the expression—technically and philosophically inappropriate, but vernacularly and socially precise; since if it is true that it expressed a confusion, this same confusion is already a social phenomenon that it was important to clear up. And later, in the course of my essay I tried to go on to separate, within the class called *brujos*, the functions of priest, doctor, and diviner and, afterwards, the criminal elements that at times could manifest themselves in those activities: not only strictly *brujos* or practitioners of 'black magic' but the 'anti-social' practices of charlatans and quacks—found among blacks and whites." (See Ortiz 1937 and Ortiz 1973b[1906].)

cabildo: (Spanish). From the Latin *capitulum*, it refers to a 'body or community of an ecclesiastic order of a church . . . '; 'the *ayuntamiento* or corporation of municipal government'; a 'group of brethren of certain *cofradías* [religious brotherhoods]'; or a 'corporate group or guild [of] mutual aid' (Real Academia Española 1984:229). The Afro-Cuban use of *cabildo* partakes of all of these senses. Grouped by putative African ethnic identity (*nación*), Africans and their descendants gathered in mutual-aid/religious societies called *cabildos* beginning as early as the sixteenth century in Cuba. (See *nación* for discussion of *cabildo* policy as articulated by the authorities). Argeliers León writes that the 'blacks called them *cabildos*, choosing this word that had great significance in the colonial Spanish government. The term *cabildo de negros* came to mean [also] an assembly of blacks' (León 1984a:11). Strictly speaking, the term *cabildo* did not always refer to a *religious* organization, but could also refer to a social 'club' or mutual aid society, whereas the term *cofradía* specifically pointed to a more or less official religious brotherhood associated with a particular church and its patron (León 1984a:35). However, in Cuba the term *cabildo* was more commonly used, and could encompass both senses. With respect to the African identities of the various *cabildos*, Rafael L. López Valdés writes, 'The names adopted by the *cabildos* evoked the African origin of their members, utilizing ethnic denominations in currency in the discourse of the slave trade: the Cabildo Arará Magino (Mahi, Fon) is the oldest known, since it already existed in 1691.' During the eighteenth century, documents mentioned *cabildos* of the Apapá (Ibibio, 1714), Mina Guagui (Watchi, Ewe, 1731), Yolofe (Wolof, 1738), Lucumí (in great measure groups of conglomerated Yoruba, 1778), Carabalí Isuama Begre Abate Singlaba (Isuama, Ibo, 1783), and Carabalí Isuama Isieque (Isuama, Ibo, 1792; see López Valdés 1987:9–10). Historically, the Cuban *cabildos* were modeled upon the traditional corporations (*cofradías* and *cabildos*), which had organized Spanish society under the Church since the fourteenth century in Seville. In the minds of the Cuban colonial government authorities, grouping the slave population into separate *cabildos* represented a 'divide and conquer' strategy (see *nación* below), which had cultural, as well

A Carnival procession with a *cabildo* queen under a ceremonial umbrella preceded by *diablitos*. Detail from Victor Patricio Landaluze, *Día de Reyes en La Habana.*

as political, dimensions. As a hegemonic cultural strategy, the gradual, projected Hispanicization and Catholicization of *cabildo* members would serve the purposes of long term social control. As early as 1755, the Church in Havana instituted devotions of Catholic saints in numerous *cabildos*. Such saints as Santa Barbara and Santa Rita in Cuba, and Our Lady of the Rosary and São Benidicto in Brazil, became their official and overt patrons, while African deities may have remained their more covert patrons (see Ortiz 1921; Brown 1989:ch.1, Thompson 1983:18). Pedro Deschamps Chapeaux reproduces the banner (*bandera*) of a Lucumí *cabildo* bearing the date 1820 (currently housed in Havana's Casa de Africa Fernando Ortiz Collection): 'La Sociedad de Socorros Mutuos Nación Lucumi de Santa Barbara, Año 1820' ('society of Mutual Aid, Lucumí Nation of Santa Barbara, 1820'). The Yoruba thundergod, Changó, was, undoubtedly, the *cabildo's* covert patron. If the organizing of the *cabildos* 'from above' sought control through the divide-and-conquer strategy, it had the effect of preserving and reproducing African-based and counter-hegemonic values. Africans utilized this 'new social framework'—the legally legitimate corporate grouping of the *cabildo*—to reconstruct and transmit ethnic identity and cultural/religious practices, not to mention to organize insurrectionary movements (see Bastide 1978:chs.2,5; Mintz and Price 1992[1976]; Brown 1989:ch.1; Scott 1985:264–278). The *cabildos* were internally organized in hierarchical fashion, headed by leaders who inherited, or were elected to, titled offices ('kings' and 'queens'), and they were established in their own houses. As a 'mutual aid society,' this institution provided in times of sickness and death, held masses for deceased members, collected funds to buy nation-brethren out of slavery, and also held regular dances and diversions, and sponsored carnival processions (*comparsas*) on saints' feast days. *Cabildo* leaders – 'kings'—guided, disciplined, and inspired members, who were their immediate 'subjects'; the kings were 'accredited ambassadors' representing their 'nations' to the island's governor, the Captain General. In effect, this subordinated political structure recalls West African colonial 'indirect rule,' which opens the question of a negotiation of power and interdependence between the government and *cabildo* administrations. *Cabildo* leaders were supported by a 'court' consisting of a 'queen' or two (second in rank) and lower-ranking chiefs such as the *abanderado* ('standard bearer') and *mayor de plaza* ('chief of ceremonies') whose titles derived from formal military hierarchy. Later, many *cabildos* adopted the titles of republican government and civic organizations: 'President,' 'Vice President,' etc. Either the king or a specially-elected *tesorero* ('treasurer') collected, guarded, and disbursed *cabildo* funds which came in the form of monthly dues (*cuota mensual*), donations, alms, bequests, and fines (*multas*) imposed on wayward members by the elected leader. Treasury funds were often used to purchase nation brethren out of slavery (Bremer 1853,II:380–81). Public feast days, such as the 'Day of the Kings,' meant the 'coming out' or 'outdooring' (Marks 1974) of internal *cabildo* organization, authority, and codes of loyalty under the distinctive *banderas* of the nations, representing, in Marks' terms, the 'Africanization' of the streets. With the cessation of the slave trade (1865–70, though illegal after 1820 in the Spanish possessions) and emancipation (1880), the ethnic makeup of the *cabildos* changed and their functions shifted (see Scott 1985 for the best description and analysis of this transformation). It is clear that *cabildo* organization offered the foundation for the consolidation and emergence of the Afro-Cuban religions (Santería, Ifá, Palo Monte, Arará) and the Abakuá brotherhoods. By the twentieth century, the old-style *cabildos* were transformed into the Afro-Cuban 'houses' or 'house-temples' (*casa-templos*) of religious practice, in which 'ethnic' identity gave way to initiatory rites of passage and fictive kinship as the criterion of membership (Bastide 1972:95; Brown 1989:73–83; Murphy 1988:33; Palmié 1993). The term *cabildo* is often still used among Afro-Cubans to refer to religious 'houses.'

Canga Cafú: (possibly creolized Yoruba, exact origin unclear). In Ortiz's 'Dia de los Reyes' text, this figure appears as a masquerader who Escolástico Gallardo describes as a 'black buffoon' that dances the 'half-frenzied' *o'-ñaña-'o*. Ortiz's *Glosario de Afronegrismos* defines *Cafú* vaguely as a 'personage of afrocuban folklore.' The compound term looks to be related to others Ortiz provides in the entry for *Cafú*: *Cafunga*, *Cacafú*, *Cacanfú*, *Canfu* and *Cacanfunga*. Ortiz claims that the Lucumíes in Cuba used the expression, 'murió como Cacanfú,' that is to say, 'he died valiantly.' He suggests that the term passed to other groups, where, for example, among the *mandingas*, *achantis*, and others, *kanfú* is a 'title that is given to persons of great respect,' including to priests, and often connoting 'prophet.' Ortiz suggests, at the same time, that the word resonates with other African lexicons from the Mandinga and Congo (Ortiz 1924:86–93). Ultimately, however, the salad of etymology here does not bring us any closer to understanding the nature of the *Canga Cafú* as a carnival figure in Cuba. If the figure bears any relation to the Yoruba-Lucumí, it would seem unlikely that his dance would carry a name that, in other contexts, was apparently linked to the Abakuá of Efik/Ejagham origin (see *ñáña* and *ñáñigo* below).

capataces/reyes del cabildo: (Spanish; lit. 'boss' or 'overseer'/'kings and queens of the *cabildo*'). These were the leaders and organizers, elected or hereditary, of the Afro-Cuban religious mutual aid societies (see *cabildo*).

Carabalí: (West African/creolized Cross River). The generic ethnic rubric applied to enslaved Africans who embarked from the West African port of Old Calabar near the mouth of the Cross River. Their actual origins likely extended westward across the Bight of Bonny to the Niger Delta, eastward into Cameroon, and some distance inland. Linguistic creolization transposed the consonants 'r' and 'l' to produce 'Carabalí' from Calabar. The term was usually suffixed with a specific subgroup name, such as Isuama, Olugo, Bibí, Brícamo, Briche (alt. Brichi), Efó (Ekoi-Ejagham), Efí (Ibibio-Efik), and Orú (Oron). Subgroups with compound names had their own *cabildos* in many Cuban cities. For example, there were the Cabildo Carabalí Isuama and Carabalí Olugo in Santiago de Cuba, and the Cabildo Carabalí Brícamo Apapa Efí of Havana, out of which emerged the first Abakuá lodge, Efik Butón, in 1836. (See Ortiz 1987[1916]:45 and Sosa Rodríguez 1982:ch.2.)

carabela: (Atlantic creole term with African, Spanish, Portuguese roots). During the slavery period in Cuba it referred to Africans who came on the same slave ship, and was used as a term of fictive kinship comparable to the Afro-Jamaican understanding of 'shipmate' and the Suriname Maroons' term *sippi*, 'first used between people who had actually shared the experience of transport in a single vessel; later it began to be used between slaves who belonged to a single plantation, preserving the essential notion of fellow sufferers who have a special bond. . . ,' according to Sidney Mintz and Richard Price. "Today 'sippi' (now 'sibi') continues to designate a special non-biological dyadic relationship with very similar symbolic content." *Sippi* and *mati* (pron. may-ti, as in 'mate'), also found in Suriname, and *batiment* in Haiti, are pidgin/creole terms based in English lexicon, while in Brazil and Trinidad the terms *malungo* and *malongue*, respectively, are apparently African-based terms (Mintz, Price 1992[1970]:43–44). All would be synonymous with the African-American figurative use of 'brother' and 'sister,' not to mention the African-American special understanding of the expression: 'we come from different places but we're all in the same boat now.' All of these help us gloss the Afro-Cuban *carabela*. Ortiz traces the term etymologically to a Congo phrase, *Kala-belo*. *Kala*, according to Ortiz's breakdown, means to 'be,' 'live,' 'inhabit,' 'reside,' and *bela* 'part of a population,' a 'grouping of houses in a city' or 'neighborhood.' Thus, 'kala-belo' could have meant 'neighbor of a barrio,' and corresponds to the term 'paisano,' in Ortiz's reckoning (Ortiz 1983b:124–25). Still, if the term can claim some African origin, it may also have 'remodeled'/been remodeled by the Spanish and Portuguese term *carabela* (or *caravela*), meaning a boat or craft (Real Academia Española 1984:269). This interesting possibility nicely carries Ortiz's etymology in the direction of the 'shipmate' connotation. Finally, *Carabela* is frequently used by practitioners of the Kongo-Cuban religions to refer to certain Congo spirits—the spirits of deceased Africans who, of course, endured the Middle Passage (my fieldwork, and personal communication with Judith Bettelheim, fall 1989). A *carabela*, in this last sense, is symbolized by a skull and crossbones, or represented by a picture or statue of an 'old African,' often dressed in burlap.

Celador: (Spanish). A guard. Apparently a particular unit or class of the Cuban colonial police.

cohetes chinos, saltapericos, siquitraques: (Spanish) All three are types of fireworks, forms of carnival's 'popular pyrotechnics,' in Ortiz's terms. The first is a 'Chinese rocket'; the second is a 'deafening rocket' that 'creeps and skips'; the third is a 'rocket that explodes and bursts with repeated detonations.' The last was called in standard Spanish *triquitraque* (Ortiz 1983b:442,448). Such explosives may have been connected to the growing Chinese presence in Cuba (for exapmle, Chinese rockets); however, both the Abakuá and Palo Monte rites feature the use of exploding gunpowder—the Congo as a form of divination, and the Abakuá as a form of *rompimiento*, breaking open the road for ceremonies.

collares de hormillas de botones: (Spanish). These necklaces strung with 'buttons' were essentially disks of wood or bone or seeds. The latter is a very common form of African necklace, such as the Yoruba *lágídígba*, a heavy dense strand of black disks (Abraham 1946:401) derived from a particular seed sliced crosswise.

collares de maní: (Spanish, object of African origin). They are necklaces strung with a kind of peanut (*maní* or *manises* [pl.]; in Cuba, the particular peanut was *Arachis hypogaea*, Lin. of the Leguminosa family, see Rodríguez Herrera 1959,II:226–7). Ortiz's *Glosario* reports *maní* as a Congo term, and that it was a plant imported from Africa to the Island (Ortiz 1924:322–323).

In Cuba, the street vendors of toasted *maní* (*maniseros*), with their colorful *pregones* (calls), inspired many a popular tune (Rodríguez Herrera 1959,II:226–27); and, according to some researchers, *maní* also referred to a popular martial art cognate with the Afro-Brazilian *capoeira* (personal communications with Robert Farris Thompson and C. Daniel Dawson). In the Lucumí religious setting, the *maní* is sacred to Babalú Ayé (deity of skin disease and patron of the poor and infirm), where it is called *epá* or *efá*. In the Kongo-Cuban ritual language, it is called *mindo* and *gúba*. *Maní* is used among Afro-Cubans to combat epidemics and as an aphrodisiac (Cabrera 1983[1954]:484). *Gúba* is cognate with the African-American secular usage of *goober* for 'peanut,' and, in the religious setting, as part of *goober-dust*, a magical powder.

comparsas: (Spanish). According to Judith Bettelheim, '[a] *comparsa* is a larger group of *conga* drummers accompanied by paired male and female dancers as well as by smaller groups of line dancers performing a specific choreographed routine' during carnival (A *conga* is a 'small group of musicians who all play the same rhythm and are followed by neighborhood residents, who dance through the streets with identifying flags or banners'). 'A *comparsa* often includes elements of the *cabildo* . . . such as a King and Queen and decorated banners and *farolas* with specific, identifiable iconography. In Santiago de Cuba, the older, traditional Carnival groups are known as *comparsas*, while new groups are called *paseos*. *Comparsas* are traditionally organized by neighborhood, and are united by ancestral ties. . . . A *paseo* is a special sub-category of *comparsa*. Usually produced and directed by an individual, the *paseo*'s name is 'owned' by the individual director/producer who can alter its organization, hire different musicians, and manage its income' (Bettelheim 1988a:137).

congado: (creolized Kongo term; also *congada*). Roger Bastide writes of this carnival form in Brazil: It is a '[f]olk drama on African themes (tribal warfare, embassies, death and resurrection of a prince). Mario de Andrade has described these as dramatic ballets interspersed with songs and spoken dialogue' (Bastide 1978:473). Noted as early as 1721 in Brazil, it was associated with the feast day of Our Lady of the Rosary (Nossa Senhora do Rosario), at which time elections of the black kings and queens of the religious brotherhoods (*irmandades*) were held. 'The dances that accompanied the coronations were known as *congadas*, *cucumbys*, *ticumbi*, or *turundu*, depending on the region. They amounted to a theatrical performance consisting of several parts': A.1) the entrance of dancers and the arrival of the king; A.2) a royal procession through the streets, dancing outside the church and the houses of the dignitaries; B.1) the 'embassy': 'Queen Ginga . . . sends an ambassador to the king, sometimes on a mission of war, sometimes of peace. Even if their intent is peaceful, the clumsiness of the king's ministers and the hot-headedness of Prince Suena precipitate war between the Congo and the army of Queen Ginga. The Prince is taken prisoner and sentenced to death'; C.1) 'The third act recounts the death and resurrection of the prince. The queen, grieving over her son's death, summons the *feiticeiro*, (priest-magician) who goes in search of his body"; C.2.) In the final act the fighting begins again. . . . The festival ends with more dancing in which the Immaculate Virgin of the Rosary is of course not forgotten' (Bastide 1978:120–125).

Congo: (alt. Kongo [see Thompson 1983:ch.2]). A generic ethonym used in Cuba to refer to 'Bantu' Africans from Central West Africa, that is, present-day Congo-Brazzaville/Republic of Congo (former Zaire)/Angola. During the slave period it bore suffixes to indicate more precise ethnic identity, including 'Congos Reales' (Royal Congos), Mumboma, Musundi, Mondongo, Cabinda, Mayombe, Benguela, Loango, and even Mozambique (Bantu east Africa; see Ortiz 1987[1916]:45–46). Many had their own *cabildos*. The term 'Congo' also is/was used to refer to the ritual language used within the Afro-Cuban religion called Palo Monte (see Cabrera 1984). 'Congo(s)' also refers to the spirits of deceased Africans who were Congos 'in life,' and may have 'worked' within the Palo Monte (or Mayombe) religion. Such spirits populate the Afro-Cuban-inflected practice of Spiritism (*Espiritismo*). These *muertos* (spirits) often have names such as Tomasa, Francisca, Simona, Francisco, Tomás, and Negro José. Those Congos who are 'very material,' or 'grounded' (*fundamentado*) in sacred ceramic vessels or iron cauldrons, called *prendas*, *ngangas*, or *nkisos*, 'work' with earths, sticks, relics of the dead, plants, and sacrifices (see Cabrera 1986b; Brown 1989:chs.5,6; Thompson 1983).

Congos Reales del Santo Rey Melchor: (Central African, Spanish) 'Royal Congos of Holy King Melchor.'This group, in the context of the 'Day of the Kings,' refers to the name of a particular Congo *cabildo* under the patronage of Melchor (alt. Melchior). Melchor was the Black figure—in some depictions—among the 'Three Wise Men' or 'Three Kings' (Gaspar, Balthazar, Melchor), who brought gifts to the baby Jesus on 6 January—Epiphany—the moment represented as the Adoration of the Magi—the very calendrical celebration on which the Day of the Kings was enacted. Pedro Dechamps-Chapeaux discovered that in Cuba the Congos had 'preferably . . . Holy King Melchior' as their patron, while the Arará often had the Holy Spirit, the Carabalís Saint Christopher and the Holy Trinity, the Lucumís Saint

Barbara, and the Mandingas the Virgin of Regla and the Immaculate Conception (1968). (For more on Melchior, the Three Kings, and the transformation of Epiphany by the *cabildos*, see *rancho de reis/reisado* below). Lydia Cabrera defines 'Congo Real' as the name given to the 'Portuguese Congos,' who, in the Congo-Cuban language, were called 'sikongo Lundebutúa' (1984:55) or 'Congo Mumdamba' (54).

Corpus Christi: (Latin). The 'Body of Christ.' The name of this Roman Catholic festival refers to the honoring of the Eucharist—the communion, the Roman Catholic sacrament renewing Christ's propitiatory sacrifice of his body and blood—observed on the Thursday after Trinity Sunday, in late May or June, that is, the second Thursday after Pentecost, which comes 50 days after Easter. Instituted by Pope Urban IV in 1246, its obligation as a holy day, as well as the accompanying dramatic events, including festive processions, were established and embellished across the medieval European Christian world. Processions included 'flowery floats and pageantry' as well as elaborate religious dramas (Apostolos-Cappadona 1994:85). Though first set apart as a holy day in 1264 by papal bull, Corpus Christi was officially authorized in 1311 by Pope Clement V at the Council of Vienne. The procession of the Host was directed by Pope John XXII in 1318., Important for our understanding of the popular transformation of all Church-initiated festivals is the dynamic cultural development the hegemonic overlay produces. It involved an inevitable secularization, and the 'carnivalization' of Corpus Christi. If originally the liturgical dramas were enacted in church, they began to be organized by participating Guilds and performed by lay actors on moveable stages at stations on the street and in the marketplace *en route* during the procession. Contemporaneous reports of the Day of the Kings in Cuba, in tone and letter, refer to such 'licentious' elements, as well as 'irreverent and indecorous' behavior. White Cuba's sense of the Day of the Kings as a fearsome festival, during which respectable people stayed off the streets, may derive from its association with the presence of the 'devil' in historical Corpus Christi dramas, who appeared in Cuba, to them, in the form of Africanized maskers.

costumbrista: (Spanish, m/f). A writer of the Literature of Manners , that is, one who depicts the typical customs of a country or region (Real Academia Española 1984:392). Ortiz frequently drew upon the writing and illustrations of such nineteenth century *costumbristas*—witness the long quotes and figures in his text(s). Ortiz was particularly fond of the Basque artist, Victor Patricio de Landaluze, who illustrated Afro-Cuban life, ritual, and festival in painted and print media with an extraordinary sense of 'realism,' for example, in his prized 1881 volume of lithographs depicting diverse Cuban social 'types' entitled *Tipos y costumbres de la isla de Cuba.* As late as 1953, Ortiz, who collected Landaluze's work, lamented that Cuban middle class society would have nothing to do with these *cosas de negros* ('black things'), and only recently have such works been recuperated as precursors to important aspects of a Cuban national ethos and artistic modernism (see Landaluze 1881; Ortiz 1953; Blanc et al 1992:53–56; Martínez 1994:79–80). The contemporary Cuban painter, Pedro Álvarez, incorporates the types and scenes of Landaluze's work in semi-comic/semi-tragic ways to critique aspects of Cuban society, such as racism and nationalism.

cuadrillas: (Spanish; lit. carnival 'blocks;' a carnival band). A theme-group of carnival participants. According to Argeliers León, they may have been 'integrated by outlandish masks, painted faces and bodies, with feathers on the head simulating Indians. There were acrobats, contortionists, those mounted on stilts (*zancos*), they carried flags (*banderas*), instruments. . . .' (León 1984b:25). Today, at least in Santiago Carnival, the larger *paseos* are divided into different *cuadrillas*, each with its own sub-theme. Cuadrillas are not separate and independent groups but must be part of larger bands.

cucumby: (Central African, Spanish, and/or Amerindian origin; also spelled *cucumbi.* See *bacumby* and *Gombay*). It is the 'name used for certain forms of the *congada* in some regions of Brazil, notably Bahia,' says Bastide. The *congada* is a 'folk drama on African themes (tribal warfare, embassies, death and resurrection of a prince)' which included songs, dance, and dialogue (Bastide 1978:473).

Culona: (Mande or Cross-River region). Ortiz identifies the *Culona*, through his nineteenth-century sources, as 'a *diablito* who dances with a wide ring around the waist, which sustains a skirt of vegetal fibers,' for example raffia. The *Culona* costume might further be distinguished by horned and/or feathered crowns and adornments or shakers around the wrists (see 1960[1920]:32–33, figs. 6,7,8). The the 'ring' around the waist was often of a flat disk shape, like a large metal washer, covered in cloth, as also seen in recent Havana carnivals. For Ortiz, the *Culona* costume, along with those of other *diablitos*, represented the adornments of a '*brujo* [sorcerer] and the savage taste of his dress.' This hypothesis—that the *diablito* was a sorcerer or fetishist—was reinforced by the 'partially religious character of the *cabildos*' (Ortiz 1924:152). It was also reinforced by Ortiz's etymology of the term *Culona*, was traceable not to the Spanish, but precisely to the Malinké and Mandinga adjectives, *kulona* or *lonna*, which mean 'wise' and 'well-educated'—e.g., a wiseman and African religious traditionalist (see 1960 [1920]:32 and 1924:152). (Ortiz admits that he once thought *Culona* derived from the vulgar Spanish term, 'big-assed woman' [from *culo*; see 1973b [1906]:72 and translator's note 'f' to Ortiz's article in this volume, p.36]). More recent scholarship raises questions about Ortiz's etymology, which also implied the origin of the costume. Robert Farris Thompson argues that the masquerade at hand, though he addresses neither the term *Culona,* nor its etymology, derives from the 'hoopskirted Calabar *Aban* dancer' (1983:266–67). That is, the *Culona* would, in this hypothesis, share with the Abakuá an origin in the Old Calabar, Cross River region of Eastern Nigeria, rather than in the Western Sudan among the Mande-speaking peoples.

diablito: (Spanish). It has been most generally defined as a "black dressed as a *moharracho* [individual masker] who on the 'Day of the Kings' goes about the street dancing" (Real Academia Española 1984:492). Literally meaning 'little devil,' the term came to refer in Cuba to virtually all individual carnival figures in an 'African' manner (for example, decked out with horns, wooden masks, and vegetal matter). Ortiz and other observers considered the *diablitos* to be the fetishists and sorcerers, that is, *brujos,* of the African nations—indeed, he said, 'they were the *babalaos,* as we would say today,' or the *uangas* of Louisiana, or the *ngangas* of the Congo [in Africa] (Ortiz 1973b[1920]:32; see also *Culona, brujo, babalao, nganga*). It also could refer to non-masked figures, such as carnival's elegantly dressed black kings and queens. A January 1866 calendar distributed by a Cuban cigar maker featured an illustration (*marquilla cigarrera*) of two grotesquely stereotyped blacks wearing crowns and dancing in the street. It was captioned with the admonition: 'Los Diablos Coronados/Castigarán Tus Pecados' ('The Crowned Devils/Will Punish Your Sins'; see León 1984a:72 and Kutzinski 1993:55). Their racialized status as 'devils' located them as evil, atavistic figures opposed to true religion and the Cuban social order; as well, perhaps one might avoid their 'punishment' by promptly giving them *aguinaldo* on festival day (see above). Notable among the masked figures was the festival representation of the *íreme* spirit figure of the Abakuá brotherhood—descended from the 'leopard societies' of the Cross River region of West Africa. The masquerader is known for his close-fitting suit of burlap, ticking, and/or more luxuriuos materials, often designed with geometric, diamond or sawtooth patterning. The Ejagham of the Cross River call their leopard society's masked representations *okum-ngbe*; the Efik societies call them *idem-ikwo*—it is possible that *íreme* descends from the Efik *idem* (see Leib and Romano 1984:54). In Cuba, as in Africa, the costume featured a raffia-fringed conical hood with two large eyes, a small flat hat attached behind (*sombrereta*) to give the spirit clairvoyance,

A hooded Abakuá figure (íreme) asks for an *aguinaldo.* To the right two *cabildo* drummers play tubular single-headed Kongo-Cuban *ngomos*, similar to Afro-Cuban *yuka* drums. Detail from Victor Particio Landaluze, *Día de Reyes en La Habana.*

while the hood, limbs, and joints featured fringe, often of palm fronds. Representing the forest 'leopard' double of the riverine sacred fish (Tanze) at the heart of the Abakuá society, the *íreme* danced in feline, angular movements (see this volume's illustrations and Cabrera 1970:42, fn. 2; Ortiz 1954:1–2; Castellanos 1928; Dumoulin 1962; Thompson 1974,1983:ch.5). However, given that the first Abakuá lodge was established in 1836, one wonders how early the *íreme* figure first appeared on carnival day. Unsurprisingly, the old 'Day of the Kings' festival was, according to Ortiz, in fact, called the 'festival of diablitos.' Ortiz asks why. Perhaps, he speculates, because the whites who referred to it thusly 'found in the motley disguises of the [A]fricans, in their leaps and gambols, in their horns and masks, a certain analogy with the *diablitos* or *diabillos* . . . or masks simulating devils, that in years past used to accompany the Catholic processions of Corpus Christi in Cuba, as in Spain and other countries' (Ortiz 1983b:224). The *diablito-íreme* would be reviled as the hallmark of *ñáñiguismo* (social delinquency), and was persecuted heavily by the colonial and Republican governments from the mid-1870s through the mid-1920s (see Roche y Monteagudo 1925). The term persists in contemporary Cuba to refer to the miniature Abakuá *íreme* dolls that are sold in tourist stores.

dientes afilados: (Spanish). 'Filed teeth.' Ethnologists and observers noted this characteristic among members of certain African nations and their creole descendants in Cuba, including members of the early nineteenth-century black subculture called 'Los Negros Curros' (the 'showy-' or 'gaudy-blacks'). Through a review of the Africanist literature of his time, Ortiz identified this practice among more than a dozen ethnic groups, but noted that it was among the *Carabalíes Bibis* (Ibibio) that this custom continued most directly in Cuba. He hypothesized that the filing of teeth was a religiously inspired practice, a totemic representation of certain clan animals. Abakuá informants told him, he says, among other things, that teeth were filed to points to recall those of the crocodile, which, along with the leopard, constituted central animal avatars of the Abakuá rites and riverine mythology. Abakuá practitioners referred to the practice as *irenten* (*irén* = 'teeth'; *ten* = 'pointed'). (See Ortiz 1927:291–298; reprinted as Ortiz 1986:53–57; Ortiz 1929; Sosa Rodríguez 1982:406.)

Egungun: (Yoruba, *egúngún*). Egungun are masquerades representing important patrilineal ancestor figures in West Africa (Southwestern Nigeria, the Republic of Benin, Yoruba of Sierra Leone), as well as in some of the Nago Candomblé houses of Salvador, Bahia, Brazil. There exist many types (see *African Arts* special issue April 1978). The most massive and complex costumes are the 'Elder Egun' (*Egun Agba*), comprising many layers of cloth strips, a mirrored-and-embroidered front apron panel, and, most recognizably, a 'faceless' (Robert Farris Thompson's term), proscenium-like apex from which the cloth panels and strips hang. Fernando Ortiz claims that 'the Lucumís or Yorubas, who maintained their submerged religion in Cuba, knew the cult of the Egungun, or spirits of the dead, which were made to reappear on earth personified by masked *diablitos* covered from head to foot. This cult originated annual ceremonies, when all the Egunguns appeared, dancing extravagantly, first before the king and after for the whole population. . . .' He states that 'still, from time to time, the *Egungun* are danced by the Yorubas in Cuba.' Ortiz's claim suggests that an elaborated Yoruba Egungun cult of the distinct type that persists in Brazil developed in Cuba. Some corroborating evidence is found in one of Lydia Cabrera's footnotes. A tradition of 'dancing Egun' and Olokún cult masquerade were carried on by Havana *babalawos*, beginning with the famous Adechina (Ño Remigio Herrera), who died in Regla in 1905 (Cabrera 1980:27; see also J. Mason 1996). The last Olokun masquerades were performed in Regla as late as 1963, directed by Quintín Lecon Lombillo, the grandson of Adechina's close colleague, Atandá Ño Filomeno García. The Olokun masquerade, danced to special drums, consisted of carved wood masks and *saco* covering the body (from my Havana fieldwork). However, the presence in Cuba of Yoruba/Candomblé type Egungun masquerade is supported by little evidence. One would expect to find such costumes in one of the several major Cuban ethnographic collections if it were true—given that just about everything else has turned up, including Olokun masks (such objects were regularly confiscated by the police). Today, Santeriá ritual ancestors are venerated with altars and prayer, but they do not manifest themselves in elaborate masked costume; however, 'masks,' of eclectic types, as symbols, are associated with some deceased spirits and with the Lucumí *orisha*, Oyá, the mistress of the dead. One could hypothesize that the annual carnival procession provided an available 'niche' (Bastide 1978:58) for the reconstitution and persistence of aspects of Egungun cult practice, specifically their public veneration and spectacle, in nineteenth-century Cuba, a practice that might then have disappeared with the banning of Carnival in the 1880s. For description and analysis of Egungun in West Africa and Brazil, see dos Santos and dos Santos 1968; Thompson 1974:ch.3, pt. 6).

farola: (Spanish). In Cuban carnival, it refers to a tall, pole-like adornment, often 10 or more feet tall, which resembles the classic gas streetlamp from which its name derives (*farol*). Often decorated with multicolored paper or cloth, foil, and streamers, as well as exaggerated in scale, it is carried by the comparsa's *farolero*, who spins and waves the *farola* for kinetic effect. The term's figurative meaning refers to bragging, boasting, and showing off: a *farolero* is someone who is boastful, a bluffer.

fotuto: (alt. **Botuto**; origin debated—Amerindian and/or African). Ortiz defines it as a 'rustic wind instrument, made from a sea shell [conch shell], cut at the point of the spiral' (1924:206–207). Employed at carnival time during the Day of the Kings, it was also, according to sources, blown by peasants in the countryside to report a fire and as a musical instrument during Easter and Christmas Eve festivals (1955:317). Ortiz reports that 'some believe that it is an African word; all believe that it is onomatopoetic'—spelling out the breathy but dark trumpeted sound it produces. Earlier writers believed *fotuto* was derived from the South American Indian word for Sacred Trumpet (*botuto*; 1924:206–207). In his later work, Ortiz elaborates that the conch shell was utilized as a wind instrument on the Gold Coast of West Africa to prevent storms, in other regions of Africa to foment rain and fertility, throughout the pre-Columbian Americas by native populations in rites of passage to adulthood, as well as in the Mediterranean, to represent gods of the sea (1955:312–327). In short, given its virtually world-wide use, the term *fotuto* could have as its origin the Quechua *pututú* or the Kongo *etuto* (319,313). Finally, Ortiz notes the use of the instrument in Haiti by followers of *vodou*—much of which has the same African origin as the Cuban Arará religion (1955:322). Moreover, its use in the Haitian Lenten *rara* celebrations is amply documented, celebrations intensively connected to *vodou* rites (see Courlander 1960:plate 76; McAlister 1995). Traditionally, the shell, called *lambí*, has also been used to 'call the *coumbite*'—the rural, musically-driven, collective work regimen (Courlander 1960: plate 9). The *vodou* priest Boukman, believed to be the spiritual catalyst of the Haitian revolution, is said to have used this shell horn for communication on the eve of the Revolution in 1791. The *lambí* is integral to the national symbol of Africanity and freedom-through-revolution: a statue of the powerful Nègre Marron (Black Runaway), with chains broken and conch shell raised, stands in front of the National Palace in Port-au-Prince (sculpted by Albert Magonaise and inaugurated 6 December 1968). More recently, the conch shell was used by peasants and slum dwellers during the 1980s and early 1990s political upheavals. The great jazz trombonist, Steve Turré, recently revived the conch shell, incorporating a range of sizes producing different tones into his orchestra; during the December 1999 Havana Jazz Festival, he reintroduced the *fotuto* into the Cuban musical setting when he accompanied a rumba group with his 'shells.'

Gangá: (West African). Ortiz, (1960:24, fn. 33), citing Binger, appears to say that the Mossi '[we]re those called *gangás* in Cuba.' In earlier work (1987[1916]:48–49), Ortiz defined the Ganga nation ambiguously, referring to a range of anthropological sources, locating their origin anywhere from the Western Sudan to Kongo-Angola. In any case, the Mossi (Mosi or Moshi) of what is now Burkina Faso were historically divided into four independent kingdoms. 'Two of these, with capitals at Wagadugu and Yatenga, date back to the eleventh and twelfth centuries, and from the fourteenth to the sixteenth centuries were strong enough to attack the Mali and Songhai empires' (see Bascom 1973:41).

Gombay: (African origin; also *gombey* and *gumbay*). A pan–Afro-American term, today it refers in Bermuda to a pre-Lenten, Christmas-season festival, as well as to its masquerade dancers. In Cuba and Jamaica it is the name of a specific type of drum, yet it was also observed in the mid-nineteenth century among 'John Kooner' (Jonkonnu) masqueraders in North and South Carolina. Judith Bettelheim reports that Bermudan Gombey masquerade traditions were imported from St. Kitts and Nevis with migrant laborers in the early twentieth century; however, in the nineteenth century, the Bermuda celebration was called *gumba* or *gomba*, and mention was made of a small, sheepskin-covered drum, called *gombay*. Gombey performers in Bermuda today mask exclusively as 'Wild Indians,' yet the drum called *gombay* is apparently no longer found. In a footnote in *Día de los Reyes*, Ortiz pointed out the phonetic similarity of *gombay*—which he understood to be a Bermudan celebration—to the Afro-Hispanic term *cumbé*, defined quite generally as a 'certain old dance' (1960[1920]:23, fn. 22). Four years later, in his 1924 *Glosario*, he defined *cumbé* more specifically as a 'certain dance of blacks,' noting that it had generated several vernacular Afro-Cuban verbs and nouns: *cumbanchar*, *cumbanchear*, and *cumbancheo*. Ortiz's etymological research pointed to origins in several African languages, as well as to early

Seville (*cumbé*, whose origin could still have been African), and noted its presence in the Caribbean and South America. Among the 'congos,' *kumba* signified 'to make noise, yell . . . scandalize,' etc., and, drawing on Bentley's Kongo dictionary, Ortiz suggested that *nkumbi* referred to a certain 'drum.' At the same time, *ekombi* among the 'Carabalís' referred to a 'certain dance of women.' The term *cumbé*, additionally, resonated with the terms *cucumby* and *bacumby*, names for Afro-Brazilian festival dramas (Ortiz 1924: 154–155). In short, these references together delineate a dual sense of the term/related terms as both drum and dance/performance. In 1952, in his famous *Los Instrumentos de la Música Afrocubana*, Ortiz reported that, in Santiago de Cuba (city in eastern Cuba), a *gumbé* drum is played, and that its form is exactly like that found in Jamaica. With regard to Jamaica itself , numerous writers in the late eighteenth and early nineteenth centuries observed drums constructed of a skin stretched over a frame or box. Edward Long's *goombah* (1744) was played with sticks; Bryan Edwards saw the same thing, but heard it as *gombay* (1787); William Beckford's *gomba* (1790) was struck with the hands; I.M. Belisario's description and lithograph depicted it as partly hung around the neck and played with the hands, the drum itself consisting of skin stretched over a rectangular frame (1837). Bettelheim suggests that it is plausible that, while the term *gumbay* derived from a Central African source, the term was not always related to a drum type. And, while frame drums with similar names have been noted in the last 50 years among the Fante of Ghana and others of neighboring regions, it is not clear at all that the Jamaican drum type has an African source. Indeed, the reverse is suggested by the evidence. Frame drums and music variously called *goumbeh*, *gome*, and *gombe* are found in Nigeria, Sierra Leone, and Ghana, not least among participants in Creole urban festive societies among descendants of repatriated slaves (See Bettelheim 1988:79–82; see also Ortiz 1954:375-376).

ígis: (Yoruba: *igi*; Lucumí: *iguis*, *iggis*). In Yoruba, the word means tree, wood, or stick. Used in the Lucumí ritual context in Cuba, it can refer to the trees, 'sticks,' and branches of *el monte* (the sacred forest), which embody spiritual power and have medicinal uses. It is also used to refer to the figurated and cloth-and-bell-adorned wooden staffs used in ancestor (*egun*) rites in the Lucumí religion (*iggi-iku*: 'stick of the dead'). (See Abraham 1946:287; Cabrera 1986a:155–156).

Illamba: (Abakuá term, of Cross River derivation, also found in Cuba as Iyamba). The Iyamba is the society grade considered to be the highest (or sometimes second highest) and most powerful office (*plaza*) in the Abakuá brotherhood (Leib and Romano 1984:50 found the *iyamba* to be the 'head priest' of the 'leopard society' of Babong, the most 'traditional' Ejagham village they visited during their fieldwork. There, the *iyamba*, in the secret temple, keeps the "leopard spirit...in captivity with a 'chain around his neck to lock [him] while sleeping'" [54]). In Cuba, the Abakuá Iyamba office-holder is in charge of the sacred *ekue* drum, a friction instrument which, when consecrated and played (*fragayar*) within the inner sanctum (*fambayin*) of the Abakuá temple (*fambá*) by Iyamba, reproduces the 'Divine Voice'—also called *Ekue*—of God (see Sosa Rodríguez 1982:ch.5). (The Abakuá term *ekue* is a creolized version of the Ejagham *ngbe* and Efik *ekpe* societies, that is to say, 'leopard societies.' The leopard—and the *íreme* masquerade dancer that serves as its representation—is the forest double of the sacred 'fish' [Tanze], the original embodiment of *ekue* [from my fieldwork in Regla; see also Leib and Romano 1984:52]). Enrique Sosa Rodríguez describes Iyamba as the 'chief of the priesthood because he produces the Voice': that is, Iyamba has the unique authority to make *ekue* 'speak.' He is in charge of all "beginnings, openings, births . . . of the ritual commencements that the 'wild' (*bronco*) sound of the drum authorizes. Iyamba shares with Isué the function of keeping watch over the good functioning of the society and inspires respect by his serious, serene, and reposed character. Iyamba carries, as do four other dignitaries, an adorned staff (*itón*). Iyamba's *itón* is associated with Peace and Justice. The dignitary or *plaza* called Mosongo is also close to Iyamba, for Mosongo's *itón*, made from a segment of hollow *caña brava* (a wide bamboo), contains the sacred palm ribs (*yin* or *güin*) used by Iyamba in sounding the *ekue* friction drum (data from my fieldwork, Regla, 1992–1994). In some versions of Abakuá myth, Iyamba is the 'Father of Sikan,' the woman who first discovered the 'Voice' (*ekue*) as manifested in the sacred fish, Tanze. In Cuba, Iyamba means the 'fin of the fish' (the *ala*, *flanco*, *aleta*, *del pez*). Its root is the Abakuá term for 'fish' and 'mother' (*iya*; see Sosa Rodríguez 1982:ch.5; Cabrera 1970:161–166; Cabrera 1975:181–182). Between the end of the nineteenth century and 1942, when the Abakuá brotherhoods controlled wharf labor in western Cuban port cities and towns (e.g., Havana, Regla, Matanzas, Cardenas), labor contractors (*contratistas*) for the dockworkers often simultaneously held the Iyamba position within the brotherhoods, granting jobs to their respective members (López Valdés 1985).

Isué: (Abakuá term of Cross River origin). Referred to as the 'Bishop' of the Abakuá hierarchy, this *plaza* occupies the third highest grade in the brotherhood. Isué is in charge of the four-plumed *sese* drum, considered to be the 'Holy Sacrament' of the Abakuá. Plumed and crowned, the drum is said to represent the 'Head of Sikan'. The *sese*, among the Efó (Ejagham) branch of the Abakuá, is a sealed goblet form, charged with sacred medicines and, it is said, the blood and bones of Sikan. In contrast, the *seseribó* or *sese ndibo*, of the Cuban Efí (Efik) branches, means 'empty *sese*': it is a single-headed, tapered cylindrical drum that may contain packets of sacred medicines (from my fieldwork in Regla and Havana, 1992–1994). Both *seses* are 'silent' drums, and represent the 'foundation' of the Voice of Ekue (the Divine Voice of God). It is said that *sese* keeps/guards the voice when *ekue*, the friction drum played by Iyamba, is not sounding. Cabrera reports that Isué is also the priest of Abakuá initiation ('baptism'), the supervisor of the initiatory oath to the fire of life—a ritual passage in which the neophyte sustains a candle in his hands while Isué officiates. (See Cabrera 1970:168–174 and Sosa Rodríguez 1982:ch.5; Thompson 1983:ch.4.)

juegos: (Spanish). While one of its literal dictionary definitions is 'games,' it can be used in Spanish to mean an integral set of things that go together and apparently was also used at one time to refer to 'festivals and spectacles' (Real Academia Española 1984:801). In the Afro-Cuban idiom, *juegos* is used in three distinct senses: 1) to mean *ritos* ('rites' or 'rituals'); 2) meaning a 'set' as in *un juego de tambores batá*, that is, a set of (three) *batá* drums; and 3) with respect to the Ñáñigos or Abakuá, *juego*, as seen in Ortiz's text, refers to the membership group of a single Abakuá lodge, consisting of 25 fundamental officers (*plazas*) followed by other initiated members (*obonekues*). Therefore, in the Abakuá and carnival settings, 'games' is an inappropriate translation of the term. In Ortiz's text, *juegos* appears in a phrase owed to Enrique Fernández Carillo, who wrote the companion piece to Victor Patricio de Landaluze's famous 1881 oft-reproduced lithograph of the hooded *íreme* figure. Those carnival groups, then called, *ñáñigos*, at first were 'divided . . . in *tierras* (much later in *juegos*)' (1960[1920]:31; this phrase is mistranslated in the 1993 edition of the present volume [p. 30, as 'in bands, later sets']). In the Abakuá idiom, *juego* is sometimes used interchangeably with *tierra* (and sometimes with the term *potencia*). First let us look at the terms separately and then consider the article's intended meaning. Sosa Rodríguez, writing on the Abakuá, speculates that *juego* might have been borrowed from the Spanish, 'perhaps as a result of comparing its representations with the *juegos escolares* (scholarly groups or cells) of medieval Spain, with which were associated dramatic spectacles of liturgical character, and in which acted prodigious personages who used a peculiar form of expression reserved exclusively to initiates' (Sosa Rodríguez 1982:43). Sosa defines *tierra* in Abakuá discourse as referring to one of the several ethnic areas or lands of origin in Africa: Efí (Efik), Efor (Ejagham), Oru (Ibibio). *Potencia*, in contrast, refers to the 'essential magical foundation, all powerful, of the group of drums, scepters, liturgical garments, and sacred personages' owned by each *juego* (Sosa Rodríguez 1982:43). Later we will see that *tierra* also refers to the actual walled Abakuá temple grounds. Ortiz's temporal distinction between the *ñáñigos* first being 'divided . . . in *tierras* (much later in *juegos*)' is not clear on its face. However, if *tierra* is understood: 1) as *nación* (African 'country' or 'land' of origin, that is to say, 'ethnicity' (Sosa Rodríguez [1982:45] uses *tierra* in the sense of 'Carabalí ethnic group' of origin), and 2) that the *naciónes* were established institutionally in *cabildo* organizations, the use of *juegos* 'later' becomes clearer. The various Carabalí-descended groups (Efik and Ejagham) first processed with their respective *naciones/cabildos* (of origin), and 'later,' after the system of Abakuá lodges was established (as of 1836), *ñáñigo* participants and *diablitos* marched with these latter organizations—their own *juegos*. Ortiz's mention of the 1836 establishment of the 'first group of *ñáñigos* in Havana' refers to the 'birth' of the Abakuá lodge, or *juego,* Efik Butón (alt. Efik Acuabutón, Efik Acabatón), the first autonomous branch of the Ekpe society of the Efik people of the Cross River, from the 'cabildo Carabalí Brícamo Apapa Efí' more three-quarters of a century after the largest numbers of 'Carabalí' were brought to Cuba (see Palmié 1993:344; Roche Monteagudo 1925:4; see also Deschamps Chapeaux 1964:97). It should be understood that the socio-ritual organization of the Abakuá brotherhood turns not principally on individual initiation, as is the case in the Afro-Cuban *religions,* but on corporate groups. Individuals may be initiated into a group/lodge once it has been established, but a whole group/lodge must first be 'born' itself with the minimum number of 13–25 office holders and the requisite secrets (*potencia*) transmitted from an 'older' sponsoring lodge. To reiterate, prior to 1836—there were only various groups of 'Carabalí' organized by *cabildo,* with no established Afro-Cuban lodges. The festival participants to which Ortiz's source refers at first processed in the 'Day of the Kings' festival as part of their larger *tierra/cabildo* and later, as would other Abakuá participants, processed with their individual *juegos* or lodges.

kindembo: (Kongo origin; alt. *quindembo*). According to Ortiz's *Glosario de Afronegrismos* (1924:400), it is an 'Afro-Cuban dance brought by the Congos' to the Island. It is danced to the sound of three drums: *yuca*, *mula*, and *caja*, drums that would comprise the *tambor de yuka* ensemble for Kongo-Cuban ritual (i.e., Palo Monte; see León 1984a:64–92, esp. 74). Ortiz suggests that the term also could have referred to a personage and, additionally, that it was heard as part of a popular expression, *murió quindembo* (lit. 'it died *quindembo*'), meaning 'the matter is finished' (*ha terminado el asunto*). Ortiz, citing the works of Bentley and Johnston for Central West Africa, relates it to the Congo term *ndembo*, 'one of the most powerful secret societies . . . among the congos.' In that context, the term *kindembo* referred to the newly incorporated initiates, who have just 'died' and been reborn into the society (Ortiz 1924:402).

Los Tres Juanes: (Spanish). 'The Three Johns.' They are the three figures in the boat beneath the image of La Caridad del Cobre, the local manifestation of the Virgin Mary as Our Lady of Charity of [the town of] Cobre in Eastern Cuba. La Caridad del Cobre later became the patron saint of the island of Cuba, and was associated with the riverine *orisha* Ochún in the Cuban popular religious imagination. According to the local legend of the image's miraculous discovery (reproduced here in a loose translation from Lydia Cabrera's *Yemayá y Ochún*, "two 'indios'—Juan de Joyos and Juan Moreno—and one black creole, Rodrigo, had gone by foot to seek salt at the bay of Nipe. Embarking there in a canoe, they saw, at daybreak, a form that whitened out the distance in the sea. Rowing toward what appeared to be a figure, they encountered the image, carved from wood, of the Holy Virgin Mary, which floated . . . over a tablet. Our Lady carried in her left arm the Child Jesus, and a gold cross in her right hand. 'I am the Virgin of Charity [Virgen de la Caridad],' read an inscription in the tablet, which the indio Juan de Joyos read. Her iconography continues to reproduce the moment in which the two indians and the black, 'Los Tres Juanes,' a representation of the two enslaved races, kneeled in the canoe in order to worship the miraculous apparition of the Divine Mother, for whom all men are her sons, and, preferred [among them, are] the most impoverished [,who] are the most loved" (Cabrera 1980:57). The *cabildos* of the African nations, and, later, of free Africans and creoles, owned highly adorned statues of the saints—among them La Caridad del Cobre—that corresponded to the principal Lucumí *orishas*, carrying them in procession on each saint's calendrical feast day (La Caridad, 8 September).

Lucumí: (Yoruba, Lucumí). The generic designation during the slave-trade period for the members of the many Yoruba-speaking ethnic groups that embarked from the Bight of Benin. The Yoruba historically have occupied the area of southwestern Nigeria. However, the ethonym 'Lucumí' is believed by scholars to be derived from the greeting, 'my friend' (*oluku mi*); according to one scholar, it is common in the Ijebu-Yoruba dialect (personal communication with native Yoruba speaker Antonia Folarin, Spring 1987; see also Bascom 1951; Castellanos 1996). 'Lucumí' was suffixed with specific ethnic subgroup names, some of the major Yoruba-speaking subgroups being 'Eyo' or 'Oyo,' 'Egua,' 'Egguado,' 'Yesa,' 'Yebu,' 'Anagó,' 'Ekiti,' 'Ife,' 'Ilorin,' and 'Ketu (Ò̱yó̱, Ifè̱, Ègbá, È̱gbádò, Ìjè̱sà, Ìjè̱bu, Ànàgó, Èkìtì, Ìlo̱rin, Kétu). However, 'Lucumí' was often also applied, erroneously, to distinct groups from bordering areas, such as Kingdom of Dahomey (Benin) to the west and the Tapa and Nupe. Rafael L. López Valdéz found in Cuban archives references to at least 137 different subgroups categorized under the 'Lucumí' rubric, such as Lucumí-chanté (Ashanti), Lucumí-Popo, and, as mentioned, Takua (Tapa; López Valdéz 1986:72–73; see also Ortiz 1987[1916]:50–52; Lachatañeré 1961). Since before the turn of the century, the term 'Lucumí' has referred also to a particular Afro-Cuban *religion*, which reconstitutes principal patterns of the Yoruba. Under the Lucumí religious rubric fall two major orders *(regla)*, La Regla de Ocha (also known popularly as Santería) and La Regla de Ifá. The former comprises the priests and practices of the Yoruba-Lucumí pantheon of *orishas*; the latter comprises the male diviners of the Ifá oracle, the *babalawos*, whose patron is the *orisha* Orunmila. The reconstitution of selected Yoruba religious traditions occurred within the colonial-era Lucumí *cabildos*, as well as the numerous independent 'house-temples' of worship that have spanned this and the last century. (see Murphy 1988:33; Palmié 1993). See *cabildo.*

Macombo: (correct spelling: *Mokongo* or *Mocongo*; Abakuá term of Cross River origin). Ortiz's 'Day of the Kings' text identifies this figure as the 'supreme Chief' of the Abakuá society. Given variations in practice and conflicting evidence discovered by Sosa Rodríguez—as found in the notebooks of various Abakuá practioners—sometimes Mokongo, and sometimes Iyamba, are accorded the role of 'supreme Chief'; moreover, each has been identified as the 'Father of Sikan' (a mythological princess who accidentally captured the sacred fish, Tanze, that embodied God's Divine Voice, *ekue*). Sosa Rodríguez is certain only that the two are among the highest-ranking four Abakuá offices *(plazas)*: Iyamba, Mokongo, Isué, and Isunekue. His sources (in great part Ortiz's own archives) regarded the Mokongo as a 'valiant warrior, tribal chief, and judge.' And, affirming Ortiz's reporting in 1920, the Mokongo is also called the *abanderado*—flag bearer—by virtue of his particular staff *(itón*; see Sosa Rodríguez 1982:154–158). Lydia Cabrera reports Mokongo to be the 'father of Sikan' and the 'great warrior of the Efor [Ejagham]' people; Mokongo 'personifies in the society the concept of absolute and unlimited power, justice, and service to the hidden force of Ekue.' He is a kind of 'Abraham' of the Abakuá, the 'oldest' and most respected man in the tribe (Cabrera 1970:166–168). The first documented Mokongo in Cuba was Margarito Blanco, who was detained by the police in 1839, and identified himself as the 'Ocongo of Ultán,' undoubtedly one of Havana's earliest lodges (Deschamps Chapeaux 1964:97ff.).

maestra: (Spanish). In the text, Ortiz defines *maestra* as the *cabildo* queen—a kind of 'mother superior'—who comes out in triumph on 6 January (Epiphany) in an entourage and procession composed of the nation's officers and members. The *maestra* would be among the hierarchy of *cabildo* officers elected or otherwise chosen (for example, through heredity) by the membership (see *cabildo*). Ortiz reported, in his 1921 article 'Los Cabildos Afrocubanos,' that *cabildo* queens emerged on feast days and the Day of the Kings in extraordinary finery, including bejeweled tiaras, puff-shouldered dresses and petticoats. As documented in the paintings of Landaluze, attendants held decorative umbrellas over their heads; finely dressed *cabildo* officers and *diablitos* preceded them, performing dances and collecting *aguinaldo* (see Ortiz 1921:6–9 and this volume's Landaluze illustrations).

Malinke: (West African). A major ethnic group of the Western Sudan, they are encountered in present-day 'senegal, Guinea, and Mali, as well as parts of Ghana and the Ivory Coast. The Malinke established the great Mali empire, with its capital at Kangaba on the upper Niger between Bamako and Siguiri. The Mali empire, after which the [present] Republic of Mali takes its name, excelled all others in the Western Sudan in size, power, and renown.' Like the Bambara, the Malinke 'speak the language of the Mande branch of the Niger-Congo' group (Bascom 1973:35–36,31–32). If Malinke turned up in Cuba, as did some of their Bambara neighbors (see Ortiz 1987[1916]:43), they would have been grouped under the 'Mandinga' ethnic rubric (see Ortiz 1924:317–318).

mamarrachos: (possibly Hausa or Arabic; see *moharracho* below; lit. 'tramp,' 'scarecrow,' 'clown'). Ortiz, in his Day of the Kings text, defines *mamarrachos*, historically, as 'masquerading figures accompanying the Corpus Christi procession in Seville, opening the way through the crowd, making people laugh.' Judith Bettelheim finds that, in Santiago de Cuba today, the term *mamarracho* usually refers to an 'independent costumed individual who marches and dances alongside the costumed groups or *cuadrillas*' (personal communication 20 February 1992). Argeliers León writes that *mamarrachos* 'dressed outlandishly, used all types of kitchen utensils to make noise, preferring the use of pots and saucepans (*saltenes*)' (León 1984b:8).

Mandingo: (Mande language branch; alt. Mandinga). A generic ethnic designation for Africans taken from the Western Sudan, from Senegal to Liberia. They would have included peoples from the many Mande-speaking groups, including Islamicized Africans; the term 'Mandinga' apparently was quite encompassing, and its boundaries were unclear (Ortiz 1987:52). Scholars and practitioners of the Afro-Cuban religions have raised the question as to why no 'Mandinga culture' persisted in Cuba, when, apparently, it was so visibly rich during the largest festival of the colonial period. The Mandingas were 'luxurious with their wide pants, jackets...turbans of blue or pink silk, and bordered in *marabú*' (1960[1920]:11). As one 'old informant,' Calazán Herrera, exclaimed to Lydia Cabrera, 'the Mandingas, so many of whom came [to Cuba], proud of their straight hair, without large lips and with their Saint Alá [Allah] that had the miraculous book, they taught the creoles; when they were finished they didn't leave a *cabildo* or a language or a music. Who still speaks Mandinga? No one....' In an ironic flourish, which testifies both to the erasure and the influence of the Mandingas in Cuba, Cabrera caps her text with the oft-heard Afro-Cuban phrase (for example, in musical lyrics), "'Kikiribu mandinga!'...an expression that is employed in order to signal the end of a matter" (Cabrera 1994[1954]:380). Nevertheless, many an Afro-Cuban religious practitioner has affirmed the potency of 'Mandinga' herbal magic, and some believe that the Lucumí *orisha Osain*, the master of herbalism and owner of the sacred forest, *el monte*, originated among the Mandingas (Angarica n.d.:22). Indeed, in northeastern Brazil, among the practioners of Capoeira Angola, an African-derived martial art, *mandinga* refers to efficacious trickery and spiritual protection as provided by secret charms (*bolsa de mandinga*; alt., *patuá*) and orations, as well as to one's secret, personal, and tricky manner of executing the *ginga*, Capoeira's foundational dance movement.

marabú: Marabou or marabout, 'a soft feathery fluffy material prepared from turkey feathers or the coverts of marabous and used esp. for trimming women's hats or clothes' (*Webster's* 1997:710). The marabou, a native of Africa, is a bird similar to the stork in build—a meter and one-half in height—with beautiful black, ashy-gray, and white feathers (Real Academia Española 1984:874). In Ortiz's Day of the Kings text, the *marabú* reference is to the elaborate costumes worn by the Mandingas, which were bordered with *marabú*. (See Mandingo). However, in his 1924 *Glosario de Afronegrismos*, Ortiz defines *marabú* as a plant (*Dicgrostachys nutans*. Benth.), which is 'dangerous to cultivated agriculture.' He supposes that the term is African or Arabic (*marabut*), where it means 'holy' or 'ascetic'—though the latter would seem to be out of character with the festive material and sensibility described above. It is probable, Ortiz says, 'that *marabú* would have been brought to Cuba by the Mandingas, Fulas, Hausas, Yolofes and, in general, those from the zone that circumscribes Senegal and the Niger, the old coast called Guinea, because through their contacts with the northern muslims and the extension of Islam among those Africans, [the material] came to be known as religious *marabús*' (1924:325).

Commander Evelio Figueredo of the Cabildo Carabalí Isuama playing the *marugas* during the 1986 Festival of Caribbean Cutlure, Santiago de Cuba. In his position within the *cabildo* he is known as a *rumbero* or *chachero.* © J.B.

maruga: (alt. *maraca*; *erikundí; acheré*, depending upon type and context). In his *Glosario de Afronegrismos*, Ortiz defines *maruga* as 'a rattle formed by a hollow sphere filled with little stones and agitated to produce a sound. It is also called *maraca*' (Ortiz 1924:329). This 'hollow sphere' was, undoubtedly, a small gourd (*guira*), either mounted on a stick (Spanish: *maraca*; or Lucumí: *acheré*) or attached to the wrist (*maraca de muñeca, de tobillo, de manilla, de pulso,* or *de pulsera*). Such shakers (also called *ensansi*, in the Kongo-Cuban idiom) were worn by the drummers of Kongo *cabildos*, who beat *yuka* drums for religious celebrations called *toque de makuta* (Ortiz 1953,II:88). Such a wrist shaker-and-drum combination is also seen, for example, in a painting by Landaluze depicting Day of the Kings festivities, illustrated in this volume. However, what is more commonly called *maruga*, I believe, was/is encountered as a conical or cylindrical shaker of plaited fiber, topped with a circular or semi-circular handles, ranging from perhaps five to 12 inches in height. Commonly, these are called, in Spanish, *maracas de canasta* ('basket'; these are called *caxixí* in Brazil, and are employed within the Capoeira martial art orchestra). In Santiago de Cuba, the plaited shakers are called *chachá* , and among the Abakuá of western Cuba, they are called, in the ritual language, *erikundí.* At the same time, the Abakuá apply the *erikundi* term to double and cruciform gourd shakers, which are used by the officer called Moruá to direct and communicate with the *íreme* masqueraders.

Abakuá *maracas de canasta/erikundi* are commonly adorned, like the *íreme* costumes themselves, with raffia, cloth, or paper fringe (Spanish: *empitada*; Abakuá: *beleme* (Ortiz 1952,II:97–111). A drawing reproduced by Sosa Rodríguez (1982 [unpaginated appendix]) shows the participant in an Abakuá procession holding two such characteristic Abakuá rattles; he is referred to as the *cafande maruga.*

moharraches: (alt. *moharracho*; see *mamarracho*). Ortiz finds this as synonymous with *mamarracho*, and suggests Hausa or Arabic as the word's origin (from *moharrech*; see Ortiz 1924:340).

mojiganga: (possibly Central African origin). *Mojiganga* is conventionally defined in Spanish as a 'public festival made with various ridiculous disguises, especially men masked in the figures of animals' (Real Academia Española 1984:919). Ortiz used this definition as his starting point. The 1924 *mojiganga* entry in *Glosario de Afronegrismos* offered little specific data on this carnival figure, other than that of the Real Academica Española. Yet he did cut one suggestive etymological path to the Kongo term *nganga*, which would be affirmed by later research. Ortiz hypothesized that the compound term related to *moci-nganga*, 'a person belonging to the *ngangas*' (Ortiz 1924:343–344). In 1951, in his famous *Los bailes y el teatro de los negros en el folklore* (reprint 1985:473–476), Ortiz wrote that one of the most extravagant masks of inarguably African character consisted of a mask with artificial arms over and above the head of its wearer, supported on a framework resting on the shoulders, while the rest of the body was covered by a skirting of cane fibers, strings of garlic and rag tatters. However, the costume type most properly identified as *mojiganga* consisted of a masquerade that simulated a horse and rider. The wearer was surrounded by an armature covered in raffia-type fiber, bearing, to his front, a light construction of a horse's head. The performer/'rider' holds a set of reins with his hands, while artificial little legs dangle at the sides. The performer's actual legs propel the horse-and-rider in a spectacle of equestrian motion. Furthermore, critical to the *mojiganga* costume, historically, was a diminutive passenger, a doll (*muñeca*), attached to the frame in a sitting position just behind the human rider, its little arms seeming to hold on to the rider's torso. In Ortiz's illustration (1985:476 and this volume), both rider and passenger wear short feathered crowns, which were, at the time of his 1920 writing, considered to be the headgear of religious priests, or sorcerers (*brujos*; see Ortiz 1973b[1906]:67). The masquerade costume, as a whole, Ortiz wrote, was believed to have symbolized a religious initiate (*engueye*—a Kongo-Cuban term for initiate) in the state of possession. The costume, however, takes its name from the doll itself, seen to

Identified by Fernando Ortiz as a '*mojiganga montada*', which represents a 'religious initiate (*enguege*) in the state of possession' [presumably the individual is the horse 'mounted' by a spirit].

A member of the theater group Cabildo Teatral Santiago performing as a *zaldiko* or *burroquite.* He elicits much laughter when as a doctor, he gives an 'injection' to female members of the Cabildo. This character is often confused with the Afro-Cuban version of the rider and the hobby horse known as *mojiganga.*© J.B.

be a spirit 'messenger entity.' That is, Ortiz found the term *mojiganga* or *mujiganga*, as applied in Cuba in its original meaning, to refer to a type of wooden doll that served as a spiritual messenger or *nkisi* (alt. *nganga*, a powerful charm or spirit-embedded cauldron), which is subject to the control of a *tata-nganga* or Kongo Cuban priest. Ortiz points, as evidence, to a *mayombero* (Kongo-Cuban practitioner) in the town of Guanabacoa, who used a magically charged horn [*mpaka*] atop which was a doll that he called *mujiganga*. The festival mask, according to Ortiz, by its association with the doll, took the latter's name, *mojiganga*. At the same time, Ortiz qualifies, 'we mustn't suppose that all the details of an object are of African origin.' A mask consisting of the 'grotesque figure of a man simulating the riding of a horse was already found in Europe by the fifteenth century,' and one would suspect that such masks were to be found throughout the New World (Ortiz 1985[1951]:474–475). For example, the historical *burroquite*, a horse-and-rider costume, is found among the 'traditional masks' of Trinidad Carnival (see Crowley 1956), and I have seen such a mask represented as a manifestation of Venezuelan traditional festive culture. Still, Ortiz categorizes the mask under the general, more inclusive rubric of *mamarracho*—that is, an independent, individual masquerader—with its 'outlandish form' that entertained onlookers (Ortiz 1985[1951]:474–475). Likewise, Ortiz's student Argeliers León applied the term *mojiganga* to both the horse-and-rider mask and other kinds of 'solitary masqueraders . . . individuals dressed with a suit completely reversed [back to front], or with big old frock coats or suits of jute sack (*saco de yute*) with enormous patches of colored cloth, but with faces painted blue, mixing indigo and powdered eggshell (*cascarilla*) or other facial powder. Masked thusly they are found described in the carnival festivals of Santiago and other countries in the Americas.'

moka jumbia: (African origin; alt. *moko jumbie, moco jumbie, moco jumbo*). The term refers to the carnival stilt dancer (alt. *zanquero*), clearly seen in the c.1830 Day of the Kings group illustration by Pierre Toussaint Frédéric Mialhe in this volume. This tradition of stilt dancing, of African, and, possibly also, European, origin is found historically and contemporarily throughout the Caribbean: e.g. in Cuba, Trinidad, St. Vincent, and Jamaica. In the Anglophone Caribbean, as reported by Daniel Crowley for the historical Trinidad Carnival, Moko Jumby was played usually by men on stilts as high as 10 or 15 feet. "The stilts were brightly painted in stripes, and the masquer wore a long full skirt and a jacket or 'eton' of brightly-coloured satin or velvet. His hat was made of tòshô, the dried pulp of the wild cucumber (*Luffa aegyptiaca*) which was fashioned into an 'Admiral's' hat with long peaks in front and back, and with the crown of the hat decorated with feathers. Moko

Jumby was sometimes accompanied by a dwarf in similar costume without stilts, to accentuate Moko's height. He danced all day through the street, collecting money on a plate from the people crowded into second-floor windows and balconies. Thus he tapped an audience out of reach of the street maskers. His dance was similar to a jig, and he either used the music of any passing band, or was accompanied by a drum, triangle, and flute" (Crowley 1956:198). In Trinidad, it is believed that *moko jumbie* became extinct in the twentieth century, when electrical wires came to dominate these same heights above the city streets of Port of Spain . Meanwhile, the pan-Caribbean term *jumbie* arguably descends from Bantu-wide lexicon related to spirits of the dead, such as *kiyumba*, which means a spirit-embodying skull relic, and *nfumbi*, which means dead spirit, in the Afro-Cuban Palo Monte tradition (Cabrera 1983[1954]:131–132,1984:56). Still, the precise origin of the term has been debated. As Judith Bettelheim notes, many observers traveling in Africa remarked, from the 1730s onward, on the presence of a tall masquerader with a costume of shredded bark as connected with a regulatory society called 'Mumbo Jumbo' in the Senegambia region. In the Caribbean, as early as 1791, Sir William Young observed a Christmas stilt dancing figure on St. Vincent, called 'Moco-Jumbo,' and asserted that the term was derived from 'Mumbo Jumbo of the Mendengoes,' drawing on the Senegambian account of Mungo Park (1790s). At the same time, by 1765, the term *mumbo jumbo* also named a fearsome figure of popular English folk tales. But *moko jumbie* is not always associated with stilt-dancing in Africa . For example, among the Dan of Liberia and northwestern Ivory Coast, stilt-dancers are called 'long spirits' (*gle gbee*; see Thompson 1974:166–169). Bettelheim provisionally suggests that a variation on a Mande term joined the African masquerade practice of stilt-dancing in the Caribbean, resulting in numerous variations, among them *moko jumbie*, *moco jumbie*, *moka jumbie*, *moco jumbo*, and simply *jumby* . However, in a footnote to the discussion of this masquerade in *Caribbean Festival Arts*, Bettelheim suggests that the origin of the terms *moko* and *jumbie* is Ki-Kongo. As suggested above, *jumbie* in the Caribbean relates to spirits of the dead; in Jamaica, for example, it is associated with the practice of Obeah (Beckwith 1929:88). Today, *jumbie* is frequently heard in Jamaican Reggae songs, which draw from Rastafarian religious tradition, but with a twist: the spirits of the dead (*jumbies*) and their associated idolatrous rites are antithetical to the living essence of the one God, Jah, in the monotheistic Rasta religion. Returning to the stilt-masquerade in Cuba, more historical documentation than Ortiz provides is hard to find, though stilt dancers are integral to Havana's 'traditional' and now folkloricized *comparsas* (such as the Alacrán group), and a lively group of teenage *zanqueros* (stilt-dancers) trains at the the Casa Cultural of Central Havana.

Mokho missi ku: (African/Arabic origin). The figure appears simply as a 'black masquerader,' for which Ortiz, in 'The Day of the Kings', cites the work of Gustave Binger, *Du Niger au Golfe de Guinée par le Pays de Kong et la Mossi* (Paris, 1892), vol. 1, p. 378. No further information has been uncovered.

nabikém: (African origin, possibly Cross River). References to this term outside of Ortiz's text are hard to find. Citing only his own *Glosario de Afronegrismos* (1924:25) in the 1960 version of the Day of the Kings, Ortiz says only that 'it is possible to see the origin of the *anaquillé* in Africa in the effigies of Old Calabar in the biennial festival to drive out the devils, where the figures or images are called *nabikém'* (1960[1920]:40; see *anaquillé*).

nación: (Spanish; lit. 'nation'). A term used throughout the African Diaspora to refer to ethnic groups or 'tribes' of African origin in the New World, often institutionally organized into 'clubs' and religious brotherhoods. In Cuba these were called *cabildos* (see above), and, in Brazil, they were called *irmandades.* Among the major 'nations' in Cuba were the Lucumí (Yoruba), Arará (Ewe-Fon-Mahi), Carabalí (Ibo, Ibibio, Efik, Ejagham), Congo (numerous), and Mandinga (see alphabetical listings above). Such nation names, as applied by slave-traders and contemporaneous observers, were often larger regional (though geographically-erroneous) designations, or were derived from the name of the port of embarkation of the enslaved person (for example, Carabalí from Old Calabar at the mouth of the Cross River) rather than from local African ethnic origin. The discourse of the slave trade associated each ethnic tag with a set of inherent traits, which, presumably, affected the relative desirability of a particular individual sold in the market in human beings. For example, as the Swedish traveler, Fredrika Bremer noted in 1853, 'The Congo negroes, called the Frenchmen of Africa, are a vivacious, gay, but vain people; they have depressed noses, wide mouths, splendid teeth, and high cheek-bones; they are strong and broad built, but not tall of stature. . . . The Luccomées . . . the noblest of these coast tribes, are tall of stature, with handsome and often remarkably regular and even noble features, the expression of which is grave. . . . The Luccomées are a proud and contentious people; they are difficult to manage in the commencement of their life of slavery. . . . The Callavalis, or Caraballis negroes, are also a good people, although more lazy and careless . . .' (Bremer 1853, II:313–314). Roger Bastide and others have suggested that, in places such as Brazil the slave population was administratively factored into distinct nations as part of a divide-and-conquer strategy, yet with unintended consequences: Africans seized the opportunity to consolidate ethnically-similar personnel in order to recreate, conserve, and transmit, intergenerationally, distinct

African-based cultural practices. With respect to their precise composition and boundaries of identity, Monica Schuler suggests that the New World 'nations' were, in fact, 'facsimiles' of tribal/ethnic membership as it existed in Africa itself; that is, they were reconstituted ethnic units . Given evidence of intermarriage between members of different nations, a question could be raised as to the nature of ethnic identity and its conservation over time. What nation—what ethnicity—would be claimed by a child born to Lucumí and Mandinga (for example, my Cuban godmother claims 'Lucumí and Mandinga' heritage) or an African-born and a creole of mixed parentage? If 'pure' nation-identity ever existed in Cuba during the slavery period, it is clear that by the last decades of the nineteenth century—with the era of emancipation (1880s) and the cessation of the illegal slave trade (1820 to the 1870s in the Spanish Caribbean), demographic changes had already occurred that made the reckoning of ethnicity more difficult. According to Rafael L. López Valdés, 'even though the *cabildos* conserved a certain ethnic profile until their disappearance—that was already notable at the end of the last century, the social and religious facets present in them were replaced, gradually, by an ethnic belonging more and more imprecise.' Intermarriages, he says, 'began to take place from a very early date and continued occurring in the course of the century' (López Valdés 1987:11). The suggestive term here is 'certain' ethnic profile. If interethnic marriages began 'tak[ing] place from a very early date,' what was the nature and composition of nation membership? Could it be that, in some measure, *cabildo* membership itself figured into the reckoning of one's nation identity, rather than the other way around? In other words, was nation/ethnic identity 'constructed'—at least partly—through organizational affiliation? Drawing on Fredrik Barth, Stephen Palmié favors the idea of a constructed and 'marked' ethnicity, both in Africa and in the Diaspora. Ethnicity is subject to construction and reconstruction over time, a idea opposed to the essentialist notion that the 'New World *naciones* represented transplanted segments torn from clearly bounded African tribes existing as *tantum sui similia gentes* since time immemorial' (Palmié 1989:12–15,1993:343). With respect to continued use of the term 'nation' itself, it is still used in Brazil (*nação*) to refer to the African origins of particular Candomblé houses and ritual practices (*Nago* [Yoruba], *Ketu* [Yoruba kingdom within Dahomey], *Gege* [Dahomey], *Angola*, etc.), and in parts of Haiti (*nanchon*) to refer to distinct pantheons of gods with different putative origins (Nago, Ibo, Congo etc.). see Maia 1985:21–22; K. Brown 1989:100–102; Courlander 1960:19–29,317–331). See *cabildo*

negros de nación: (Spanish). The term indicated a person's birth on the African continent, as opposed to the term *criollo* ('creole'), which denoted birth on Cuban soil. This difference figured as one important criterion in a consciously articulated system of classification and governmental philosophy, specifically instituted to divide and conquer—that is to say, control—the massive black population in Cuba. Mid-nineteenth-century colonial Cuban decrees intended to insure that *negros de nación* remained 'divided [by] *cabildo*,' insisting that 1) "each *nación* must have their exclusive *cabildo*; 2) free blacks were not to 'mix' (*mezclar*) with slaves; 3) 'whites were not permitted to attend gatherings of blacks'; 4) 'and neither were *negros criollos* to be together with those *de nación*'; 5) 'nor should Africans or *bozales* [recently arrived and 'unseasoned' blacks] be able to associate among [whites or *negros criollos*]" (Superior Civil Governor of the Island of Cuba [1843] and the Regente de la Audiencia y Real Cancillería de Puerto Príncipe as quoted in López Valdés 1987:7).

nganga: (Kongo: 'ritual expert': priest, diviner, healer, manipulator of *minkisi* 'medicines' connected to the dead—literally, *nkisi* (singular) means "the artificial object [or container] in which there 'is' a spirit dominated by man" (MacGaffey 1986:137); Cuba: cauldron or pot charged with sacred medicines and relics of the dead). *Nganga* is of pan-Bantu origin, in usage in many areas of Central Africa. If there it refers to ritual experts and 'magicians' , in Cuba it came to refer to the spiritually-charged pot or cauldron of the Palo Monte or Mayombe religion controlled by the priest, though Lydia Cabrera's informants also defined *nganga* as a spirit of the dead (*muerto*, 1984:104). This suggests, as a practitioner recently explained to me, that the spirits of the dead contained in the cauldron were, perhaps, 'in life,' ritual experts of African origin themselves. In Cuba, the term *nganga* is also called *nkisi*, *nkiso*, *prenda*, or *caldero*. *Ngangas* contain a relic or relics, often the skull (*kiyumba*), of a deceased person (*nfumbi*), with whom the Kongo-Cuban priest (*ngangulero*, *tata-nganga*, *padre nganga*, *brillumbero*, *mayombero*, *palero*) enters into a contractual relationship in order to perform 'strong,' very 'material,' and, sometimes, 'dirty,' spiritual work. Like a 'general,' Lydia Cabrera's sources revealed, the *nfumbi*, in turn, marshalls other key natural forces to solve problems, forces embodied in a variety of *nganga* contents: sticks (*palos*) and herbs, animal bones and skulls, various metals, stones and earths from various natural places on the landscape, etc. Still, if the *nfumbi* represents a spirit of the dead, the particular composition of each *nganga* corresponds to a particular *mpungu*, or class of spiritual energy, analogous to the way in which the *minkisi* of Central Africa carry distinct names and functions (Cabrera 1986b:126–129; MacGaffey and Harris 1983:87–101,1991). However, in Cuba, the distinct *mpungus/ngangas* were 'pantheonized' into a series of nine or more principal types, such as Siete Rayos, Sarabanda, Tiembla Tierra,

Madre de Agua, Mama Chola, Centella Ndoki, and Cobayende, which were cross-indexed with the Lucumí *orishas* and the Catholic saints (for example, Siete Rayos, Changó, and Santa Barbara; see Castellanos and Castellanos 1992,III:138). Though of different character, each *nganga*, given its range of constituent parts, which are tied, through synecdoche, metonymy, and metaphor to multifarious forces in the spiritual, natural, and social domains (MacGaffey 1988), is said to represent 'the world in microcosm'—over which the priest can exert control and execute transformations. To this end, a variety of sacrifices are offered the *nganga*, which is, ideally, kept in contact with the earth and/or under the stars, either beneath a tree outdoors or in a shed .

Nochebuena: Christmas eve: in Cuba, a traditional time of family celebration, and one of the several principal moments in which the slaves were given a margin of liberty to celebrate.

ñáñigo/ñáñiguismo: (possibly Cross River origin). The term *ñáñiguismo* was applied during the nineteenth and early twentieth centuries, often indiscriminately, to numerous forms of social behavior and organizations considered to be 'delinquent' and 'criminal' by the colonial authorities, and, later, the government of the Republic (estab. 1902). *Ñáñiguismo* was associated by the white cultural mainstream and nationalist theorieticians with despotic irrationality, teeming Afro-Cuban *barrios*, malicious gangs, murder, savage black men with filed teeth, and dissipated white men fallen into primitive atavism and the lure of black women . When applied more precisely, *Ñáñigo/Ñáñiguismo* designated the initiated members/ 'society' of the Abakuá of Cross River origin (see *Abakuá, diablito, Illamba, juegos, Macombo*). The Abakuá society was ferociously persecuted by the authorities from 1874 through 1920, at other times tolerated, but always kept under surveillance and restriction (see Ortiz 1973b[1906]; Wright 1910:147ff.; Roche Monteagudo 1925; Sosa Rodríguez 1982; Cabrera 1970:chs.1,2,3). Though rarely used in Cuba today, because of its pejorative connotations, *ñáñigo* itself appears to be of African origin. Ortiz suggests that the term has an 'etymology of congo origin, even though the *ñáñigos* themselves do not.' He breaks down the term into '*ñaña*' + '*ngo*,' meaning '*mysterious, cursed, magic* leopard' (*ngo*) (Ortiz 1924:376). In 1952, Ortiz reported that *ñáña* was a term used by the Abakuá officer, Moruá Yuansá, who, with his *erikundí* rattle in hand (see *maruga*), musically called the masked *íreme* figure, saying the word *ñáña* to the latter. 'some believe,' Ortiz writes, "that *ñáña* is a name for the *íreme* or '*diablito*'; but perhaps it might be nothing more than a figure of speech, since *ñáñá* in the Efik language means a type of *maraca* (rattle), and in the mouth of the Moruá can refer to his own ritual *maracas* or *erikundé* and not the personage of the *diablito*. We will not add more explication here except to say that *ñáña-ngó* is 'the fearsome ghost [*fantasma*] or spirit of the leopard'" (Ortiz 1954:3; see also *ó-ñaña-ó*). However these definitions hold up, it is, nevertheless, clear that the powerful and fearsome leopard of the forest was/is a central avatar in the Cross River Efik and Ejagham regulatory societies (*ekpe* and *ngbe*, respectively) that preceded the Cuban Abakuá, gerontocratic juridical and slaving organizations popularly referred to as 'leopard societies. The leopard, as a focal avatar, remains central to Cuban Abakuá iconography and performance, particularly in the angular, feline movements, and the geometrically-patterned costume, of the Cuban *íreme* masquerade. The costumes often bear the stylized pattern of leopard spots or pawprints, as in the *ukara* cloth and masquerades in the Ekpe/Ngbe societies; Leib and Romano 1984:52–54; Thompson 1983:260–66). Other key symbols of the Abakuá lodge, its sacred staffs and drums, are often adorned with leopard skin. Also, the *ekue* friction drum that reproduces the 'divine voice' (*uyo*) derives from the Ejagham/Efik terms for 'leopard,' as well as being synonymous with the 'corporate group' of the society and the 'body of religious beliefs' themselves (Leib and Romano 1984:48). At the same time, in Cuban Abakuá mythology, the figures of Sikan and Tanze (the Efó [Ejagham] princess and the God-embodying 'Lord Fish') appear to have an equivalent, if not more foregrounded, narrative place than the leopard—though the latter is clearly considered the forest double of the riverine iconography and sacred ecology of Sikan and Tanze, as well as the 'secrets' of the temple, both in Cuba and Africa .

Ologboijeun: (Yoruba). Ortiz describes this figure as a '*diablito* of the Lucumí cult . . . the personification of the deity Ologboijeun, masked and threatening with a sword.' In the written Yoruba, it is spelled *Olóògbó ìjéùn*. According to R.C. Abraham, among the Ẹ̀gbá Yoruba, the Olóògbó of *ìjéùn* is the custodian of the *ògbó*, the latter being the main *òrìsà* of Abéòkúta, and having the form of a masked man with a drawn sword. The Aláké (this custodian) is the supreme head of all the *òrìsà* cults in Ègbá country (Abraham 1946:483).

ó-ñaña-ó: (creolized Cross River). The term is found in a quotation from Escolástico Gallardo in Ortiz's text to refer to a dance performed by a masquerader called Canga Cafú, among others, a dance of probable African origin, which the observer perceived as comprised of 'contortions, half lascivious and half frenetic' (1960[1920]:16). '*Ñaña*' relates to part of Ortiz's own etymology of *ñáñigo* (see above), wherein *ñaña* may mean 'mysterious,' and refer to the *diablito* (masquerade figure) himself, or the rattle used among the Abakuá to call him. Sosa Rodríguez (1982) provides data that resonate with the observer's description of the dance, and affirms part of Ortiz's etymology of *ñáñigo*. He defines the Efik term, *nyan-nyan*, as 'erratic' (401), and the Cuban creolized Abakuá term, *ñaña*, as *íreme* and *diablito* (408). However, as I suggested in the *Canga Cafú* entry, if the dancing figure has any relation to the Yoruba, it would seem unlikely that his dance would bear a name that, in other contexts, has clearer linkage to the Abakuá of Efik/Ejagham origin. Still, the term, *ó-ñaña-ó*, could have crossed boundaries in public festive space, becoming a more generalized Afro-Cuban or popular 'creole' exclamation/expression, which could be applied to any masquerader's dance—just as the popular term *diablito* was applied to all such masqueraders.

Pardos and Morenos: (Spanish). Nineteenth century Cuban terms of color classification relating to racial codes of blood content and 'purity' (i.e., 'mulatto' and 'negro,' respectively). In Cuba, up to the twentieth century, *pardo* referred officially to persons of mixed parentage (*mulato*); *moreno* was the term applied to people of African descent (i.e., 'negro race'). Rodríguez-Herrera says the term *pardo* was applied 'without rigorous precision' to a man or woman *de color*, so white [light] that only his [or her] hair is capable of announcing his [or her] mixed origin. Some evauate [these characteristics] as '*mulato blanconazo*' (1959,II:342–43). For *moreno*, Rodríguez-Herrera comments that, in Cuba, it was a 'euphemistic form that educated people used in order to designate the black [*negro*] by his [dark] color, knowing that he is his brother, according to the Martí Doctrine, and in accord with Christ' (1959,II:279; the 'Martí Doctrine' derives from José Martí's famous 1891 work, *Nuestra America*: that '[t]here can be no racial hate, because there are no races'; see Kutzinski 1993:5–6). Accordingly, Church parish volumes documenting baptisms, marriages, and deaths, for example, were divided into 'Pardos and Morenos,' on the one hand, and '*blancos*' (whites) on the other hand (see Martínez-Alier 1974:15–22). Characteristically, *pardos* would be listed as *naturales* ('natives') of this or that Cuban locale, while *morenos*, if African-born, would be listed—or list themselves in any kind of official document—as *naturales de Africa*, and as belonging to a particular African 'nation,' e.g., Lucumí.

peseta: (Spanish). A Spanish and Mexican denomination of currency (25 cents in Mexico).

peso: (Spanish). An old silver coin of Spain, which carried different values (at different times); it is the origin of the present *peso* as a unit of money in Spain, and Cuba, where it is officially equivalent to the U.S. dollar.

rancho de reis/reisado: (Portuguese). The terms are used by Ortiz in a citation of Raimundo Nina Rodrígues' Brazilian ethnography. In Brazilian carnival, according to Roger Bastide, the *rancho* (*de reis*—'of the kings') was a '[g]roup of men and women who celebrate Christmas with singing and dancing. Originally these groups symbolized shepherds on their way to Bethlehem to worship the infant Jesus'(1978:479). (*Rancho* in Portuguese means, literally, 'strolling [processing] persons.' *Ranchos*, along with *cordões* ('cordons') and *blocos* ('blocks'), were the carnival parade groups in Brazil , analogous to organizing principles of the *comparsas*, *paseos*, *tangos* or *cuadrillas* in Cuba, the last being closest in meaning to 'blocks.' The *rancho de reis* of Salvador, Bahia, Brazil included events similar to the Cuban carnival performance called 'the killing of the snake' (*matar la culebra*), in Ortiz's reading of the sources, as the former 'consist[ed] essentially of a pantomime strubble between animal or *rancho* totem object and the dancers' (1960[1920]:41–43). The 'killing of the snake' on the Day of the Kings, Ortiz believed, could be interpreted in relation to African ophiolatric rites, including the supposed 'driving out of the devil' (sometimes through human sacrifice) in Nigeria and the Gold Coast, the annual 'killing of the sacred [totem] animal' in the ancient rites Ortiz found in Sir James Frazer's work, or as a 'collective rite of purification' such as 'the expulsion of the demons' in many festivals around the world (1960[1920]:42–43). The *matar de culebra* is still performed by the Havana Comparsa Alacrán. Emphasizing its African, apparently Kongo-Cuban, origins, a 1999 media guide to Carnival explains: "Its theme was taken from a story of African origin, in which a strange animal bit the slave María Josefa, who was being helped by the sorcerer Ta-Cuñengue, who succeeds getting rid of [the animal]. This story is none other than a variation of the old pantomime dance called 'The Death of the Snake' [Matar la Culebra]". A *reisado*, according to Bastide, was a '[g]roup of singers and dancers (particularly in Alagoas) who perform dramatic ballets on various themes, usually on Epiphany, the Festival of the Three Kings' (1978:479). Thus, these processions would seem to represent two consecutive key moments in the liturgical drama around Jesus' birth: the 'Adoration of the Shepherds' and the 'Adoration of the Magi.' According to Diane Apostolos-Cappadona, in the New Testament, the 'shepherds' story 'implied the recognition of Jesus by the lowliest of the Hebrews and signified his domain over the products of the earth and . . . animals'; the 'Three Kings,' or 'Magicians,' were 'a Persian sacred caste who were skilled in astrology and the occult [who] followed a singular star to Bethlehem in search of its source—Mary and the Christ Child . . . . This event [the Epiphany] signified the first manifestation of Jesus Christ to the Gentile world.' Yet, by the seventh century in Europe, this 'Adoration of the [Three] Magi' narrative (three representing the number of gifts, the three ages of humanity, and the trinity) was transformed, and the 'Three' Magi or Kings were indentified as Caspar, Melchior, and Balthazar (see *Melchior* above). During the Medieval period, one of the Magi was identified as black; later, during the Age of Exploration, at least one, if not also another, 'began to take on the facial characteristics, skin color, and dress of the varied lands 'Christianized' by Europe, including the Americas, Africa, China, and Japan. As Ortiz notes in the text, "the three 'races' of the Three Magi were to symbolize the white, yellow, and African races" (1960[1920]:22). In Renaissance art, the Adoration of the Magi and the Adoration of the Shepherds became fused into one adoration scene" (Apostolos-Cappadona 1994:16–20). In this historical explanation are seen the performative possibilities, and results, of the transformation of a Roman Catholic liturgical series of festivals by Africans and indigenous peoples throughout the Americas—particularly in such populations' identification with the lowly, the mystical, and the royal. Thus, Ortiz's citation of the Brazilian *reisado*, given the same Epiphany setting as the Cuban 'Day of the Kings'—in which the African nations' *cabildo* courts and dancers processesed through the streets—was an apt diasporic comparison. As Roger Bastide argued, the calendrical Roman Catholic Festival and its associated organizations and liturgical narratives became important 'niches' and points of departure (1978:160) for the reconstitution of African-based practices .

real: a Spanish denomination of silver coinage, valued at one quarter of a *peseta* (that is, 25 *céntimos* or cents; Real Academia Española 1984:1148).

Reyes Magos: (Spanish). The (Three) 'Wise Kings,' 'Wise Men,' or 'Magicians,' who brought gifts to the Baby Jesus in Bethlehem. This biblical event was the basis for the observance and annual Cuban carnival celebration of the 'Day of the Kings' (Día de los Reyes) on 6 January (Twelfth Day/ 'Epiphany') in Cuba.

Salvaguardia: (Spanish). Guard. A unit of the Cuban police.

Santa Rosa de Lima: (Spanish). St. Rose of Lima, whose feast day is 30 August, was 'the first saint of the New World to be canonized.' Born in Lima in 1568 of a Spanish middle-class family, her life was said to have been 'wholly given over to voluntary penance and prayer, the former of a nature so extreme as to appear inhuman.' She deprived herself of sleep and food, 'at pains, it seems, to humble herself by methods that would impair her great natural beauty and render her unattractive' including 'rubb[ing] pepper on her cheeks to produce a blotchy complexion,' placing her hands in lime, etc. She joined the third order of St. Dominic, took a vow of chastity, and chose to model her life after her patroness St. Catherine of Siena. She died in 1617 after a long illness. (Apostolos Cappadora, 1994:296.)

tambor: (Spanish). A general term for 'drum,' which also came to name a ritual drumming event (see Ortiz 1952–1955 and León 1984a for comprehensive documentation and classification of Cuban and Afro-Cuban drums, of which there are numerous types). Afro-Cuban drums include the Lucumí double-headed *batá*; the tubular, single-headed Congo *yuka* or *makuta* drums; the wedge-tuned Abakuá *nkomo* and *bonkó* drums; and the goblet-shaped, peg-tuned drums of the Arará of Matanzas (the principal set including the *Ñonofó, Aplintí, Aché-bolisá, Guegue, Klokló*: see Ortiz 1952, III:345). Afro-Cuban drums and drummings are classified by function and ritual or festive need. For example, in the Lucumí tradition, drums and drummings are classified as *tambor de fundamento* ('sacred') and *tambor aberinkula* ('profane'). Consecrated *batá* drums are used in the former, while unconsecrated *batá* are used in the latter. Other profane ensemble types include the *guiro* orchestra (one or two *congas*, three gourd shakers [*guiro*], and a bell or hoeblade).

tambora: (Spanish). A particular type of large, double-headed drum, such as the the *bombo*. This drum, used in carnival orchestras, resembles a moderately sized marching-band bass drum, hung vertically on the chest with a strap and played with a stick. Ortiz says that the *bombo* belongs to the music of the 'whites,' especially military bands, but the blacks of Cuba, as of the United States, 'converted it into a drum for their folkloric music...[such as the] *bombo criollo* [of] the Carabalí *comparsas* of Santiago de Cuba that come out during carnival' (Ortiz 1954,IV:348–353, 390–391).

tamboril: (Spanish; from *tamborín*). It is a small drum held in the left hand and played with the palm of the hand or a stick, and often accompanied by a whistle; played for popular dances . This definition suggests that the *tamboril* might be cognate with the Afro-Brazilian *tamborim* of the Batucada orchestra. Unlike the American 'tambourine,' it is diminutive and hit hard with a stick.

tangos: (Kongo origin). In Ortiz's 'Day of the Kings,' the term appears as interchangeable with *cuadrillas*, which are organized carnival groups, or 'blocks'; yet, he qualifies that such *tangos/cuadrillas* were formed by males ('the stronger sex'), who cared little about the elegance of their dress, but, instead, concentrated on performing gymnastic and grotesque movements. Such *tangos* could be composed of *diablitos* or stilt dancers, for example (see 1960[1920]:13,16). In terms of their size, the *tangos* apparently consisted of individuals more numerous than other small bands, called *tandas* (four to six persons), the members of which sang, danced, and played instruments (small drums, horns, and jugs) as they shouted for *aguinaldo* (gifts of money; the 1993 English translation omits the term *tanda* in this discussion of size). The inference given here by the passages Ortiz quotes is that, in Havana, the *tangos/cuadrillas* were simply among the larger carnival groups (1960 [1920]:12–13). In his 1924 *Glosario de Afronegrismos*, Ortiz produces a general and rather unsatisfying definition of *tango*, as a music and a 'festival and dance of the blacks' and other common people in the Americas. He elaborates only that the term was used much in Spain and in its colonies—including Cuba—to refer to an 'African dance.' He suggests that the term is probably of African origin, citing West African terms such as *tamgu* and *tuñgu* ('to dance'), which are found in Eastern Nigeria and the Cross River (Ortiz 1924:447–448). Given the more recent scholarship of Argeliers León and Odilio Urfé, one is able to understand *tango* more clearly as: 1) an organizing institution of carnival festivity on the Day of the Kings, 2) a specific musical and dance form of Kongo origin, and 3) a term of Kongo origin. Robert Farris Thompson's research affirms the last two of these conclusions (from Yale University undergraduate lectures, 1983–1988, that is, his 'structure of the New York Mambo' course). Argeliers León suggests that several terms—*cabildo*, *tango*, and *rumba*—the first for the Afro-Cuban mutual aid society, the second and third for specific dance forms, were applied in common usage to festive black gatherings. The expression *cabildos de negros* came to mean a gathering of [blacks], as also did the words *tango* and *rumba*. While the word *tango* has gone out of use, one still says that one is going to 'a *rumba*,' meaning an Afro-Cuban dance party (with the characteristic *rumba* orchestra of *clave* sticks, three *congas* and/or *cajones* [wood boxes], *guagua* [hollow bamboo or log beat with sticks], *maruga* or *maraca*, solist and harmonizing vocal chorus; see Daniel 1995:79–83). With respect to the socio-institutional and spatial meanings of the term *tango*, Argeliers León writes that, on the Day of the Kings, the *cabildos* would come out (*salir*) into the streets; some of them were permitted to process in marked and controlled routes to the Captain General's Palace for *aguinaldo* (see *aguinaldo*), while 'many remained circumscribed to a [mere] coming-out procession (*salida*) within their own *barrios* (neighborhoods). This [latter] festivity gave rise also to the formation of the heterogeneous black *tangos* (*tangos de negros*); some included wind instruments, which produced prolonged sounds that some chroniclers compared with the sounds of the bagpipes; and other [participants] made sounds with pieces of metal.' Many of the participants were elaborately masked, with faces painted with ochre, red noses, military hats with sabers in the hand, etc. (León 1984b:36). The wind instruments mentioned undoubtedly included the *fotuto* that Ortiz describes. The tenor and type of festivity in León's account appears similar to that described by Ortiz; however, León is able to situate the *tango* more specifically in the structured and spatially marked social landscape of Havana Carnival on the 'Day of the Kings.' The *tango*, a particular cultural dance form that seems to have prevailed in those *barrio* festivities, came to be applied, it seems, to the festivities themselves. Urfé writes that 'the tango was one of the favorite musical forms during the festivities of the day of the kings' and, he stresses, 'everything seems to point to its Congo origin. In this essay we refer to it as the Congo tango especially as part of the rumba' (Urfé 1984:173). In mapping out the 'Congo musical and dance legacy' in Cuba, Urfé delineates the 'original Congo *tango*' as a specific foundational form, the rhythmic base for such forms and national genres as the *contradanza*, the *habanera*, the first musical *danzones* by Miguel Failde, and the Afro-Son. At the international level, the Congos generated the Argentine *milonga* and *tango*, and the blues of the African-American composer William Christopher Handy; all of these assimilated the rhythm of the Afro-Cuban Congo *tango* (Urfé 1984:176).

tierras: (Spanish). Refers in Afro-Cuban discourse to 1) a geographic African region or land of origin classified within the colonial-era 'nations' system: for example, 'Tierra Lucumí' being Yorubaland or even more specifically 'Tierra Oyo,' Ife, Iyesa, etc; 'Tierra Efí' and 'Tierra Efó' being the Efik and Ejagham areas, respectively, of the Cross River Region, etc.; 2) those 'nations' as socio-spatially established in the Afro-Cuban *cabildos*, e.g., as Ortiz used it: "the *ñáñigos* first being 'divided . . . in *tierras*'" meant specific Carabalí nation-subgroup *cabildos* (see *juegos* above); or 3) the enclosed physical grounds of an Abakuá lodge or religious 'house.' In Brazil, similarly, the Candomblé houses—large enclosed grounds with multiple dwellings for the deities and priests or smaller compound homes and even apartments—are called *terrieros* with the same sense applying. In Brazil, *terrieros* are categorized by the putative ethnic/regional African origin of their ritual traditions, such as Ketu (Ketu-Yoruba), Gege (Fon), Angola (Kongo-Angola), etc.

uanga: (Kongo origin; alt. *guangá*; in the Day of the Kings text, he uses the term to name magico-religious practices in Louisiana, see *Culona* above). Ortiz defined the term as *brujería* or *hechizo* ('sorcery' or 'witchcraft'; 1924:468). It could be associated with ritual 'works' of malign intention, that is, to bring sickness or misfortune, and which could be introduced into the body through the skin or in food. Similarly, writing on Haiti, Alfred Metraux associates the term with malign religious practices. *Wanga* in Haiti 'inflict transitory trouble and curable illnesses. . . .' The "term . . . is applied to any object or combination of objects which has received, as a result of magic procedure, a property that is harmful to one or more people. *Wanga* are also called 'poisons.'" Embodying spirits, "[m]any *wanga* are objects which have been 'arranged' [*rangé*] by a sorcerer in such a way that a mere touch from them is enough to produce their desired effect—generally illness. Not least of their marvellous properties is that of being harmful only to the person who has been marked down for the sorcerer's attention. *Wanga* are said to be used by priests to destroy the reputations of their rivals, by dimming their ability to effect cures and, consequently, by turning away prospective patients" (see Metraux 1972:285–87, 76).

vegigante: (Spanish). A large, inflated animal bladder, carried by a masquerader, or attached to a costume. It is used, playfully, to hit passersby, and, perhaps, open the way for succeding maskers, during public festivities. It derives from European Carnival practices (see Nunley and Bettelheim 1988:37, and see fig. 13 in that text).

Virgen de Regla: (Spanish; the Virgin [of the town of] Regla). She is an important local manifestation of the Virgin Mary, in what was once a small fishing village that became a bustling port town eastward across the bay from the City of Havana proper. Her church overlooks the Bay of Havana. She became the patron of the Port of Havana on 23 December 1714, and was historically seen to control marine storms and the fortunes of fishermen, seamen and dockworkers. The Virgin became associated with the *oricha* Yemayá, a deity who, in Yorubaland (Y̱em̱o̱ja), is considered to dwell in the Ogun river, and whose principal shrine and epicenter of worship is Abẹ́òkúta. "A goddess of rivers and streams[,] her sobriquet is 'yé-o̱mo̱n-e̱ja' ['mother of the child of fishes']... One day [her son] raped [her] and she ran away with water gushing from her breasts and forming a lagoon." From her, it is believed, are descended major *òrì̱sà*, including S̱òngó, Ògun, Olóòkun, O̱ya, Ò̱bà, S̱ònpònnòn, and O̱sóòsì (Abraham 1946:680). In Cuba, she represents not the river ('sweet water') but the Sea ('salt water'), the symbol associated with motherhood and life. Her festival day is 7 September, when, prior to the Revolution, the *cabildos* of Yemayá / Virgin of Regla came out in procession, carrying the Virgin, playing *batá* drums, and making stops to pay respects to the elder Lucumí priests and priestesses of Regla (see Cabrera 1980:9–19 and ch. 2).

Virgen del Cobre: (Spanish; Nuestra Señora de la Caridad del Cobre). In English: Our Lady of Charity (of the town of) Cobre. Originally a local manifestation of the Virgin Mary in the copper mining town of Cobre in Eastern Cuba, where she is ensconced in a beautiful church overlooking the mines, she was declared the Patron Saint of the Island of Cuba on 10 May 1916. The Virgin wears a yellow mantle. In the Afro-Cuban cultural and religious context of Western Cuba, she has long been associated with Ochún, the

Above left, the Basilica of La Virgen de la Caridad del Cobre, Oriente Province. Also known as the Brown Virgin and celebrated as the *oricha* Ochún, she is the patron saint of Cuba. © J.B. *Above centre*, the interior altar. © J.B. *Right*, popular twentieth century chromolithograph of the Virgen del Cobre and 'The Three Johns' (see entry for 'Los Tres Juanes'). *Right*, scores of women attended a procession for the Virgen of Regla on September 7, 1999. Carrying a statue of the Virgen, this woman is also holding a 'doll' recalling the colonial '*anaquillé*' discussed by Fernando Ortiz. © David H. Brown.

copper-skinned, riverine *oricha* (deity) of sweetness, love, fertility, reproduction, fortune, etc. In Yorubaland, the Ò̱sun River, which flows through Ibadan Province, was named after her – as it was believed to be the river where she swam. The symbols of her worship include pots full of small stones and her devotees wear brass beads on their necks. It is believed that any woman drinking water from this river will conceive. In the town of Ò̱sogbo, the site of her major shrine, a fish of the Ò̱sun River that causes pregnancy is worshipped with sacrifices. In Cuba, the calendrical festival of Ochún is September 8.

en zancos (Spanish). 'On stilts.' This refers to carnival stilt-dancers found throughout the Caribbean, where they are often known as '*moko jumbie*.' (See *moka jumbia* above.)

Zarambeque: (Spanish). Defined by the Real Academia Española simply as a 'black rhythm and dance, happy and riotous' (1984:1411).

Carnival in Santiago de Cuba

Judith Bettelheim

Introduction[1]

In both 1991 and 1992 Carnival in Cuba was cancelled. As I write this introduction (1993) I wonder when Cuba will again rejoice and play; when will the carnival spirit permeate the hot July days of celebration? Cuba is in the midst of a severe economic crisis, and Carnival costs money, money that at this time must be saved for more immediate and essential needs. For example, *paseo* La Placita from Santiago de Cuba receives a yearly budget of approximately 30,000–40,000 pesos (approximately $27,000) for its annual carnival production.[2] They use this money to hire contractors and different workshops which create the costumes, headdresses, accoutrements such as banners and *farolas* (a lantern-like construction on a long pole), and the float, all to be used in the carnival parade. Today, there is not enough money to buy oil for public transportation or for cooking.

During the summer of 1991 the Pan American games were held in Havana and Santiago de Cuba. The international community of spectators and participants needed food, transportation, housing and entertainment. Carnival was cancelled, but certain carnival groups participated in the cultural activities scheduled around the Pan American games. And in certain neighborhoods of Santiago de Cuba and the surrounding towns, block parties were held. Carnival-time was celebrated quietly, with dancing to recorded music and limited quantities of alcoholic refreshment.

At the opening ceremony for the Pan American games in Santiago de Cuba the largest *paseo* in Santiago, La Placita, performed a highly stylized and choreographed almost three-quarter hour long routine, complete with acrobatic stunts and synchronized dancing with hoops. I watched on a television set in the home of friends in Havana, wondering how many people around the world also were watching La Placita perform, and wishing those same people could have seen them perform on the streets of Santiago during carnival itself. Maybe five hundred costumed dancers stretched for blocks along the carnival route. Coordinated in colors and theme, La Placita always presents a spectacle, a *fantasía.*

La Placita was already in rehearsal for their Carnival 1991 performance when finally rumors became fact and carnival was officially cancelled. (Rehearsals usually begin two months before carnival.) Ironically, on July 26, the day that the parade participants would have been resting from their night-long carnival spectacular, I interviewed the artistic director, Pablo Estrada Pérez, and some of the star dancers. As Pablo explained, "The theme would have been 'Fantasy Under the Sun,' with the sun as the universal element that illuminates all of us, especially for Latin America. . . . Our premise, and what we hoped to accomplish for America . . . a sense of this unity. . . . [We were going to] dance to popular music from each country, some of it recorded and some played by our own 30 piece orchestra."

Before I left Santiago for Havana I attended a week-long series of cultural performances supported by the Dirección Municipal de Cultura. Entitled 'Noches de Folklor, Magia y Música en el Santiago Panamericano,' these events were directed at tourists and entrance tickets were sold at all tourist hotels. Out of the seven scheduled events, three were held at Afro-Cuban Focos Culturales[3] (government sponsored meeting halls) and others were scheduled at library patios and downtown theaters. The three Afro-Cuban cultural groups permitted to perform included the Tumba Francesa, members of the traditional dance group of the Foco El Tivolí (see below), and members of the musical corps of the powerful *conga* Los Hoyos. All week I watched performances of traditional dances, religious rituals, and religious songs with their musical accompaniment. I was so grateful that I knew a lot about what I was watching, because most of the tourists at each performance were simultaneously moved and confused. Some to whom I talked asked questions about the dances, the costumes, the obviously narrative performances, and the 'scenery,' the altars and backdrops constructed for the occasion. Others simply enjoyed the spirited dancing, playing, and singing.

I remember my discomfort during these performances. At least during Carnival itself the number of Cubans watching and commenting on the parade far outnumbered the tourists. Here, these cultural performances were substituting for carnival and there were hardly any Cubans in attendance. This was a production for tourists. I recall a conversation I had with the newly appointed director of Cultura Municipal, Eliades Acosta.[4] He proudly showed me plans and diagrams for a new center of Santiago culture, complete with temples for the major religions, and musicians and drum lessons for the visitors. There were even plans to include performances of religious ceremonies on a daily basis, so that tourists could see the religions functioning publicly, supported by the government. In this way the mostly Afro-Cuban practitioners would receive a salary for their work at the cultural center, and the government would receive badly needed currency from the tourists. This is all part of a larger Cuban project to use culture to economic advantage. As Rex Nettleford (1988:187) has astutely observed, 'Cultural tourism is after all important to several Caribbean governments, for whom it is a major source of national income.' Yet Cuba's economic crisis is so severe that Carnival has been cancelled two years in a row. This is not the first time in the twentieth century that a crisis cancelled carnival celebrations. It happened in 1912 and 1913 when Afro-Cubans in Oriente resorted to an armed uprising led by the Partido Independiente de Color; and in 1917 when a general uprising led to U.S. armed intervention; and in 1930–33 Carnival was suspended by the government of Gerardo Machado; and in 1942–44; and in 1958 during the Revolution; and in 1969 there was no Carnival, in support of Castro's program of La Zafrade de los Diez Milliones, or the sugar cane harvest of 10,000,000. I can only hope that soon carnival music, dance, and innovation again will heat up the streets of Cuba in July.

History

Carnival's cultural history has been nuanced by a wide variety of interests and influences. My aim in this essay is to provide information relative to specific aspects of Cuban history and to propose reciprocal associations within Carnival culture that may clarify both Carnival and other festival celebrations. How, within the communal act of Carnival, and its antecedents such as the parading of *cabildos* [neighborhood mutual aid associations], does power get expressed either by ethnic groups or by ruling governments? The history of Carnival is a history of negotiations, of constant shifts and nuances. The institution of Carnival has created its own internal flow. As Stuart Hall (1990:222) has suggested, "Perhaps instead of thinking of identity as an already accomplished fact, which the new cultural practices then represent, we should think, instead, of identity as a 'production,' which is never complete, always in process, and always constituted within, not outside, representation.' During slavery, when power discrepancies were greatest, reports describe 'wild' celebrations of African Caribbeans. Today, control has been established, but does ethnicity still play a major role in Carnival? Some carnival organizers deliberately restate in performance specific components of African Cuban culture. To what end? Carnival is an expression of shifting power negotiations among various aspects of Cuban society.

Contemporary carnival celebrations in Santiago de Cuba, Camaguey and other Cuban cities derive from festivals honoring various Catholic saints accompanied by the special public processions permitted the African slave population. Today, carnival organization also extends and perpetuates the organization of another historic Cuban festival, the Día de Reyes celebration ('Day of the Kings,' Epiphany, January 6). The following late-nineteenth century accounts of processions in Santiago underscore African Cuban participation and the importance of royal regalia in establishing authority during public processions.

> An important *comparsa* [a special festival association] of Congo negroes of both sexes is passing in procession along the street. They have just been paying their respects to no less a personage than his Excellency the Governor of Santiago. . . . The troupe is headed by a brace of blacks, who carry banners with passing strange devices, and a dancing mace-bearer. These are followed by a battalion of colonels, generals, and field-marshals, in gold-braided coats and gilded cocked-hats. Each wears a broad sash of coloured silk, a sword and enormous spurs. These are not ordinary masqueraders be it known, but grave subjects of his sombre majesty King Congo, the oldest and blackest of all the blacks: lawfully appointed sovereign of the coloured community. (Goodman 1873:137)

Despite the colonialist and ironic tone of this description, it is obvious that the parade was an expression of power enacted in public and aesthetic terms. This is underscored by another account: 'The black *cabildos* stand out because of the luxury of the colorful decorations and the luxurious outfits that the queens of the different nations wear. The slaves' masters participate in these parades to the rhythm of songs and drums, with sounds from *almirez, botijuelas*, and *maracas* [brass mortars, jugs, and rattles]. They liked to decorate the bodies of the pretty black women with gold bracelets, diadems of precious stones, diamond necklaces and earrings, and exotic embroidered shawls. The queens in their thrones were carried on palanquins' (no original source given: Villarreal 1960:142).[5]

There is even ample documentation of African Cuban *cabildos* during the 1700s. An announcement for a slave sale of 1799, for example, identifies a '22-year-old Mandinga negra' by the location of her *cabildo* meeting house (Ortiz 1921:17). By 1792 these *cabildos* had become so potent that government regulations attempted to control the time and place of their public processions.

The institutional foundation of Carnival today is rooted in urban history, in *cabildo* history.[6] As a type of corporate club, the *cabildo* owned its own land and buildings, administered the inheritance of the slave population, disciplined its members, and provided neighborhood police services. *Cabildo* power often rivaled civic authority and *cabildo* public processions proclaimed ethnic and neighborhood solidarity. Today the *cabildo* maintains a powerful institutional and socio-psychological presence whose fluctuating public presence and power is reflected in the attitudes of Carnival organizers. As the artistic director of the carnival group, the *paseo* La Placita, explained, La Placita is like the '*gran cabildo*' [great cabildo]:

> Because during Carnival we see, in our *barrio*, the barrio of La Placita, the coming together of grandparents, fathers, sons, nephews, etc., from different places. There are a few of us who stay here; we are the Santiagueros. There are others who have gone to work in different places, but when the time comes, they all come back here; we meet here. It's like finding the great *cabildo* family.[7]

Today, three types of carnival groups exist in Santiago and each is rooted in the urban history of the *cabildo*. A *conga*, the most traditional and quintessentially Santiaguero of carnival groups, consists of a small group of musicians playing a special conga rhythm on drums and metal percussion instruments. Santiago *congas* are accompanied by large circular drums called *congas*, brake drums, and lead by the *corneta china*, a double-reed horn played in a staccato wail. *Congas* include some costumed performers, but they do not perform a choreographed routine and most *congas* are accompanied by neighborhood residents carrying identifying flags and banners. The second type of group, the *comparsa*, includes *conga* musicians and others playing well-known Cuban tunes. Santiago *comparsas* include the famous bands of *caperos*, or male performers wearing elaborately decorated capes and hats. *Caperos* do not dance, but rather run in an undulating line while forming intricate figure eight patterns. The third and newest type of group is the *paseo*. Larger and more elaborately choreographed than the *comparsa*, the *paseo* can hire different groups of musicians and seems to have more flexibility in its costuming and routines. Although a *comparsa* may include male and female paired dancers, significant female participation in Carnival is provided by the *paseo*. *Paseos* boast between 100–500 male and female costumed dancers and are known for their varied costumes.

Carnival and its relation to power centers has changed over time. These changes are best understood when put in the perspective of *cabildo* history, a fluctuating history of recognition and underground activity, which I will summarize briefly. In 1823 the *cabildos de nación* (*cabildos* based on African nation of origin) first were given permission to perform publicly in Día de Reyes

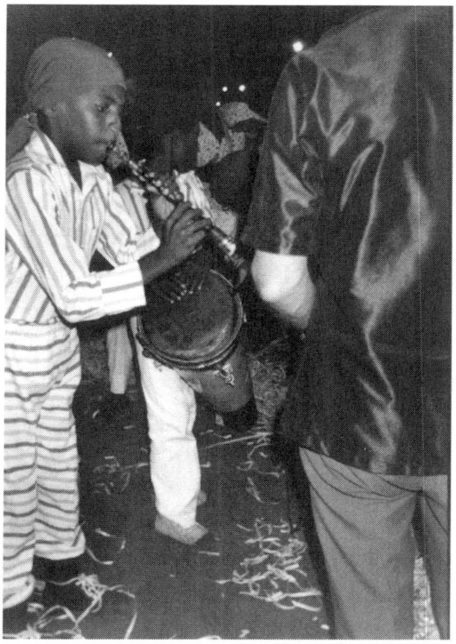

A young musician playing the *corneta china* with the children's section of the Comparsa San Agustín during Carnival 1989, Santiago de Cuba. These children will inherit their fathers' roles in the *comparsa*. © J.B.

celebrations.[8] It is reported that on this day each cabildo 're-enacted' an important homeland celebration beneath the official saint and banner of the *cabildo*. Converging on the Government Palace in Havana, the official representatives of each *cabildo* received a monetary holiday bonus and the spectators also gifted them. Eyewitness accounts of mid-nineteenth century Día de Reyes celebrations stress the 'fantastic' costumes worn by the Black participants and the fact that each parading group was led by a solitary Black masquerader, dressed either as a '*tambor mayor*' [a drum major] or in military fashion. These accounts also mention that each group elected a king and queen (who were actually of the royal lineage of given *cabildos*), who often paraded beneath a parasol. *Cabildo* hierarchy and authority was/is apparent in the use of courtly and/or military dress. These and other *cabildo* regalia, such as identifying flags and certain musical instruments,[9] publicly announce the *cabildos*' capacity for social commentary and activist behavior. In public performance the authority of the *cabildo* was/is demonstrated in visual terms, giving ritual activity both aesthetic and social actuality, comprehensible to those who could/can read the language of its performance.

In Santiago today *cabildo* royal authority is still respected. During the Carnivals I attended, in 1987 and 1989, the Cabildo Carabalí Isuama and the Cabildo Carabalí Olugo (both groups descended from original *cabildos de nación*) paraded in their courtly attire, accompanied by apprentice royalty (children) and musicians. Rank and authority were not being imitated in these carnival performances, but rather publicly displayed. The authority of women is underscored in *cabildo* lineages which pass through the female line and the public performances of these *cabildos* attest to the importance of women in Santiago cultural life (see below). In their costumed appearances we may be looking at an Afro-Cuban appropriation, not imitation, of a royal European style that dates to at least the mid-1600s. Are these contemporary *cabildo* members making the same statement as their seventeenth-, eighteenth- and nineteenth-century brothers and sisters? By retaining the regalia of the courtly entourage and parading during Carnival are they asserting their continued presence and perhaps subversive authority in Cuban society today?

There is ample documentation that in the past *cabildos* provided organizing centers for uprisings, such as the 1812 'Aponte Conspiracy.' In Havana another occurred in 1835 and was led by Juan Prieto, the foreman of the Cabildo Lucumí known as Ello y Oyo, referring to the ancient Yoruba kingdom of Oyo.[10] Throughout the 1800s different *cabildo* groups resisted authoritarian control and persisted in rebellious behavior.[11] The *cabildos'* potential for attracting free Blacks and freed slaves posed an ongoing threat to official stability. Their existence was a threat to any government, so officials began demonstrating less and less support. On December 19, 1884, by official decree both public processions of *cabildos* and Día de Reyes celebrations, which officially lasted from 1823–1884, were prohibited in Havana.[12]

Cabildo performances in Santiago de Cuba were never prohibited, as they were in Havana. In Santiago the Carabalízona de Santa Lucia was registered by 1884, and in 1894 the Baracoa Brothers officially named the new organization Cabildo Carabalí Isuama (Pérez 1982:12). The Carabalí Isuama, like the other important twentieth-century Santiago *cabildo*, the Carabalí Olugo, pays homage to ancestry from the Igbo area of Nigeria where the Isuama live next to the Elugo (Olugo?), north of the area of the Kalabari Ijaw.[13] Carabalí Isuama operated on two levels: as a public *cabildo* that danced and marched during street festivals, and as a private *cabildo* that supported the *mambises*[14] against the Spanish in the Wars of Independence (1868–1895) and that held private religious ceremonies. By the second decade of the twentieth century Cabildo Carabalí Isuama had become a permanent presence in the summer festivities for Saint Santiago (St. James) and Saint Anne, on July 25 and July 26 respectively.

Although their public presence in festivals was severely restricted, *cabildos* continued to exert an influence on Cuban society. For example, during the War of 1898–1902 the Cabildo Carabalí Isuama used its drums to carry illicit weapons and medicine to freedom fighters and even transmitted coded warnings with drumbeats. These covert warnings played a role analogous to the

Members of one of the oldest documented cabildo groups in Santiago proudly proclaim their powerful African roots (most probably from the Bight of Biafra) by appropriating the courtly dress of Europe. Cabildo Carabalí Olugo, Carnival 1989, Santiago de Cuba. © J.B.

coded Abakuá secret script, *anaforuana*, used in Afro-Cuban uprisings as early as 1812.[15]

The Cabildo Queen, who often performed publicly during festivals and performed more selectively during religious ceremonies, plays an important role in cultural life today and has a long history among African Cubans. In April 1853, during the week following Easter, Frederica Bremmer was in Havana and visited a Lucumí Cabildo (Yoruba).[16] There were seats for the king and queen under a canopy on one side of the room. 'The customary dancing was going forward in front of this seat. One woman danced alone, under a canopy supported by four people. Her dancing must have given great delight, for all kinds of handkerchiefs were hanging about her, and a hat even, had been placed upon her head. The women danced on this occasion with each other, and the men with the men. . . . These Cabildos are governed by queens, one or two, who decide upon the amusements, give tone to the society, and determine its extension.'[17]

In Santiago de Cuba, the Cabildo Carabalí Isuama (probably Igbo related) was registered officially by 1884. Although as registered the direction of the *cabildo* was the five Baracoa brothers, the subdirection was controlled by women, who were in charge of the altar and ritual activities. These women were always *miembros proprietos*, or membership through lineage. In Santiago during Carnival and special festivals, when two *cabildos* met on the street during public performances, they performed special rituals. The first section

The royal lineage of Cabildo Carabalí Isuama during Carnival 1989. Left to right: King Euclides Rodriguez; Queen Angela Lugo; Bastonera Caridad Lugo; and Duchess (Mother of the King) Joaquina Caballero. Santiago de Cuba. © J.B.

of the performance always referred in song to their lead dancer as 'the dancingest black woman of the *cabildos*.'[18] The Cabildo Carabalí Isuama still maintains a seated royalty whose lineage descends through the female line: Queen Angela Lugo; Duchess (mother of the King) Joaquina Caballero; Bastonera Caridad Lugo; and King Euclides Rodriquez. They performed during Carnival 1987 and 1989, and their queen and the queen of the Cabildo Tumba Francesa presided over the performance of the Tumba Francesa that I attended during July of 1991. Both Queens directed the dancing and drumming from the sidelines, seated regally in costume and carrying small batons.

After 1884 in Havana and other western centers the public processions of *cabildos* were outlawed, but private meetings and celebrations continued. Officially the *cabildo* began losing whatever power it had accumulated. It seems that by the turn of the century, in some areas, traditional African Cuban culture was already moving toward a folklorized public presence. In the Matanzas Carnival of 1875 the big hit was the *comparsa* called 'Los Negros Congos,' organized by the mulatto Andres Solis, and composed of twenty couples performing a choreographed routine.[19] By 1900 *comparsa* groups had also added small floats, with decorated messages from their commercial sponsors, to their public processions.[20]

The Duchess of the Court, Joaquina Caballero, performing with the Cabildo Carabalí Isuama during Carnival 1989, Santiago de Cuba. © J.B.

However, in Santiago some of the most African (*'el más negro'*) of the carnival groups, those today that are known as *congas*, continued to come into direct conflict with the authorities. On June 19, 1919, the main newspaper in Santiago printed an announcement, known as the Edict of Mayor Camacho Padro, prohibiting '*comparsas carabalís* with African style dancing and drumming' from appearing in Carnival.[21] As a result of the public outcry, journalists and others began a campaign against the Edict. For example, one of the most 'African' of the carnival groups from the *barrio* of Los Hoyos dared to come out and perform, singing the following: 'Camacho doesn't want African *congas*; but I am coming with my trombone; until they give me the prize . . . bon! bon! bon!' (Brea and Millet 1987:112) This expressive popular outcry contributed to the rescinding of the Edict.

By the mid-twentieth century many *cabildos* developed into and integrated with other social groups to form *comparsas*. These *comparsas*, especially those incorporating masquerades and processional street dancing, were relegated to the neighborhoods where they originated, and at times were banned.[22] After a period of sporadic outings, during the period of increased tourism in the 1930s and 1940s, they were allowed to function again. For example, in Havana in 1937 the mayor's office authorized the resurgence of *comparsas* in that year's Carnival, since in the previous few years they had been forbidden 'for the fear that their patriots would use them to . . . disturb the order.'[23] Still, official newspapers carried sensationalistic and derogatory stories about 'cult activity' and the harmful presence of African-derived societies, often accompanied by related stories of the kidnapping of white Cuban children for these activities. (The implication being that these African Cuban organizations were 'cults' in the pejorative sense maintained today.)

Many scholars and informants from Havana credit the influence of Fernando Ortiz[24] with the diminished restrictions against pre-Lenten *comparsa* outings in the capital during the 1930s. In fact, Ortiz's influence around Havana may have helped promote the continuation of African Cuban *comparsas* and the related Abakuá brotherhoods there.[25]

Today in Havana, neighboring Matanzas, and Santiago de Cuba, Carnival is celebrated from the 18th to the 27th of July, in honor of the Revolution, with the final complete Carnival parade held on the 26th. This date commemorates Castro's assault on the Moncada barracks in Santiago de Cuba, on July 26, 1953, which was specifically planned to coincide with traditional Carnival in that city. It is not unusual for governments to officially change the date of carnival celebrations. In Bermuda the traditional Gombey festival used to take place between Christmas and the New Year, but today most Gombeys come out in August during the national holiday for Cup Match. Nassau's Junkanoo parade is held on Boxing Day so as to not compete with

Trinidad Carnival in February. And in Luanda, Angola, carnival has been moved to March 27, celebrating the date of South African withdrawal from Angola during the second war of liberation, 1975–76 (Birmingham 1988:96). Breaking away from the Christian calendar and establishing a political date for carnival celebrations, in order to institute a more contemporary nationalistic and/or political caste to these celebrations, is becoming more and more common. But Cuban carnival history is a little more complicated, especially in Santiago de Cuba, Cuba's second largest city and the city with the largest African Cuban population.

Until the 1920s there were two types of carnival celebrations in Santiago. When it was celebrated in relation to the Catholic calendar, Carnival was held in February or March, during the several days prior to the Lenten period. This celebration in Santiago de Cuba was called Winter Carnival and was private in nature, supported by certain organizations and their clubs, like the Philharmonic Society, the Club San Carlos, the Club Catalonia, or the Club Galicia. (These clubs were firmly rooted in Santiago social life by the 1860s.) Membership was restricted. Most of these organizations had their own buildings where they could meet, rehearse, and sponsor galas. Winter Carnival was nicknamed Carnival for the 'blancos Cubanos,'[26] meaning Cubans with more Spanish than African heritage.

But there was also a Summer Carnival, a Carnival Santiaguero that originated during the slavery period. Held after the sugar and coffee harvest, Summer Carnival originally was intended as a period of rest and divertissement for the laborers (the Blacks) and was eventually nicknamed '*Carnaval* de las clases bajas' (or Carnival of the lower classes) or the Carnival of the *mamarrachos*,[27] which also coincided with the celebration of Saint Santiago (St. James) day on July 25.

By the 1920s Winter Carnival celebrations were abandoned and Summer Carnival remained the only Carnival in Santiago de Cuba. On Fridays, Saturdays and Sundays during the month of June, everyone in Cuba knew one could go to Santiago to party. It was the pre-Carnival season. The major patrons of these summer festivities were local industries: Polar, La Cristal, and Hatuey beer; Bacardí rum, and Edén tobacco.[28] Many of the participants in Summer Carnival were the newly unemployed sugar and coffee workers, who were quite willing to remain in Santiago de Cuba after the harvest and work for these commercial patrons in the jobs that the festival season created. This combination—the unemployed and the commercial sponsor—contributed to the popularity of July Carnival.

During the 1940s and early 1950s especially, Carnival in both Santiago de Cuba and in Havana became increasingly commercialized. The 1959 Revolution altered the previous patronage and the structure of the Carnival parade.

Carnival today does not meet stereotypical expectations of parading agit-prop-style street performances. The themes are rich, eclectic and even raunchy. In Santiago de Cuba in both the 1987 and 1989 Carnivals, the five-year-old *paseo* Textilera, composed of factory workers and their friends, included two hundred and fifty dancers whose performances of choreographed cabaret routines were accompanied by a live drum ensemble and recorded popular music. Other groups included the *paseo* La Kimona, with kimona-clad dancers and men dancing as *ninja* spirits.

During my 1989 fieldwork in Santiago de Cuba I was aware of growing controversy regarding the degree of government support given to the various carnival groups.[29] The newly formed *paseo* Textilera has an entire textile factory and its workers at its disposal. They have ample rehearsal space. During Carnival 1989 I noticed that all the female dancers, perhaps over 100, wore matching leather shoes, quite an accomplishment in Cuba where it is often difficult to find a supply of shoes at all! Why does such a new carnival group merit such strong government support? The position of this particular textile factory in government hierarchy most certainly affected patronage. As with *cabildo* history, the official support and recognition given to various festival groups influences not only their public visibility, but their aesthetic demeanor. Government support and recognition is as much a power issue today as it was in the nineteenth century.

Prior to the Revolution the thematic organization of each group's carnival performance was characterized by eclectic internationalism. Since the Revolution this international flavor has been highlighted by homages to socialist equality and subcultures within Caribbean/Latin American unity.[30]

A brief history of the *paseo* La Placita, Textilera's constant rival, will suffice as a capsule of carnival history. Celebrating its 50th anniversary in 1988, La Placita is also substantially supported. Many credit this to the neighborhood's political history. La Placita's history is rooted in Santiago's history and the *paseo's* development can be used as a case study in twentieth century Carnival. La Placita is located in a neighborhood famous for its revolutionary fighters and subsequent political leaders, and a neighborhood adjacent to the infamous Afro-Cuban barrio of Los Hoyos, which supports its own Carnival *conga*. In fact, *paseo* La Placita was born out of Los Hoyos as a breakaway group in 1938. During the dictatorship of Governor Gerardo Machado (1924–1933) activists from *barrio* La Placita worked to overthrow the government and by 1931 many had affiliated with the Communist Party. General Antonio Maceo, a leader during the Ten Years War (1868–1878),[31] and the Independence War of 1895, known as 'Cuba Libre,' was born in this *barrio*, and his home became the meeting place for subsequent political leaders.[32] Again in 1952 two famous *placiteros*, people from the neighborhood

Paseo La Textilera's float with cabaret-style performers posed as 'the stirrer' in a cocktail. Santiago Carnaval July 1989. © J.B.

of La Placita, Lester Rodriguez and Pedro Miret, joined Fidel Castro in the storming of the Moncada barracks in Santiago. The *barrio* became an arena of armed rebellion and today it is known as 'Placita de las Martyres' in honor of its history of activism for a free Cuba.

During the political turmoil of the 1930s, Carnival was suspended although a few groups came out in 1934 and 1935. When La Placita marched in the Carnival parade of 1938 it was sponsored by the Edén Cigar Company, the soap company Crusellas, and the Cuban branch of Colgate-

Palmolive. During this period La Placita directly competed with its neighbor Conga Los Hoyos. On its parade route La Placita often took a detour to perform in front of the central office building of Edén cigars.

By July 1948 La Placita was fully organized as a *paseo* and paraded during Carnival as 'El Paseo Los Sultanes' which presented a panorama of 'Arabic culture.' The women on the float all wore face scarves and long flowing skirts, while the men wore turbans, scarves, and baggy pants. The fact that by the 1940s female participation in certain carnival groups was publicized as a welcome innovation underscores another aspect of carnival history. Integral to the category of *paseo* is the organization of groups with sections of couple dancers or a chorus of female dancers. And concomitantly, these dancers are costumed according to a generalized theme, rather than as individual characters. While many Santiago carnival enthusiasts bemoan the popularity of the *paseo*, with its recorded music and contemporary choreography, it is through the *paseo* that female participation in Carnival has become guaranteed. (A parallel historical development is evident in Trinidad Carnival where 70% of the performers are women.)[33]

Aside from the women who belonged to the lineage of the historical *cabildos*, with their established courtly entourage, in the twentieth century only a few women have been able to achieve solo recognition and penetrate the performing aspect of Carnival. (Almost all the costume designers and seamstresses are women.) The most famous of these, Gladys Linares Acuña, died in about 1986. Her participation as a *campanera*, playing the *campana macho*, the by now pan-Caribbean percussion instrument made from the brake drum of a car, is legendary in Santiago de Cuba. Beginning at about the age of 15, she displayed so much talent and determination that she was permitted to apprentice to Conga Los Hoyos, the oldest, Blackest, and most famous *conga* in Santiago. She played with them until her death at the age of 49. Known affectionately as La Niña or Ma-Fi-Fa, she achieved such special status that Los Hoyos created a *bandera*[34] in her honor, which hangs permanently in their Foco Cultural. Anyone who asks will hear the by now standard story about Ma-Fi-Fa:

> She was a delicate woman, very short, thin, in other words, tiny, slender. It was inconceivable that among all those black men, that a woman that delicate and feminine, a woman who had no masculine characteristics . . . Astonishingly, when she died the two men who performed the autopsy reported that she was a virgin. [This] is really hard to believe, that among so many men . . .[35]

Gladys Linares Acuña's participation as a *campanera* was inspirational. In the early 1980s an all-women *conga* was founded by the cultural worker Gladys Gonzalez Bueño and functioned for about two years, although they never competed in Carnival. Gonzalez contends that the participants were mostly *paleras* or *santeras* (priestesses of the religions Palo and Santeriá), but that community pressure forced the group to disband despite its special status. Other carnival groups permit young girls to train as musicians and perform during Carnival, but they stop playing when they begin an active social life in their mid-teens. Of course, women can always participate as singers. (Certainly the corollary between Acuña's reputation and her virginity [real or imagined][36] and the status of young girl musicians is parallel to women's participation in ritual activity world over, when the 'contamination' of menstruation or childbearing restricts participation.)

Female authority in Santiago cultural and religious life is not at first apparent. Following a pattern reported by fieldworkers throughout Africa and the Caribbean, initially I was introduced to male Carnival leaders and male spiritual leaders. But consistently after repeated interviews and visits with certain cultural groups, I would meet the women in charge. This is especially true in my research with artists working with religious groups or with performers whose affiliation was with 'religious' societies. As Gladys Gonzalez Bueño explains (and certainly this is nothing new to students of Africa and the African Diaspora):

> They [men in *congas]* accept or reject women based on a special and unique socio-cultural phenomenon that exists here in Santiago, and especially here in this neighborhood of Los Hoyos. There is matriarchy. I'm the boss here; he is not the boss here, and I'm not even from Santiago. It is a unique phenomenon that exists in the homes of Santiago. Men in this neighborhood are known for being somewhat tough, macho, goodlooking . . . but as soon as they step through the door the one in charge is the woman.[37]

This story of male public authority and female private authority is reflected in the most famous *cabildos*, Tumba Francesa and Isuama, as well as in many *casa-templos*, or private religious societies, throughout Santiago.

During Carnival 1989 a group of Swiss and Germans had come to Santiago to apprentice with musicians at the Teatro Cabildo, a contemporary folkloric theatre company. At least half were women, and they participated as drummers in Carnival as a special European (white) *conga*. During Carnival the reaction of Santiagueros was of surprise and amusement, and I heard comments and debated questions about talent and appropriateness. But women have slowly begun to infiltrate male dominated Carnival throughout the Caribbean. In the realm of music there are female pan players in Trinidad, especially with the smaller pan bands that travel on wheeled platforms along the Carnival route, and in Martinique women are now included in the marching bands as percussionists, often playing gongs or sticks.

Highly trained dancers performing a cabaret style routine with Paseo La Placita during Carnival 1989, Santiago de Cuba. Although this style of performance is controversial, La Placita is the fastest growing *paseo* in Santiago and most popular with participants in their teens and twenties. © J.B.

Both in Cuba and in Trinidad the structure of Carnival groups had to change to accommodate the many women who want to participate as dancers. (It is important to distinguish between female participation as dancers, and females who are/were chosen as 'queens,' who simply sit and wave to onlookers. The first Queen of Carnival in Santiago was sponsored by the newspaper 'Diario de Cuba' in 1919. Her name was Ruby Ramsey and she had blonde hair and blue eyes. Since the early 1970s there have been no elected or appointed carnival queens.) For example, one of Santiago's carnival groups most known for its sumptuously costumed female dancers, La Placita, first acquired that reputation in the 1940s when local commercial companies, such as Crusellas soap, began to give substantial monetary donations to major groups. La Placita created a character 'Panchita jabon Condado,' a laundress, who had a solo dance role and danced a narrative about getting clothes clean.[38] (In my research on Santiago Carnival history I have noted an unspoken distinction being made between women who participate in Carnival by posing or dancing on floats and women who actually march and dance in the streets during a parade. In the first instance they are showcased and away from contact with onlookers, in the second the women's aura is considered more immediate and more powerful.) It was not until 1950 that La Placita established an entire carnival section which featured about 50 dancing women. The theme was 'Los Turistas' modeled after a 'typical North American tourist.' The men wore 'baseball' caps, flowered shirts, white pants, and sunglasses. The women wore circle skirts and flowered blouses, with straw hats. As a special feature, the float was a new American automobile with a *corneta china* player on the hood. During the 1950s, despite the profound political turmoil created by Batista's coup d'etat and Castro's attack on the Moncada barracks, La Placita continued to establish sections with choreography that supported female participation. Each year's theme was structured around a different 'Fantasía': Cubana in 1951; Guajira (*campesinos*) in 1952; Gitano-Húngara in 1953 and Escocesa (Scotland) in 1955. La Placita did not compete in 1954 as too many young men from the *barrio* had left to join the freedom fighters. In 1956 the theme was 'Fantasía Brasilera,' and the women were costumed with Carmen Miranda style outfits complete with fruit salad headresses, the float decorated with palm trees and oversized pineapples. Again in 1957 and 1958 the *paseo* didn't parade because of increased political tensions in the city. With the Triumph of the Revolution in 1959, Carnival began again and La Placita's theme was 'Fantasía de Cuba.' Their float was decorated with sugar cane and fruit and received a $200 prize from La Reforma Agraria.

Each year since the Revolution La Placita dedicates its theme and concomitant aesthetic overview to various aspects of pan-Caribbean or pan-socialist culture, from 'Fantasía Staliana' in 1960 to 'Fantasía Czechoslovak' of 1964 to 'Fantasía Indochina' of 1970 to 'Fantasía de Cuba en el CAME' (Council for Mutual Economic Assistance) of 1976 and 'Fantasía en el Cosmos' of 1984. Since 1967 each La Placita carnival parade has included a special section of costumed paired male and female dancers who lead the *paseo* and have become its special trademark. In the 1960s they were directed by two local, well-known dance instructors, Gloria and Maria Rodríguez. By the mid-1980s the artistic director and choreographer were both men. Beginning with only about ten dancing couples, the 1989 outing that I witnessed included about seventy-five couples and at least 100 solo female dancers, in addition to the hundreds of other participants. The entire *paseo* performed a summary of their previous themes, from the homage to Hungary of 1949 to the present. To lead off this eclectic 1989 melange a section of about 100 female dancers performed, costumed in white cabaret-style leotards and colored wings: blue, green, black, and white. This particular section was lead by a couple performing a *pas de deux* in complete cabaret-style. All other sections of the carnival performance were highlighted by scantily clad cabaret-style dancers bumping and grinding in front of a banner announcing each section. (These female performers were initially frowned upon by post-Revolutionary authorities, but since the rise of tourism in the 1980s they are once again a popular part of carnival parades.)

★★★★★

As I reread my fieldnotes from this particular performance, I realize that I imposed my own sense of North American irony on the performance as I noted the rich juxtaposition between the semi-nude dancers performing an impeccable bump amd grind underneath a billowing Soviet flag in the section 'Fantasía Soviética.'

My own ironic and confused reaction to these luscious Cuban dancers has prompted another avenue of research and self-reflection. When I started working in Cuba in 1985, something started nagging at me. I finally knew I had to confront an aspect of Cuban culture that was not only perplexing, but that I was ill-equipped to deal with: the sexy lady, the Tropicana dancer, the bumping and grinding dancers on the carnival floats. As Jeannie Forte has written: 'Women performance artists expose their bodies to reclaim them, to assert their own pleasure and sexuality, thus denying the fetishistic pursuit to the point of creating a genuine threat to male hegemonic structures of women' (1990:252). Although the particular Cuban situation I am describing does not dovetail with all of Forte's remarks, the gist of her argument merits serious consideration. As Donald Cosentino commented in a review of a paper I delivered in 1990, 'The 'Red Hot Mamas' of Cuban Carnival, like the screaming Igbo market women in the Aba riots of the '30s and the Yoruba cash madams of the '70s, had found the brazen flaunting of their sexuality a source of strength. Their flesh could absorb and refract the gaze.'[39]

During a recent trip to Santiago de Cuba I was able to interview some of the dancers I had photographed during Carnival 1989. These dancers performed in cabaret style and two were featured on the Cubanacan float. (Cubanacan is the recently established Cuban Tourist Association.) Moraima, 22 years old in the summer of 1991, had been dancing for three and a half years at a local hotel show and was delighted that I had photographed her. 'I was eager to learn to be a show dancer. . . . My parents are proud of it. . . . They never stopped me. I see this as a normal job; it's my job and I perform it. It is my profession.'[40] As I continued this interview I attempted, tentatively and sometimes awkwardly, to ask my own inelegant questions, as much to clarify my own misgivings as to understand Moraima's position. During Carnival 1987 and 1989 I had noticed that European male visitors, especially the Soviet men who had special front row seats, gloated and gawked at the dancers and insisted on taking many photographs of themselves posed with the dancers. Although the dancers obliged, I also noted side comments and negative facial expressions passed among them. These men were behaving very differently from the Cuban men at Carnival, who were enthusiastic and appreciative, and yet simultaneously distant. After all, semi-nude dancing women in Carnival were ordinary, exciting but not exotic. So I phrased an awkward question to Moraima:

J.B.: 'Foreigners seem to react to you as something strange. How do you feel about this, as a woman?'

Moraima: 'We don't feel offended. You can't feel bad about that. It's a natural thing that comes from them and you can't judge them as bad or feel bad.'

J.B.: 'Many feminists in the U.S. feel that women shouldn't dance for men as you do. As a Cuban woman, what do you think about women in my country who say that this kind of dancing is all mixed up with machismo?'

Moraima: 'As long as there is respect toward us as dancers, even if we dance semi-nude. I think it is natural that it might be like this . . . . If you are asking me I'll tell you not to take it as something bad. It's a natural thing that occurs only when we dance; it's not forever. At the moment that we dance we respect ourselves.'

It seems obvious from the above exchange that Moraima, as well as the other dancers I spoke with, viewed their performed sexuality as just that, a performance. For them, the sexual black female is a part of their cultural heritage that they are proud of. Sexuality, and its use in performance, is inherent in and vital to many African and African-based performance traditions. For example, the Cuban *rumba* is derived from the dance the Yuka, which is often described as a 'courtship' dance during which the male dancer gives the female the *golpe de frente*, which in the *rumba* is called the *vacuno*, or vaccination. It actually consists of a kick toward the female's genital area. In the dance, sometimes the woman covers her genital area with the corner of her skirt and turns away from the *vacuno*, and sometimes she does not. The decision is hers. Sex is the performance topic. In other dances the male/female couples touch and slap each other's thighs or grind suggestively. Sexuality is performed publicly and everyone joins in. As with the Cuban cabaret style carnival dancers, they are enjoying their performance. Especially in the *paseos* that have expanded their structure and choreography to include more and more female dancers, the women finally have an opportunity to perform during Carnival, for historically their roles were restricted to 'folkloric presentations.'

Despite the hundreds of women who perform in 'modern' dances during Carnival, the pull of traditional African Cuban culture is still very strong in Cuba today. Many Carnival participants appreciate this heritage in a personal way that goes beyond folklore. For example, the 1989 performance of *paseo* La Placita discussed above was organized like a play with various acts and scenes, including a section 'Fiestas de America' with a tribute to Mexico with a Mexican 'hat dance' and a tribute to Afro-Cuba with a dance honoring five Santeriá *orichas*:[41] Changó, Babalú Ayé, Ochún, Yemayá, and Eleguá. The Ochún was particularly well performed, very convincing. I suspect that for the last section of her dance, Ochún was possessed. The choreographer ran out to support her and embrace her as he accompanied her to the side lines. Was I watching an actor or a practicioner, or a combination of both? As the director of La Placita, Manuel Fernando Quincosis, commented: 'There are people who still have these beliefs, but the dancers do it from a cultural point of view. More than anything, it's maintaining the culture. . . . There are a few, always, who believe.'[42] It is these believers who each year perform with the more traditional Afro-Cuban sections of the large *paseos*. One dancer, Carlos Cavado, admits that although he has been asked to dance in cabarets, he doesn't like them: 'I've never liked cabaret because it's a whole other thing. The branch I like is folklore, strong stuff. Cabaret is . . . it's very nice and beautiful, some really beautiful dances. But I like folklore, the Black branch, as we call it here. . . . Since that's what I like, that's what I do.'[43]

Most of the dancers performing in these folkloric presentations are confident that their participation is helping to keep that aspect of African Cuban culture vibrant. These are cultural performances, supported by centuries of practice and belief.

Carnival organizers (especially Poder Popular, a branch of city government which is officially responsible for the organization of Carnival[44]) claim an emphasis on unity, like the subtitle of the important journal 'Del Caribe' published in Santiago, 'El Caribe Que Nos Une' (the Caribbean that unites us). For them, the performed reality is equality. Carnival sub-themes emphasize folklore and ethnicity, and all components are treated equally. Distinctions within the community of the Caribbean are expressed through performance, but the performances emphasize that no one sector is more important than another. In Carnival, at least, the officially intended message of equality is successfully portrayed. For example, during the July 1989 carnival parade the crowds in the stands responded enthusiastically to the float sponsored by Cubanacan. The crowd rose to their feet and applauded as the dancers, complete with live pop music and scantily dressed gyrating women, threw paper *serpentinas*. And this same crowd applauded equally heartily when the *oricha* Babalú, from the *paseo* La Placita, was held aloft by three other male dancers. The Babalú was especially convincing, with a limp, a deformed arm, drools, and trance-like dancing.

La Placita's artistic director, Pablo Estrada Pérez, who started dancing with La Placita at 10 and who is now 41, emphatically explains the *paseo*'s commitment to a two-sided reality, a reality which he claims correctly reflects contemporary Cuba and the Caribbean/Latin America as well as Cuba's African heritage. 'In our themes we bring out our cultural ancestry as well as the modern side of Cuba. We pay attention to the *rescuing* [emphasis mine] of folkloric values; that is why there are religious, ritual, elements within the *paseo*. There are people in our *paseo* who belong to Folkloric groups and know these dances; so we learn from these people. All these kinds of groups have been created by our government in order to *preserve* [emphasis mine] the Afro-Cuban culture. So any way, there is always the modern, the Tropicana-style as you call it, and there is the folkloric.'[45]

Most carnival organizers agree with this assessment that African Cuban culture needed or needs 'rescuing' and that in post-revolutionary Cuba this rescuing process is part of the official work of cultural institutions. (This attitude and cultural agenda are shared by most Caribbean nations.)[46] Indeed, since the Revolution, the foregrounding of African Cuban culture has been official cultural policy. Argeliers León, a noted scholar and senior researcher at Casa de las Americas in Havana, was named director of the Folklore Department of the National Theatre after the Revolution, and three African Cuban 'religions'—Palo Monte, Santeriá, and Abakuá—have all been presented in dramatic productions. León and the current choreographer for the Conjunto Folklórico, Rogelio Martinez Furé, both conduct extensive fieldwork in preparation for these productions and include explanatory notes in their programs. The same is true for Rex Nettleford and Fradique Lizardo, directors of the National Dance Theatre of Jamaica and the Ballet Folklorico Dominicano, respectively. These institutions, and their parallel organizations in other Caribbean countries, emphasize this 'rescuing' process in their artistic productions.

Some carnival performances emerge, analogously, as a form of folkloric homage. Costumed Abakuá society *íreme* dancers [costumed dancers belonging to Abakuá] appeared with the *paseo* Sueño during Carnival 1987. One of the Sueño dancers, Yupy Pratt,[47] is a 24-year-old African Cuban artist who has been passionately involved with African Cuban culture since he was quite young. This and his participation in Carnival as an *íreme* exemplify the attitude and circumstances of the impact of this heritage on a child of the Revolution.[48] Yupy moved from Havana to Santiago de Cuba in 1983. While growing up in Havana he apprenticed and studied with older men who were knowledgeable about African Cuban culture, elders who were his 'godfathers,' and who claimed Kongo ancestry. These teachers taught Yupy from old, private notebooks they owned. Yupy copied these documents by hand and now uses his notes for reference and for inspiration for his designs.[49]

Yupy's father is a well-known Santiago musician and leader of the carnival group, *paseo* Sueño. Yupy serves as the *paseo*'s assistant director and assistant

Yupy Pratt wearing the *íreme* costume he designed for Paseo Sueño's Carnival 1987 performance, Santiago de Cuba. There are no Abakuá brotherhoods in Santiago de Cuba, and Pratt intended this presentation as an homage to the Afro-Cuban brotherhood. © J.B.

choreographer. Although Abakuá is primarily active in Havana and neighboring Matanzas, and to the best of my knowledge there are no Abakuá *potencias* (lodges) in Oriente Province, both men learned about the tradition

A Cuban airline poster tempting potential visitors with colorful visions of 'folklore' performances. Pictured here are costumed impersonators of the *íremes* of the Abakuá brotherhood. The *íreme* has become the most popular representation in the nationalization of Afro-Cuban culture.

at the University in Santiago, and Yupy learned more while working with the Ministry of Culture in Havana. Neither man belongs to an Abakuá *potencia*. But, as Yupy pointed out, Abakuá plays a major role in African Cuban history. 'Everyone knows the *íreme*.'[50] Surely Yupy's own intense and personal involvement with traditional African Cuban culture influenced the choice of theme for the 1987 outing of *paseo* Sueño. While living in Havana, he worked with members of the Conjunto Folklórico Nacional, who were also anxious to obtain his innovative African Cuban-based artwork. (Yupy prefers to paint his designs on cloth.) Indeed, one special book he owns, which includes motifs and translations of traditional African Cuban material, was published by the Folklórico Nacional in the early 1960s, in the first few years after the Revolution.

Abakuá *íreme* dancers are an important and colorful aspect of Cuban national folklore and are considered picturesque by many Cubans and tourists. Simultaneously Abakuá *potencias* play an active role in the daily life of their members (see above). The Cuban scholar Israel Moliner Castañeda considers the appearance of Abakuá society *íreme* dancers in contemporary public performances as a form of 'folkloric propaganda,' a superficial

The brother of the chief *houngan*, Pablo Milanés Fuentes, from Pílon del Cauto, a Haitian-Cuban settlement in the mountains above Santiago de Cuba, dancing Ogún during the 1986 Festival of Caribbean Culture, Santiago. © J.B.

reflection of a historical phenomena.[51] The same might be said of the frequent appearance of Yoruba-based costumed *orichas* in festivals, carnivals, and dance presentations all over Cuba. For example, a 1988 ballet I attended, sponsored by the Dirección Provincial de Cultura, Santiago de Cuba, was entitled 'Ercilí.'[52] The main characters were Ercilí (Erzulie) and Ogún Guerrero (Ogún the Warrior). The narrative was loosely based on the stories told in the Haitian Cuban communities located in the mountains above Santiago de Cuba (see Tumba Francesa section) and research conducted by scholars at the cultural organization, the Casa del Caribe, in Santiago.

In Santiago de Cuba during Carnival 1989 eight out of nineteen groups included tributes to traditional African Caribbean culture in their repertoires. Some recreated the courtly entourage, so prevalent at the turn-of-the-century and reminiscent of Fancy Dress Jamaican Jonkonnu. Others included choreographed routines paying homage to the *orichas* of the Santeriá religion, and still others incorporated songs and dances learned from the Haitian Cuban communities of Oriente Province. A song performed by Cabildo Carabalí

Isuama included the chorus 'Africa, Africa, we cannot forget you,' and a section of the *paseo* Sueño sang: 'My Mother, my Father came from Haiti. I dream of Haiti.'

The *paseo* Los Pinos also included a Haitian Cuban section. The performers were dressed in white with red kerchiefs and head-ties, and the Ogún 'impersonator' wore a blue kerchief and carried a machete. As he danced in the center of a circle created by the other performers, he directed attacks on the other dancers and then turned the machete on himself. Although the *paseo* did not announce the title of this sequence, its homage to the Haitian Ogou is obvious from the following description from Haiti: 'The vacillation of Ogou's anger, its tendency to switch targets from his enemies to his followers, has historical precedent. This is a facet of his character which is present in the Yoruba tradition, which the slaves no doubt brought to the island of Hispaniola. . . . Ogou's anger comes full circle and ultimately is directed against himself. This is the dimension of Ogou's character that reveals itself in the final movement of his ritual sword dance, when he points the weapon at his own body' (Brown 1989:76–77). The performance of this Cuban Ogún and of a dancer from the *paseo* El Tivolí,[53] who performed a possession ritual often associated with the very traditional Afro-Haitian Cuban Tumba Francesa groups, are both additional evidence of the vitality associated with traditional African Cuban culture.

* * * * *

As Victor Turner suggests, a cultural performance is part of an ongoing social process when people themselves are conscious of, through participating themselves or witnessing, the nature, texture, style and given meanings of their own lives. I reject an abstract structuralist model of culture which claims to approach meaning without attending to the relevance and importance of the action of a cultural performance; the structuralist model tends also to deny the real activist aesthetics that are embedded in such performances. Most conventional analyses of carnival celebrations worldwide stress the importance of what is usually called 'rites of reversal' when there is a suspension of all hierarchical ranks, privileges, norms and prohibitions during the carnival celebrations. The commoner plays king; the folk take over the streets, and as Mikhail Bakhtin (1984) so eloquently points out, festive laughter is directed at everyone, even the carnival participants themselves. But this overused formula does not apply to Cuban Carnival today.[54] In Santiago the actual Carnival parade is quite distinct from Carnival celebrations, and the costumed performers, although having fun, are serious and highly competitive. The street celebrations do not include costumed performers, but rather are dancing and eating/drinking street parties held in specially designated areas of the city. It is a common 'joke' in Santiago (where food shortages are frequent) that one cannot buy chicken in the market during Carnival, because it is being reserved for the special street vendors.

In European carnival there is often a thin line between the spectator and the participant, for carnival performances occur in public, in the open, in a town square or along a main street. Frequently the spectator is swept up into the narrative of the action. This is basically still the case in Port of Spain, Trinidad, where the *mas* bands may end up parading across the Savannah stage in front of the footlights and television cameras, but they have marched from their respective neighborhoods to Frederick Street and up the length of the street to the Savannah. Street interaction happens not only on Mardi Gras, but during the three days before. The Carnival Roadmarch of Monday and Tuesday includes thousands and thousands of revelers.

But that is not the case in Havana or Santiago de Cuba today. In Santiago the carnival groups do not dance together in the streets. Their parade is limited to a 4–5 block area of the Alameda, which is cordoned off by bleachers and grandstand. There is no street intermingling of the carnival groups where costuming (disguise, transformation) and concomitant characters permit a genre of interaction reserved for this occasion in other countries. In Santiago de Cuba even the audience is restricted (and I use the word audience very deliberately), for tickets for the carnival parade are hard to come by and certain sections of the grandstand are reserved by invitation only. It is in front of a reserved section, where the jury also sits, that the various groups actually perform for their awards. Bakhtin warns that carnival must not be confused with what he terms the self-serving festivities fostered by governments, secular or theocratic. For Bakhtin, carnival is revolution itself, while others regard carnival as a safety valve for the passions of the folk, who might otherwise lead a revolutionary uprising. But, I believe, by the late twentieth century, the definition of carnival itself is changing. In most celebrations that I am aware of, competitions restricted to special cordoned-off areas are the norm. More and more, authorities are restricting street interactions, and carnival parades resemble theatrical performances structured by a proscenium arch.[55]

In Santiago de Cuba, before the Revolution all day long costumed carnival groups would mingle with people on the major streets in town. The streets would be lined with what Santiagueros refer to as kiosks, or stalls selling food, drink, etc. As *conga* musicians marched down the street, people would pour out of their houses and join the procession. Or cars with loudspeakers would play a favorite tune, and instruct the people to come out in the streets and dance. Eventually the entire street would be packed with dancing people. Today, the stalls which sell food and drink and the music are restricted to certain hours, and the recorded or live music is limited to a stage area built in designated streets in certain neighborhoods. There are no costumed characters on the street. The intermingling is restricted to social dancing in special public areas.

In 1988 I attended Carnival in Port of Spain, Trinidad, while living with a family in the Belmont section, the home of Jason Griffith's famous 'sailor bands.' One day as we were resting from the previous night's activities, a section of a *mas* band from the neighborhood marched by. Soon the entire block was following behind the musicians. I have been told that all neighborhoods in Port of Spain support these spontaneous parades. This genre of street interaction is extremely limited in Santiago de Cuba.[56] A few times I have seen members of a theater group, Cabildo Teatral Santiago, borrow costumes and go house to house in certain neighborhoods, singing, in character, and asking for donations. Today, this is a deliberate nostalgic activity designed to help recall traditions and provide amusement. Also, in 1989 a delegation from a sister city, Santiago de Caballeros, the Dominican Republic, visited Santiago de Cuba during Carnival. Accompanied by members of the Casa del Caribe, affiliated with the Ministry of Culture, two costumed and whip-swinging masked performers danced down the major street Martí, the heart of the Conga Los Hoyos neighborhood, past their Foco Cultural, during the daytime non-carnival hours. This too was a special performance, not a carnival-type street intermingling.

Carnival embraces heterogeneous traditions. It includes religions, class structure, ancestral city identities, and popular culture. Carnival is multivalent; impersonation is balanced by self-presentation; people play others and people play themselves. The entire performance is organic, as each segment, of history or of the performing group, competes for recognition. Often history is played as a living text. Stuart Hall (1990:225) reminds us that the history of all enforced Diasporas is replete with experiences of dispersal and fragmentation. 'Cultural identities come from somewhere, have histories. But, like everything which is historical, they undergo constant transformation. Far from being eternally fixed in some essential past, they are subject to the continuous play of history, culture and power.' As the festivals of the French revolution used the model of antiquity to visually and psychologically create a new order, Cuban Carnival stresses Caribbean and Socialist unity expressed through performances that pay tribute to the history and folklore of individual nations.

The construction/reconstruction of certain performance elements can be looked at as the use of unfamiliar things in familiar settings or familiar things in unusual settings. In either case the leaders of each carnival group have deliberately chosen to, or agreed to, incorporate a specific cultural genre into a larger performance. The use of the familiar allows for a broad-based appreciation and understanding, such as the Tropicana style of dancing and undress. Remember, after Castro closed the Tropicana, popular pressure forced its reopening. Carnival's insistent emphasis on ethnic heritage is more problematic.

Ethnic or national heritage is still important in Cuba, although much of its public presentation is reserved for folkloric presentations. These folkloric elements have a long history in public performances. While Yoruba-derived religion and concomitant *oricha* worship is widespread in the Americas, there is national recognition that only in Cuba did a Cross River tradition from Nigeria implant, survive and flourish. This history is condensed into the image of the Abakuá *íreme*. Not only does the *íréme* play a major role in cultural performances, but the use of the *íréme* as a national emblem is a deliberate, self-conscious statement on the part of official cultural institutions. The Abakuá society has developed a reputation as the most socially dangerous and potentially subversive of all African Cuban groups. Yet the *íreme* is depicted on airline posters, meeting hall banners, designer fabrics, etc. *Íreme* dolls are sold at all tourist hotels.

How does an emblem of a powerful and extant African Cuban brotherhood publicly function in contemporary Cuba? Fernando Ortiz's publications have, in post-revolutionary Cuba, reinspired a new generation of festival artists. Today in Cuba ethnic dance theater or *danza folklórico* is often used as a restoring device for national pride. Do these tourist items and the folkloric performances violate African Cuban cultural values? Is there a disparity between the beliefs of this minority and national cultural values? Used as a case study, does the persistent image of the *íreme* point to the existence of multiple realities which are mediated by a common symbol, the *íreme*? Official Cuban cultural policy claims that public aesthetic display is important in resurrecting, preserving, and/or rejuvenating African Cuban culture, especially when that culture was so deprecated in pre-revolutionary society. But I wonder.

Public display often can diffuse the power of an image, especially if that image was once restricted in its use and symbolic interpretive potential. The Abakuá society used to have a secret language. In 1975 Lydia Cabrera published a book which decoded that language, and today these same once-private ideograms are used to decorate banners in conference halls and are displayed with translations. Yupy Pratt uses these same ideograms in his artwork, recombining them freely. For him they are an emblem of his African heritage, an emblem to be used proudly in a public artistic context.

Have national cultural institutions appropriated imagery from a powerful African-based Cuban brotherhood and thus perpetuated the continued demise of that social force? Certainly by incorporating the performance of Abakuá *íreme* dancers or performances by a costumed Changó or Ochún into Carnival, expressions of ethnicity get aired publicly. Where does one draw the line between public expressions of ethnicity accomplished with pride and 'folkloric propaganda'? Cuban Carnival performances present common emblems which can be interpreted in multiple ways, reflecting the existence of multiple realities which are mediated through performance and exhibition, often employed against their original intent. At this particular point in my research I believe that these images, these carnival performances, are double coded. For African Cubans they are powerful messages, reminders of an ongoing, rich and powerful reality. According to official culture they are indicators of the new status, an elevated status, of the African Cuban in post-revolutionary society.

Notes

1. The research for this article was begun during my work as co-curator of the exhibition 'Caribbean Festival Arts,' sponsored by the Saint Louis Art Museum with funding from the NEH and NEA and Rockefeller Foundation. Subsequent fieldwork was carried out with support from the American Council of Learned Societies, 1989-90, and San Francisco State University in summer 1991. An earlier version of this article appeared in *African Arts*. April 1991. xxxlv.
2. According to Enrique Bonne, the head of Carnival Commission in Santiago de Cuba, the yearly budget for Santiago Carnival is usually just over one half a million, and each carnival group must make an official presentation to receive funding. Interview, July 27, 1991.
3. In Santiago in 1982 four Focos were created for the following groups: Tumba Francesa; Conga de Los Hoyos; and the Cabildos Carabalí Isuama and Carabalí Olugo. These four were honored with the title 'centenarios,' signifying that each one was more than one hundred years old. During the next three years eight other Focos were established.
4. Interview, July 29, 1991.
5. This and other translations are by myself with the assistance of Sergio Waisman and Alina del Pino. In many cases I have been unable to find an exact translation of the Cuban, especially when phrases are part of an Afro-Cuban vocabulary or are particular to Santiago. In this case the *almirez* must be a type of percussion instrument, probably similar to the brake drum so popular today. The *botijuela* is a wind instrument created from an earthen jug with holes cut on one side. Fernando Ortiz indicates that it is known as a *bunga* by older Afro-Cubans. *Nuevo Catauro de Cubanismos* (La Habana: Editorial de Ciencias Sociales, 1985) p. 89.
6. In Cuba the *cabildo* is a mutual aid society, organized by neighborhood and ethnicity. Historically membership was structured by descent, although today other factors are influential.
7. Interview, Pablo Estrada Pérez, March 10, 1990, Santiago de Cuba.
8. Official Día de Reyes celebrations in the area of Havana were instituted during the government of Capitan General de la Isla de Cuba, Dionisio Vives, 1823–1832. Robin Moore includes an extended discussion of both Día de Reyes celebrations and Carnival in Havana in his 1997 publication. Beginning with a discussion of the controversy

surrounding the date of the abolition of Día de Reyes, he also discusses conflicting documentation on slave participation in Havana Carnaval, and the subsequent fluctuating participation of Afro-Cuban *comparsas* in Carnaval in the first two decades of the twentieth century.

9. The Carnival Museum in Santiago has in its collection a Tumba Francesa drum which is decorated with the national crest and the date 10 October 1868, the date of the beginning of the Wars for Independence. The Tumba Francesas of Oriente Province developed from *cabildos de nación*, with the law of 2 January 1887 all Tumba groups received the name of a saint to parade behind, and their King and Queen became known as President and Presidenta. Teresa Toranzo Castillo, "La Tumba Francesa 'Los Maceo-Bandera-Moncada' como Exponente de la Cultura Popular Tradicional," *Trabajo de Diploma, Facultad de Artes y Letras, Universidad de Oriente*, June 1988, p.27.
10. In Cuba Yoruba are known as the *Lucumís* (from olokumi-'my friend' in Yoruba).
11. By 1836 the Abakuá lodge Efik Butón emerged from Cabildo Carabalí Brícamo Apapa Efi in Regla across the Havana harbor and established a reputation for being the most aggressive and boisterous group in Havana (Roche-Monteaguado 1925:4). In Matanzas in 1862 the 'Cabildo Niño Jesús of the Carabalí Bríkamo' authorized the establishment of the Abakuá lodge Uriabón, which also developed a reputation as 'troublemaker' (Moliner Castañeda 1987a:n.p.).
12. Slave emancipation was a slow process in Cuba, dating to 1880 with an added six-year apprentice period.
13. In Cuba, Carabalí generically refers to the many groups arriving from the Bight of Biafra. Today, in Nigeria, Isuama is an Igbo (Ibo) group living inland (east) and upriver from the Kalabari Ijaw (Ijo) near the Niger River. The Abakuá brotherhood originated in the area of the Cross River, Nigeria. Sidney Kasfir indicates that Olu is the precolonial term for 'upcountry' (as opposed to riverine) Igbo, so the linguistic connection between eastern Cuba and Igbo country is again suggested (personal communication, April 17, 1997).
14. Fernando Ortiz (1985 [1923]:337) gives various possible origins for this word, while indicating that the most likely source based on its use in Cuba is Congo, where *mambi* refers to a vicious or dangerous man. In Cuba *mambi* can also be used to refer to a type of 'witchcraft.' How perfect for underground freedom fighters!
15. Although Robert Farris Thompson documented Abakuá *anaforuana*, called *nsibidi* among the Ejagham of Nigeria, in use as of 1839, David Brown (1989:23) has established its use as of 1812. The Abakuá brotherhood is based on an historical relationship with Ejagham societies in Eastern Nigeria, although membership is established by an admission fee and loosely constructed ethnic bonds. During recent fieldwork David Brown was told that there are at least 48 active Abakuá *potencias* in Matanzas and neighboring areas. Personal communication, December 1989.
16. (1853:183–185) She identifies this particular *cabildo* as Cabildo de Señora Santa Barbara [Changó] de la nacíon Alagua.
17. Ibid. p. 184
18. Nancy Pérez et al. (1982:16) The first dance they performed is called the Bata Armarilla, after their costume, a yellow and white long dress with full arms. I think it is important to note that yellow and white are the colors of Ochún who is associated with the Virgen de la Caridad del Cobre, whose basilica is located a twenty minute drive from Santiago.
19. Licenciado Israel Moliner Castañeda (1987b).
20. Virtudes Felu (1985:48)
21. Rafael Brea y José Millet (1987:111)
22. *Comparsas* also encompassed the neighborhood *parranda*, or groups of musicians and singers, and the *charanga*, a small neighborhood party group.
23. Administración del Alcade Dr. Antonio Beruff Mendieta (1937:6).
24. Fernando Ortiz (1881–1969) is one of Cuba's most prolific and revered scholars. His first publication on African Cuban society appeared in 1906, *Hampa Afrocubana: Los Negros*

Brujos, and he published continually until his death. A pioneer of modern sociology and anthropology in Latin America, Ortiz originated the concept of 'transculturation' which emphasizes a horizontal lending and borrowing of cultural constructs, in opposition to 'acculturation' which posits the enveloping of one cultural mode by a more dominant mode.

25. In the early 1920s Ortiz published a series of *íreme* images in a major early work on African Cuban culture. Most of my fieldwork has been in Santiago de Cuba, and to the best of my knowledge there is no organized Abakuá brotherhood in Oriente Province, although it is evident, from the interviews I have conducted, that Abakuá-based knowledge is still important for many individual Cubans there. Today in Cuba the costumed dancers representing members of the Abakuá society are called *íreme*. Traditionally these same dancers were known as *diablitos* or *ñáñigos*, the individual members of Abakuá. Ortiz's 1925 publication included the by now often reproduced mid-nineteenth century engraving by Pierre Toussaint Frédéric Mialhe, who was born April 14, 1810, in Bordeaux and was professor at the Academy of Painting in Havana, 1831–34 and 1857–61, and the 1870s and 1880s paintings of the Andalucian-born Cuban *costumbrista* Victor Patricio Landaluze, who died in Havana in 1890. Lydia Cabrera, who did most of her research in the 1940s and 50s, published her first work on this subject in 1958, *La sociedad secreta Abakuá*, which as it turns out was the last book she published in Cuba before leaving. Both this publication and her El Monte of 1954 include photographs of Abakuá *íreme*. I have recently learned that these photographs were taken by Pierre Verger, who visited Cuba with Alfred Métraux in 1957 and worked with Lydia Cabrera. It seems that Verger also took a bus trip across Cuba in 1936. I have never seen the photographs from his early trip reproduced, and have seen only a few of his 1957 photographs. Documenting Verger's work throughout the Caribbean remains an interesting project.
26. Interview with historian Nancy Pérez, July 18, 1989, Santiago de Cuba.
27. Literally translated, *mamarracho* connotes a grotesque, comic figure, usually used derogatorily. In Santiago de Cuba *mamarrachos* came to signify costumed characters who assumed sarcastic and funny poses and who participated in Summer Carnival.
28. Eladio 'Tatica' Pérez has been working with the *comparsa* Paso Franco for 35 years. He was 64 years old in 1989. Before the Revolution, he recalled that Paso Franco was supported by a variety of interests, including Edén tobacco, Bacardí rum, and city government. *Comparsa* members would sell lottery-type tickets on the streets, and in return the *comparsa* would keep the profits while the winner would receive a silver pendant with the commercial firm's name on it. Interview, July 24, 1989, Santiago de Cuba.
29. Historically, before and after the Revolution, patronage and wealth has correlated with the race and class of a given carnival group's members. The variability of government patronage merits a much deeper analysis than I can provide here, although it is relevant to remember that in Cuba all means of production are owned by the state.
30. In 1989 the *paseo* Sueño included a danced narrative about Jamaican police harassment and the Rastafarian life style in their performance.
31. The Ten Years War began in October 1868 with the 'Grito de Yara' in Oriente Province and remained a struggle restricted to the eastern part of the island.
32. Oriente Province and its capital Santiago de Cuba have consistently produced leaders and supporters in revolutionary struggles. In 1878-80 a new separatist war broke out in Oriente, but after nine months the rebellion was crushed. During the War for Independence Antonio Maceo and Maximo Gomez launched their campaign on the western provinces from the east. Maceo was killed in 1896.
33. In the late 1940s after the war, some women, who were professional hairdressers and seamstresses, brought out their own small female bands. Everyone dressed the same, and the most popular costumes were the Barbajan cooks or the Martinique dancers, dressed in long skirts with layers of lace trim, off the shoulder blouses, head ties and hoop earings. By the early 1960s younger male bandleaders began to divide their bands into sections

which permitted increased female participation. Each section consisted of female solo dancers costumed identically. By the 1980s female participation exploded. I thank Pamela Franco, a graduate student at Emory University and a scholar of Carnival, for helping to verify this information.

34. When I visited the Foco Cultural of Los Hoyos in 1986 I first saw and photographed this *bandera.* It wasn't until subsequent trips that I was able to collect her history.
35. Gladys Gonzalez Bueno, interview, July 21, 1991
36. It is not important if Acuña was a virgin or not. What is important is that this is now the official story.
37. Interview, July 25, 1991. For an important discussion of woman power behind male authority and more visible performance presence see: Anita J. Glaze (1981).
38. This and subsequent data about La Placita's performance history is from Rosario Fernández de la Uz (1987-88).
39. *African Arts.* (April 1991:8).
40. Interview, July 23, 1991.
41. The Santeriá religion is in part derived from a Yoruba religious base.
42. Interview, March 10, 1990, Santiago de Cuba.
43. Interview, July 26, 1991.
44. In existence since the mid-1970s, Poder Popular is based on an electoral system for local, regional, and national assemblies of its members.
45. Interview, March 10, 1990, Santiago de Cuba.
46. See Rex Nettleford (1988).
47. Yupy Pratt is a pseudonym. During the 1980s, while he was living in Santiago de Cuba, Pratt asked me to use this pseudonym. When I met him again in Havana in the 1990s, he asked me to switch to using his given name, Ludvik Perez Reginfo. I have an article coming out in *African Arts* that discusses his religious artistic production.
48. I interviewed Yupy Pratt for the first time in Santiago de Cuba on June 5, 1988. Before actually meeting him I saw him perform in Carnival 1987 and asked members of the Ministry of Culture to help me locate the artist who had designed the costumes for the *paseo* Sueño.
49. This reminds me of an incident in Haiti described by Zora Neale Hurston. She recalls seeing a *houngan*'s copy book with drawings of the *loas* and their attributes. *Tell My Horse* (Philadelphia: J.B. Lippincott, 1938).
50. Actually this is not true for all Cubans. While in Havana shopping for souvenirs I found that none of the younger clerks knew what *íreme* dolls were. Also, I questioned some young adults in Santiago, and they knew nothing about the Abakuá tradition; they are white Cubans with no interest in traditional culture.
51. Moliner Castañeda is the Especialista en Estudios Culturales de la Provincia de Matanzas. This quote is from an interview, July 21, 1987, in Havana.
52. This production was a joint project of the Conjuntos Folklórico Santiago and principal dancers from the Ballet Royal de Wallonie, Belgium.
53. Tivolí is the original French-Haitian neighborhood in Santiago.
54. The appropriateness of applying this formula to Brazil also is disputed hotly today.
55. It is interesting to note that in French revolutionary festivals the emphasis was on open, horizontal space, stressing lack of boundaries, while in Cuba, festival space is delineated by parallel barriers which create vertical lines of closed performance.
56. Sometimes *conga* musicians may celebrate the opening of Carnival week by parading in their own neighborhoods around their Foco Cultural, but I have only heard of this happening in two special neighborhoods, Los Hoyos and San Pedrito.
Villarreal, Juan Jerez. 1960. *Oriente: biografia de una provincia.* La Habana: Editorial Siglo XX.

Carnival in Santiago de Cuba at the End of the Millenium[1]

Judith Bettelheim

What distinguishes Cuba from other Caribbean tourist destinations is the global impact of its Afro-Cuban cultural traditions, music, dance, and religion. Haiti is deemed too dangerous for most tourists, and visitors to Jamaica most often travel to 'well protected' hotel destinations. Perhaps these tourists will visit a folkloric or nightclub-style performance, but visitors to Cuba do not rely on hotel performances; instead they go to cultural or religious centers, searching for the best places to dance and hear music. For such visitors, there is even a special category of tours called 'folklore tourism.' Of these offerings, one of the most popular destinations is the performance workshop 'FolkCuba' held by the Conjunto Folklórica in Havana.[2] Here Conjunto members teach drumming, singing, and special dances to interested visitors. This relationship between tourism and popular culture has created a commodification of 'local color' (double entendre intended) which has seriously affected aspects of Afro-Cuban culture and carnaval performances.

During the 1980s official culture often used Afro-Cuban emblems to signify what was considered the new, open and more equal Cuban society. In fact, the *íreme*, the costumed initiate of the Abakuá society, has become the most popular representation in the nationalization of Afro-Cuban culture. In the 1980s miniature *íreme* dolls were sold at all tourist hotels and a Cuban airline poster tempted potential visitors with colorful visions of 'folklore' performances, often including photographs of the dancing *íreme*.[3] (By the mid-1990s these had been replaced by miniature rumba dancers and beautifully attired women in color-coordinated dresses; some I suspect are dressed as *oricha* impersonators.) In the 1989 Santiago Carnaval, young, costumed Afro-Cubans paid tribute to the dancing *íreme*. Even though they themselves were not initiated members of the Abakuá society,[4] the carnaval participants considered this performance an homage to their heritage and to the continued role of the society in contemporary Cuban life. These examples of commodification generate many questions: Do the *íreme* tourist items and these carnaval performances mean the same thing to different segments of society, or is there a disparity in the understanding of this emblem of Afro-Cuban culture among the different segments? Where does one draw the line between proud public expressions of ethnicity and 'folkloric propaganda?' Although these questions may not produce clear answers, the question itself is on the minds of many carnaval participants and cultural leaders in contemporary Cuba. As the following discussion will demonstrate, the commodification continues to expand.

In the 1990s not only the Abakuá but Afro-Cuban religions, for some people, have also become commercial ventures. Even among religious leaders there is increased debate and controversy. Some of the religious houses I recently visited in Havana had large signs over their front doors, and charged admission to visitors wanting to visit and to photograph.[5] At another religious house in Santiago I visited, the leader handed me a business card, complete with the group's official name, address, and phone number. As Afro-Cubans attempt to participate in the U.S. dollar–based economy, they sell what they can, what they 'own'—in this case their religion, now more than ever open to the public for a fee. For instance, in Santiago, the cultural institution Casa del Caribe has opened a building dedicated to the representation of Cuba's 'non-institutionalized' religions. (That is Cuban terminology.) Each room of the converted residence is dedicated to a different religion. Permanent altars have been constructed; religious objects are displayed, and paintings have been commissioned, etc. A fee is charged to the many cultural tours or individual scholars who visit and receive docent-style lectures.[6] Here there is (ostensibly) no photography allowed.

Considering this new open policy, ironically, there were few references to Afro-Cuban religion included in the 1998 Santiago carnaval parade. Ten years earlier, in Carnaval 1989, eight out of nineteen groups included substantial tributes to Afro-Caribbean culture in their repertoires. In 1998 two groups did include a costumed dancer representing the *oricha* Eleguá dancing with his special insignia, a *garabato* or hooked staff, who cleared a path for the rest of the *comparsa*. Even though it is completely appropriate for Eleguá to take the lead, for he clears the road and opens pathways, these solo paraders seemed out of place, as the remainder of the *comparsas*' performances had no relation to Afro-Cuban culture or history.

At this point I can only guess why this change has taken place. Perhaps as the religious institutions themselves are becoming more and more available to the visitor, there is less necessity to perform the religion in Carnaval. In fact, if the previous decade's performances can be considered a way to publicly proclaim the continued power and perseverance of Afro-Cuban based religion, then the new open policy of accessibility may negate the need (or desire) to perform the religions in Carnaval. Robin Moore (1997:226) agrees in part with this assessment, noting that in the 1990s 'African derived religious expression' is more openly visible than ever before. More than ever 'popular singers and entertainers openly incorporate sacred melodies and lyrics into otherwise secular stage acts . . . countless pop singles that have been released since about 1992 contain lyrical references to the *orichas* and the religious practices associated with them.'

Certainly, the tourist industry has been expanded during the 'special period' specifically to try to fill an economic gap.[7] But in many cases the reality of the 'tourist industry' implies the manufacture of cultural identities for the 'tourist.' In this case, the tourist is predominantly a person from Canada, Spain, Italy, or Germany; in other words, the majority are white Europeans or Euroamericans. In 1997, the *New York Times* reported the following statistics: 600,000 tourists were counted in 1994; 1.2 million arrived in 1996. According to a June 1999 National Geographic article, 1.4 million tourists visited Cuba in 1998, and in 2000 about 2 million are expected, and this figure does not include the thousands of visitors who travel with academic and other non-tourist programs.

In Santiago alone in 1999–2000, the Hotel Santiago was taken over by the Spanish chain Melia, which also built the elegant Melia Cohiba in Havana. The refurbished downtown Santiago hotel Casa Grande has been transferred to the Accor chain from France, which runs the Sofitel chain in the U.S. Accor has also acquired the adjacent Hotel Venus and plans to connect the two with a grand swimming pool. Two other major hotels in Santiago, Las Americas and Hotel San Juan (until the pullout of the Soviet Union known as El Leningrado), are still majority-owned by Cuba, and each is being refurbished.[8] Each of these establishments will have a 'nightclub,' complete with the requisite entertainment or a 'disco,' with unofficial entertainment. Since 1993 the U.S. dollar has been legal tender. All over Cuba the dollar-driven economy and the dependence on tourism for much-needed dollars has had a huge impact and caused many social changes. The changes in Carnaval are no exception. Just as tourists in the 1920s and 1950s (the two previous periods of major tourist activity) were drawn to the 'sensuality' of the island and 'exoticism' of its Afro-Cuban culture, [9] today, too, increased tourism is exploiting both gender and ethnicity.

In Santiago de Cuba during the 1980s the carnaval parade was held in the wharf area and ran up the connecting large boulevard, the Alameda. Thus the parade was downtown, in a densely populated mostly Afro-Cuban barrio with a long cultural history. The small, neighboring streets of the old city were decorated and competitions were held to determine which neighborhood was most inventive in its street decorations. A central section of the Alameda was cordoned off for bleachers and the jury, and the carnaval parade was restricted to a street lined with parallel rows of bleachers set up on either side.[10] The actual parade took place in this approximately three-block-long section, and seating was limited to ticket holders and invited guests. By 1994 the parade was moved to midtown, around Parque Delores, and in 1996 the parade was moved to yet another newer midtown neighborhood along the wide Boulevard Garzon with its combination of high rise apartment buildings and family houses. This new location is away from the older, more Afro wharf neighborhood, a significant change indicative of the many more to come.

A change of venue is an important indicator of the rationale for the government's support and an indication of the government's desire for a change in the social face of the festivities. Pedro Pérez Sarduy reports that, in Havana around the mid-1970s, carnaval organizers decided to move the parade to the whiter, more middle-class Vedado section of the city. In the 1990s, presumably to cater to the tourist trade, Havana Carnaval moved again, this time to the Malecón (Seafront Drive), alongside the Hotel Nacional and other major tourist hotels.[11]Considering these historical precedents, for the remainder of this essay I will elucidate the changes in Santiago Carnaval and provide a few specific case studies.

Conga Los Hoyos, the most powerful and 'blackest' (lo más negro) *conga* in Santiago, usually had hundreds of participants and often simply took over the streets during carnaval time. Los Hoyos is one of Santiago's main '*centenarios*,' the designation given to cultural groups that have been registered for over 100 years. (I first saw them perform in 1986 during the then annual spring festival celebrating Caribbean culture, sponsored by local Cultura Municipal.) Its performances have always been eclectic and individual, usually consisting of a strong instrumental ensemble (*corneta china*, metal brake drums, three types of drums) and many singers. The community of Los Hoyos followed behind, singing and dancing in a dense crowd of non-choreographed individuals. Conga members sang and danced together, but there were no elaborate routines.

As is perhaps to be expected, considering the changes outlined above, the *congas* of Carnaval are not what they used to be. Since my visit in 1991, Conga Los Hoyos experienced a split in leadership and members of their cultural center had splintered over disagreements as to whether the center should be opened for mingling dancing by paying tourists. There were also disagreements as to the nature of their carnaval participation. In 1998 a small group performed, led by a weak Eleguá. This Los Hoyos outing also included a section of schoolgirls dancing in a choreographed cabaret style as a prominent part of the performance (see below). For many of the older community members this change constituted a complete break with tradition and they simply did not parade. Youth seemed to have taken over.

A cultural worker I have known over the years, Gladys Gonzalez Bueno, used to work with the Santiago *cabildos* and with Los Hoyos. I was surprised when I didn't see her at the carnaval parades, so I looked her up. She had quit working with Cultura Municipal and had boycotted Carnaval 1998. In explanation of her protest, Gonzalez Bueno stated that if she went to Carnaval she would have a heart attack because of the 'Blanqueando de Carnaval' or the 'Whitening of Carnaval.'[12] For her, the fact that Los Hoyos included a choreographed cabaret-style routine in their performance was an example of this 'whitening.' Others commented that the young people of Santiago were no longer interested in traditional style performances and that all the girls wanted to perform 'cabaret- style,' hoping to eventually secure a position in many of the new clubs that had opened for the growing tourist business.

Along with the changes in emphasis of the performance of Los Hoyos, many other groups had also changed dramatically. In 1998 the carnaval participants were overwhelmingly young women and girls . . . dancing girls. I can only imagine that these young girls were preparing for and even dreaming of the future, when they would be cabaret dancers hired to be dancing on the carnaval floats.

In my 1993 essay, I began a commentary on the sexy dancers of Carnaval. I noted that in 1989 *paseo* La Placita included about seventy-five couples, and at least 100 solo female dancers dressed in cabaret-style leotards and colored wings. In my 1994 essay[13] I expanded this discussion and, using examples of female resistance through performed transgressive behavior in both Africa and Afra-Caribbean society, I attempted to understand and come to terms with the performance behavior of the sexy dancer. But certain carnaval performances in 1998 have forced me to reconsider my own reactions to the sexy dancer in Carnaval and her role in the renewed tourist industry. The patterns of performance appear to mirror those of previous tourist boom periods.

Rosalie Schwartz documents the dramatic changes in Havana Carnaval between 1928 and 1931, when each year 'outspectacled the one before.'[14] By 1930, Havana Carnaval had become more of a tourist attraction than a Cuban holiday, especially after the Afro-Cuban *comparsas* were banned because of their perceived raucous behavior that the authorities contended

This first prize float in Santiago Carnival July 1998, sponsored by Cubanacan, the tourism branch of government, was designed in imitation of the 1990s Hotel Santiago. The dancers have descended to street level and are performing in front of the judges' grandstand. © J.B.

resulted in violence. It was in 1936 that the Afro-Cuban *comparsas* were again permitted to parade, mostly due to the pressures exerted by Fernando Ortiz and his associates. Joining forces with the mayor of Havana, Ortiz argued that the *comparsas,* with their costumes, music, songs, and dances, would not only attract tourists, but they would also educate Cubans about their own culture. In 1936 Havana's city council allocated funds for the *comparsas*. By the early 1950s at least ten Afro-Cuban *comparsas* performed in each carnaval parade.

A detailed report of the 1952 March Havana carnaval celebration was published in *Holiday* magazine.[15] Against the background of a military coup and the presence of armed guards at every corner, according to the writer, the city seemed to function normally and carnaval participants paraded in full force. 'By midnight nobody would have guessed there was a revolution within a thousand miles.'[16] Troupes of bicyclists, motorcyclists, and horsemen put on elaborate performances. There were many floats, one representing a Chinese pagoda complete with girls wearing bathing suits and kimonos. Of the eighteen *comparsas*, many included 'a series of full-scale production numbers so elaborate that they make the best Broadway can do seem like

The float sponsored by the Santiago branch of the Tropicana night club. The caricature-like depiction of the Afro-Cuban drummer is typical of Carnival representations and has moveable arms attached to poles and ropes manipulated by the attendants who walk alongside. Carnival July 1998. © J.B.

petty cash.' But the author, a travel writer from the United States, reserved his most detailed description for the performance of the *comparsa* El Alacrán, The Scorpion. (Pérez Sarduy includes commentary on this famous Havana *comparsa* in his essay.) About 100 men and women 'of darkish complexion' were dressed in cotton costumes reminiscent of 'the cane cutters of Cuba.' But it was not the costumes, nor the large papier maché scorpion, that attracted the writer's attention, but the powerful narrative dance performance with its live musical accompaniment. Mistakenly, but appropriately sensationalistically, referred to as a 'voodoo ceremony' directed by a 'voodoo high priest,' the narrative included a fair-skinned victim, a red-stained sheet, a sacrifice to the scorpion and piercing shrieks. What is most significant is that at the end of the narrative the 'victim' 'rose to her feet and joined the other dancers in the rumba that ushered them from the scene.'[17] Give the crowd what they want and you will be rewarded. I can just imagine the grins and laughter of El Alacrán members as they danced away.

What is significant to me about this 1952 description is the mélange of elements included in the carnaval parade, and the juxtaposition of elaborate, costumed performances and floats with the occasional more 'roots' performances of the Afro-Cuban *comparsas*. While the *Holiday* magazine writer noted the spectacles included in Carnaval, he reserved a detailed commentary for that which he perceived as an indigenous cultural performance, for he admits that after viewing carnival parades in Rio de Janeiro, Venice, and New Orleans, 'spectacles' begin to resemble one another. So, what makes Carnaval in Cuba unique today, its floats and spectacles, or its Afro-Cuban cultural performances?

As I look again at Santiago and Havana Carnavals of the 1990s, I wonder how much has changed. Carnaval iconography during the most recent boom period of tourism seems to be reinventing itself. In 1989 Santiago Carnaval I documented four floats and only one of the four exclusively featured cabaret-style costumes and female dancers. In 1998 Santiago Carnaval I documented seven floats, and six of them featured adult women, wearing cabaret-style costumes, dancing cabaret-style to recorded Dominican merengue music. The seventh float was for young school-girls and their attendants. The 'princess' on this float was interviewed by a carnaval announcer during a *desfile corta*, or preliminary parade, and the audience clapped in appreciation. The float that won first place was designed in imitation of the Hotel Santiago, a new 1990s tourist hotel in contemporary architectural style. Many of these floats received huge ovations from the predominantly local audience watching the parade and the dancers seemed to be familiar to many spectators, as they waved and threw kisses at specific groups of individuals. I was told that most were local women who had achieved status, both monetary and professional, as cabaret dancers. In the late 1980s two important cabarets opened in Santiago; one is a branch of the famous Havana Tropicana.

These floats also featured advertisements. In the 1989 Carnaval I had noticed 'commercial announcements' for various branches of Cuban government. One carnaval *paseo* included a section of dune buggies filled with Tourism employees carrying banners for Cubanacan, the government tourist division. But Carnaval 1998 was different. Along with Cuban advertisements there were foreign interests represented. One float was sponsored by the popular champagne Freixenet; a large banner with the name was attached to each side of the float. I also noted some advertisements during other performances. Members of the carnaval group Los Pinos wore tee shirts with large letters spelling CASTROL . . . a Spanish oil company. (Naively, at first I thought this was some kind of comment on Fidel, but a Spanish tourist seated next to me set me straight.)

The use of recorded music, especially Dominican merengue, is another recent change to Carnaval. I regard the exclusive use of this music as another instance of veering away from Afro-Cuban culture, particularly since Santiago has always been noted for its unique style of carnaval music. The *congas* of Santiago represent one of the oldest and most respected musical

A group of young dancers performing with Paseo La Placita during Carnival 1998, Santiago de Cuba. Note that both the female and male dancers are posed in 'proper' dance positions. © J.B.

idioms of Cuba and they are made up of, for the most part, Afro-Cubans. In Santiago young Afro-Cuban children are proud to learn the style of playing that has made their city so famous. While some may regard the 'invasion' of Dominican merengue as a typical subversive carnaval maneuver, others put it in the category of the 'whitening' or 'commercialization' of Carnaval, an element from the outside that excludes the indigenous Afro-Cuban live musical element.

Concomitant with this injection of 'outside' and commercial interests came a change in choreography and dance style. In the late 1980s an offspring of Havana's Tropicana nightclub opened in Santiago and along with it a dance school to train the performers. To a trained dancer's eye there is a difference between rehearsed steps and learning to perform by being trained to perform for others, and those moves learned by growing up dancing with one's family, friends, or cultural group. Many of the young dancers and much of the choreography in Carnaval 1998 reflected a schooled performance style. At the beginning of routines dancers took their places and 'posed' in an appropriate position. Often an outstretched leg would extend to a pointed foot, even when dancing in stylish heavy sneakers. Arms would be placed 'in position.' It is evident that these young dancers had had 'training.' Most of the audience seemed to support the performance groups by applauding and calling out names. Since so many of the groups included school-age performers, I am tempted to assume that most of the audience consisted of family and friends. None of my friends or colleagues in cultural work from the 1980s were in attendance. I can only wonder if a majority of the crowd was also very different from that of the previous decade. If most of the Santiago audience consisted of friends and relatives, that would help to explain the positive response elicited by the previously discussed floats.

I would like to summarize what I consider one of the most profound changes in Carnaval with a description of a particular Carnaval-related performance. This performance took place in central downtown Santiago, in Cespedes Park in front of the old but newly restored Grand Hotel. The two dancers, impersonating the *orichas* Eleguá and Ochún, belong to a cultural group which is funded by the Department of Municipal Culture. During the performance, the Ochún took off layers of her costume (scarves, skirt, etc.), and ended up wearing a yellow tee shirt and yellow tights. Now, Ochún is a sexy, flirtatious *oricha*, but her *oricha* clothes, during religious services, folkloric performances, and even previous Carnavals, are usually frilly, layered, and discreet. She is usually clothed in fine 'feminine' dresses, in her colors, yellow and white. By ending her performance in a yellow and white tight-fitting tee shirt and tights, this *oricha* impersonator may have been asserting her own personality, that of a contemporary liberated woman. It is quite possible to read this performance as a personal, yet public, affirmation of a certain type of female power in Cuba today. Indeed, this performer was voicing a present truth about contemporary life in Cuba, where the sensual woman is a powerful, albeit controversial, social and economic force. She performed a version of a current cultural experience. Perhaps she was also implying that her persona paralleled that of Ochún's. For Ochún is not just a beautiful woman; she is an enchanting seductress. I would certainly like to interview a cross-section of Santiago's population, especially those working with religious communities or practitioners themselves, to better appraise this performance.

Carol Boyce Davies (1998:339) has also written about her own attempts to reconcile the seeming contradictions between a display of female agency embodied in the sexy carnival dancer and sexy dancing as an example of 'carnivalized demands of entertainment.' In both Trinidad (Boyce Davies' example) and Cuba (my example), the female body has become a commodity for the tourist industry. In Cuba, this is best exemplified by the containment of the body in the space allotted on a carnival float,[18] or by specific predetermined choreographic routines that are precisely followed. Let me explain.

In Trinidad the thousands of female participants dance in the streets. They do not follow prescribed choreographic formations, but mostly perform improvised, eclectic solos. One can lose oneself in the freedom of movement.

As Boyce Davies writes: 'this is the one time that women are able to take space, to assert the sexuality which includes women *wining*[19] on and with each other and which also includes women at home in their bodies expressing with these bodies the very same sexualities which men desire and fear they cannot control simultaneously.'[20] In Trinidad Carnival, the taking over of street space is a version of carnival resistance. Yet, in Cuban Carnaval, the dancing is most often restricted, especially the 'dancing' on the floats. In a tightly contained space the women bump and grind endlessly, repeating the almost mechanized patterns of movement over and over. In fact, most floats are designed with small railings, so the women can support their upper bodies as they bend over offering a better rear view of the endless grinding to recorded music.

Ironically, although there was definitely a female spectacle, none of the floats in 1998 integrated the women into the total design. There was nothing close to the innovative design of La Textilera's 1989 float, where the dancing women were ingeniously placed within an oversized 'cocktail glass' so their dancing bodies could be read as the stirrer. (La Textilera was a powerful Santiago *paseo* in the late 1980s. Today it no longer exists, as the factory which supported it has closed.) In 1998 there was no spontaneity, no improvisation, no total body language. I got bored, but the dancing was not intended to entertain me, I think. But who was being entertained? Who was still excited by the time the sixth float passed by? I looked around and found that I could not answer that question.

These same questions came to mind as I watched certain groups of younger girls performing with various *paseos* and *congas*. The girls with *conga* Los Hoyos got down and did 'the doggie' on the pavement, on all fours with the butt high in the air—a horizontal bump and grind.

I can no longer regard the dancers on the floats as exhibiting performative transgressive behavior.[21] The younger girls who 'did the doggie' as part of their repertoire were certainly challenging norms and expectations of the elder members of *conga* Los Hoyos, for at least half of the *conga* refused to participate in Carnaval 1998. They were in part protesting the new choreographic routines, such as 'the doggie,' introduced into the repertoire. These young women were certainly taking resistance to the streets, just as the dancer impersonating Ochún in the previous discussion may have been. Here, maybe, young Cuban women were 'dancing out' their resistance. Yet, these carnaval innovations are socially and politically ambiguous. Who exactly is being entertained? Is there something more than (other than) self-expression being performed?

While I do not intend to imply that all these dancers, as individuals, want to participate in the side businesses of tourism, historically, as well as today, chorus girls and tour guides are important categories of employment. Today, in both Havana and Santiago, descriptions of the cities' streets recall earlier descriptions from former tourist boom periods: '[Havana is] one of the last unabashedly sinful cities of the world . . . It is not new and, to anyone who knows Havana, it is not news.'[22] Another controversial aspect of the dollar economy is the proliferation of *jinateras*, or prostitutes. Many are Afro-Cubans who sell for dollars that which they own, their own bodies. Many have little other means of acquiring dollars that are needed to purchase daily essentials, like food or clothes. I have been told that in the winter of 1998–99 there was a large crackdown on *jinatera* activity in Havana.

This entire topic is problematic and controversial and I am sure there will be many articles written about it in the future.[23] In Cuba today, Carnaval, as always, reflects social changes and social pressures. Women's bodies have become a site for contested notions of freedom and self-expression. And I do think there is an important difference between the female performer who executes a sensuous rumba dance responding to and controlling her male partner by flicking her skirt to cover and uncover her pelvic area, and the woman who endlessly bumps and grinds on a carnaval float.

Cuban identity has always been related to feminine identity. In her essay on Havana's Tropicana Nightclub performances, Elizabeth Ruf (1997:86) correctly contends that 'the sublimation of feminine beauty is not isolated from revolutionary patriotism but actually linked to it via a longstanding identification in Cuban cultural expression of the island of Cuba with the female body.' Along the same lines, Benítez-Rojo, in *The Repeating Island* (1992:29, 219), includes a commentary on the parallels between 'the Caribbean text' and the Caribbean's 'supersyncretic culture.' He continues by evoking the improvisations embedded within the Carnaval as the cultural means by which 'the text' consistently escapes into the excitement of the spectacle, of the performer, of the experiential. He then offers a litany of nouns, verbs, and adjectives which underscore a main thesis—that Carnaval is feminine, that the power of the culture is embedded in feminine mystique, if you will. 'There is something strongly feminine in this extraordinary fiesta.'[24] Throughout his text Benítez-Rojo also evokes La Virgen del Cobre, who is known as 'la Virgen mulata,' as a trope which explicates both the power and confusion inherent in Caribbean society, for in Cuba, in the Afro-Cuban context, she is associated with Ochún, the copper-skinned *oricha* of sweetness, fertility, seduction, etc. She embodies that aura of seduction that emulates from a rich, confusing turbulence—like that of 'the white man who loves a black woman or vice versa.'[25]

Many commentaries on Benítez-Rojo's thesis note that for him, as for many others, the potential of Caribbean culture resides in gendered circumstances and gendered phenomenon, which distill as gendered 'performance.' Benítez-Rojo continues: "[but performance is] also . . . the execution of a ritual, that is, that 'certain way' in which the two Negro women who conjured away the apocalypse were walking. In this 'certain kind of way' there is expressed the mystic or magical (if you like) loam of the civilization that contributed to the formation of Caribbean culture."[26]

This is not the place for a critique of Benítez-Rojo's musings; that has already been accomplished by many scholars.[27] Suffice it to say that, indeed, 'the mulata [has come] to be associated with illicit pleasures that were [are] rationalized on account of the mulata's supposed hedonism.' (Ruf 1997:90) But let me return to Benítez-Rojo for a moment. By evoking Caridad del Cobre he pinpoints an image of the copper-skinned woman (El Cobre is the location of an important copper mine), of female beauty, of prowess and energy that resonates powerfully in Cuban society. For practitioners of la Regla de Ocha (also known as Santería) la Caridad del Cobre is also celebrated as the *oricha* Ochún. Caridad del Cobre is Ochún; Ochún is Caridad del Cobre. I turn again to Santiago Carnaval 1998 to end this essay.

In 1998 the esteemed Cabildo Carabalí Isuama was led by two older dancers. Neither was a King or Queen or part of the royal lineage I had previously documented. One woman, in a multi-colored skirt, carried a dark-skinned doll wearing a bright yellow outfit, obviously referring to the patron saint of Cuba, the Virgen of Caridad del Cobre, whose basilica is located nearby. This is the saint whose statue was brought from the church to Santiago to be blessed by Pope John Paul II, and the photograph of this blessing was carried on wire services worldwide. It is interesting to note that when leaders of la Regla de Ocha asked permission to drum in honor of the Pope's visit, permission was denied. Therefore, the parading of this 'doll,' or, stated differently, a woman parading one of the most important women in Cuban history, during Carnaval may have incorporated multiple meanings. One of these certainly reminded government officials of the almost ubiquitous conflation of a Catholic saint and a Yoruba-derived *oricha* in Cuban religious practice and thus reminded them of the power of Afro-Cuban society.

Notes

1. I would like to thank the NEH for funding my research during the summer of 1998. During my work with Palo Monte religious leaders, I was able to revisit Santiago and attend Santiago Carnaval
2. For a fascinating study of tourism, popular culture and religious performance see Katherine Hagedorn, *Divine Utterances: The Transformation of Memory in Afro-Cuban Performance*, forthcoming 2000.
3. For a fuller discussion of this term and other related topics please see my 1993 essay in this volume.

4. See my 1991 *African Arts* article for a more detailed discussion.
5. The 'admission fee' may be included in an offer to perform a divination or subsumed in the fee charged for photography.
6. I have been told that recently this fee was declared illegal by provincial authorities. There seem to be negotiations all over Cuba regarding such official fees and tax payments.
7. 1990 marks the beginning of the 'special period,' when new laws were established to counter the effect of the Soviet pullout.
8. This information was supplied by my helpful colleague Nancy Mikelsons.
9. Rosalie Schwartz (1997:xiv).
10. Although certain neighborhoods receive permission to set up amplifiers for recorded music in the streets and the residents dance and drink beer in public, my focus has always been the costumed carnaval parade.
11. For additional details see Sarduy's original chapter in this book.
12. Interview, July 29, 1998.
13. Bettelheim, 1994, pp. 193-199.
14. Rosalie Schwartz, pp. 82-87.
15. Hamilton Basso, 'Havana,' *Holiday* magazine, December 1952.
16. Ibid., p. 70. On March 10, 1952, a military coup established army control and returned Batista to power.
17. Ibid., p. 140.
18. I am grateful to Boyce Davies for introducing the trope of street space into the discussion of gendered carnival performance.
19. 'Wining' is a specifically Trinidadian term and dance movement which incorporates gyrations of the pelvic area, often mirrored in a line of dancers holding on to one another. The same genre of movement is called 'bubbling' in Jamaica and 'wuk up' in Barbados.
20. Davies, p. 339.
21. See my 1993 essay for a discussion of 'transgressive behavior.'
22. Basso, p. 68.
23. To elaborate just a bit, in Cuba many people distinguish between a 'street prostitute' who has many partners and a woman or man who has a long term relationship with a foreigner who sends gifts, money, etc. to Cuba. In both cases this money may be used for the support of a family, or for community needs.
24. Benítez-Rojo, p. 29.
25. Ibid., p. 27.
26. Ibid., p. 11.
27. See Kutzinski, 1993.
28. 'The drumming that was denied during the Pope's visit was consistent with the fact that Afro-Cuban practitioners were not allowed to meet with the Pope when other denominations did,' writes Nancy Mikelsons in a communication 1/24/00. She suspects that this may have been a joint decision of the Catholic Church and the Cuban government.

The Tumba Francesa and Tajona of Santiago de Cuba

Judith Bettelheim

'Todo tumbero francesa fue tajonero'

Of the many carnival groups which perform annually, two of the oldest and most revered are the Tumba Francesa and the Tajona. Both are distinguished by their costumes, music, and dances, which relate to a specific type of performance, one that today is referred to as *folklórico*. These groups do not compete against the other carnival *congas*, *comparsas*, and *paseos*, but rather perform alone, as a tribute to a special and vital aspect of Santiago history, the presence of a strong Haitian French culture in eastern Cuba.

Before the war of 1895, the War of Independence, there were several documented Tumba groups in Santiago and the neighboring region. Today many people still remember the names of Tivolí, Cocoyé, Papiante, Caridad del Cobre, [1] and Alto Pino. As a tribute to their heritage some Santiago carnival groups have taken the names of these older societies, while other groups maintain an historical connection with famous Tumba groups, such as Tivolí and Alto Pino. And in Carnival 1989 the *paseo* Sueño paid homage to the strong cultural presence of descendants of the original immigrants as they sang 'Mi Mama y mi Papa vienen de Haiti; sueño de Haiti.' (My Mother and my Father came from Haiti; I dream of Haiti.)

In Carnival 1989 the *paseo* El Tivolí performed. The women were dressed in a 'Haitian style,' in white, trimmed in red, nineteenth century style dresses, and the men were dressed in white, with either red or blue bandanna-style scarves. One male dancer performed a special dance with red scarves tied on his knees and arms (see below), while another with a blue head-tie danced a tribute to the *oricha* Ogún, as he turned a machete in on himself in order to test his own power and expresses his anger as a warrior (see chapter on Santiago Carnival). Some reports indicate that El Tivolí was one of the original French Tumbas active in Santiago.

At least since the middle of the nineteenth century there has been a rivalry between neighborhood carnival groups originating in the barrio of Los Hoyos and those from neighborhoods of strong Haitian Cuban culture. For example, in the Carnival of 1845, the group from El Tivolí put on a skit about a Frenchman 'savigni' who thought he was smarter than everyone else. The group from the barrio of Los Hoyos masqueraded as 'Frutas de Cuba,' satirizing the French immigrants. The carnival group from El Tivolí was so angered by this skit that a fight broke out between the two carnival groups, and the consequences were so severe that the carnival of 1845 is always remembered as *'Las trágicas fiestas de máscaras.'* This competition between Los Hoyos and El Tivolí continues today, and is exacerbated by an unresolved historical dilemma: how much Haitian French influence is in the barrio of Los Hoyos itself? This long and complicated issue is discussed below.

By 1957, on the eve of the Revolution, the number of Tumba groups had so diminished that the remaining members had joined together to form one group, which was known as the Tumba Francesa Lafayette. The society of this latter name was first registered in 1862 and was made up of slaves and free blacks known as 'Franceses,' a term used in Oriente to signal the heritage of these individuals as originating with the immigrants who fled Haiti during that country's War of Independence in 1792. In 1905 the name was officially registered as Caridad del Cobre or Caridad de Oriente. After the Revolution, in the 1960s, the group was declared an official folkloric society and its activities were placed under the jurisdiction of the Consejo Nacional de Cultura. In 1979, the official name of this particular group, whose Foco Cultural (government supported meeting house) is located in the barrio of Los Hoyos, was changed to Los Maceo-Bandera-Moncada, in honor of the Cuban patriots and independence fighters, Quintín Bandera, Guillermo Moncada, and Antonio and José Maceo. (These latter names are actually never used, and the group is always referred to as the Tumba Francesa of Santiago.)

The most revered and well known Tumba queen was Consuela 'Tecla' Venet Danget, known as 'la Reina cantadora,' who died on March 19, 1988, in her late nineties (Castillo 1988:n.p.). Tecla is said to have been very knowledgeable of 'old ways' and knew many songs in 'dialect.'[2] (I presume this refers to the Creole that was spoken by descendants of the Haitians.) Tecla was cherished by members of all the *folklórico* groups in Santiago; it is said that at her funeral even the grave diggers cried, and that drums were played at her open coffin all night long. Tecla's mother, Nemecia Danget,

Queen Sara Quiala Venet (r) of the Sociedad Tumba Francesa and Queen Silvina Casamayor (l) of the Sociedad La Tajona during a performance of the Tumba Francesa at the Foco El Tivolí, July 1991, in honor of the Pan American Games, Santiago de Cuba. © J.B.

was a dancer and later queen in a turn of the century Tajona group, and her aunts, Yapé and Amalia Danget, also belonged to a Tumba group whose president was Gaudiosa Venet. In the Tumba Francesa's Foco Cultural in the barrio of Los Hoyos hangs an old photograph of Nemecia, who was born a free black of Haitian heritage in El Caney, now a small town on the outskirts of Santiago. It is said that Nemecia was about 115 years old when she died. Stories also are told about Tecla's grandfather, a highly respected wise man known as 'Patenten,' whose given name was close to Oristen de Ronseler or Ogisten de Ronsolé, obviously reflecting his Haitian heritage. He had been a slave, and it is remembered that he barely spoke Spanish or Creole, but a 'foreign language.' Today the queen of the Tumba is Sara Quiala Venet, who inherited her position from her grandmother Tecla. The queen of La Tajona is Silvina Casamayor, and both queens[3] presided at the combined Tumba/Tajona performance I witnessed at the Foco El Tivolí in July 1991.

The cultural performances of summer 1991 were part of the official regional cultural activities preceding the Pan American games. Because of the economic crisis in Cuba, combined with the cost of the games, Carnival 1991 was cancelled, yet certain folkloric activities were permitted and supported, both as an 'appeasement' to sections of the Afro-Cuban population and as a tourist attraction. (Tickets to these performances were sold at tourist hotels, and they were not open to the general public.)

The King and Queen (Silvina Casamayor) of La Tajona parading with members of the court during Carnival 1989, Santiago de Cuba. Groups such as La Tajona and Tumba Francesa do not compete during Carnival, rather, they parade as honorary 'folklore' groups. © J.B.

During performances it is virtually impossible to distinguish between the Tumba Francesa or the Tajona, unless of course one recognizes their respective queens or drummers. Their origins in eastern Cuba are equally similar, and some scholars simply use the two names interchangeably. Yet some of the people I spoke with insisted that Tajona is more country in origin, is really from the hills, and that their drumbeats are highly religious. Gladys Gonzales Bueno even added, 'Tajona plays *brujería* [or magic].' Certainly the Haitian roots of these groups and their consistent association with the hills, religion, and freedom fighters merits further elucidation.

The word *Tajona* itself is the name of a mill, circular in shape, that is dragged by animals and used to grind coffee. In fact the heritage of both the Tajona and Tumba societies is intimately connected to French Haitian immigration and coffee estates (*fincas*) in eastern Cuba, for the word *Tajona* was then used to refer to the festivities of the slaves on these *fincas*. It is said that the Tajonas had special songs and dances and were often given permission to travel from estate to estate during their festivities (Berenguer

The collection of Tumba Francesa instruments at the Carnival Museum in Santiago de Cuba. Three *tumbas* or drums, one decorated with the national crest and the date October 10, 1868, marking the beginning of the War of Independence, and a *catá*. Photo taken in April 1986. © J.B

1977:224).[4] Although there are some minor variations in the statistics offered by different scholars, all agree on the importance and cultural impact of the French Haitian immigration into eastern Cuba. According to the research of Rafael Duharte (1988b:79–89), most of the coffee estates were established between 1815–1836 by immigrants from Haiti and their slaves. In 1792 the population of the coffee estates was only c. 1,500, but by 1807, directly following the Haitian War of Independence and the subsequent migrations, there were at least 11 new coffee estates run by French Haitians. In 1808 the estimated population of Santiago de Cuba was 33,000 and of these at least 7,500 considered themselves 'French' (Duharte 1988a:35). The breakdown of this portion of the population is described as follows: whites 2651; free mulattoes and free blacks 2,341; and black slaves 2,457 (Berenguer 1977:224). When considering that 32% of the total immigrant 'French' population were slaves, one can realize that Afro-Haitian culture has strong roots in eastern Cuba. In addition, there has been a constant flow of Haitians into eastern Cuba since the nineteenth century, with a large number establishing themselves as laborers in the early twentieth century. Although, as a result of the 1809 expulsion order, those French Haitians not wanting to become Spanish citizens left for New Orleans, those who returned or stayed behind were responsible for the building and running of the coffee estates in the mountains of eastern Cuba; the most famous one was named 'Fraternidad' (Duharte 1988a:35). (Many of these estates were deserted during the 1895 War of Independence, as the Blacks left to join the *mambises* [freedom fighters] and others moved to the city of Santiago de Cuba. There is a restoration program in process directed by the regional government of Oriente.) By 1841 there were 604 coffee estates in eastern Cuba, with an estimated population of 27,456; the population of Santiago itself had grown to 91,512. By the 1850s an estimated 30,000 people had entered Cuba from Haiti (Guanche 1983:277).

When establishing the importance of French Haitian influence on the culture of Santiago and its immediate environs,[5] one must realize that there was both an urban culture and a rural one, and in communal public festivals these cultures would meet. For example, by 1799, just six years after fighting had broken out in Haiti, the name of a major street in Santiago was changed from Calle Gallo to La Grande Rue (Street of the Rooster to, in French, the Grand Street) because of French influence in that part of town. The French women set up private schools where they taught art, music, and dance, and a grand theater, El Tivolí, was even constructed, with a seating capacity of 300–400 (Guanche 1983:275). Another strong cultural connection was made by the Haitian slaves who worked on the coffee estates and brought the crop down from the hills to the port of Santiago, located at the border of the barrio of Los Hoyos. Thus slaves and free blacks from the French quarter, from the estates in the hills, and from the barrio of Los Hoyos could all meet in the port district in town. It is with this confluence of micro cultures that Tajona groups met Tumba Francesa groups, and other *cabildo* and religious groups.

The development and impact of French Haitian culture, and its intermingling with Afro-Cuban culture in the mountains above Santiago, is being fully studied only recently. It is a fascinating story. At the famous copper mine of El Cobre there was an important slave uprising in 1731. These runaway slaves or maroons (from the Spanish *cimarrones*) established a protected settlement, or *palenque*, in the hills above Santiago. Today, the residents of the *palenque* known as Pilón del Cauto, also located in this same area, claim to be descendants of the maroons from El Cobre (Pérez de la Riva 1975:366). But the residents of Pilón del Cauto also must have had close contact with Haitian slaves and subsequent Haitian immigrants, as they also claim Haitian ancestry and dance to the gods of the Vodún pantheon. In fact, when I have seen them perform at Festival and Carnival in Santiago, they always pay homage to Vodún deities, rather than those of Santería, and dance in an Afro-Haitian style.

Jesus Guanche (1983:295) calls the culture of the maroons in eastern Cuba '*franco-haitiano-africana.*' He states that during the first quarter of the nineteenth century Oriente became the most important center of *palenques* in all of Cuba. And in 1815, the maroons of the *palenque* Sigua invaded numerous coffee estates and cattle ranches of the Partido de Limones and liberated many slaves. Also in 1815 construction began on a road to connect this mountain area to Santiago de Cuba, and in 1823 another road was begun to connect Limones with the area of Candelaria (Guanche 1983:289). Both these roads were financed by the French-owned estates in the area. And it was along these same mountain roads that the rural Tajona groups paraded. This is extremely interesting in light of a story that I was told by at least five oral historians of carnival, the story of a special carnival Tumba (or Tajona) from the barrio of Los Hoyos, a group known as Los Brujos de Limón. And as Gladyse Gonzalez Bueno stated, 'This Tajona was the *brujería* of the *monte*' (or the magic from the mountains).[6]

There is some confusion about the origins of Brujos de Limón, but the general outline of its history links it with the barrio of Los Hoyos, freedom fighters and the mountains above Santiago. During the Wars for Independence, 1868–1878 and 1895–1898, many freedom fighters came from Santiago and specifically from the very Afro-Cuban barrio of Los Hoyos. In fact, the famous *mambi* (freedom fighter) army of ex-slaves was led by the black Generals Antonio and José Maceo, Quintín Bandera and Guillermo Moncada[7] who were from this barrio (see above renaming of the Tumba Francesa group.) One version of this history even claims that the Maceo brothers were members of the original Tumba Francesa Lafayette (Bonne 1988:n.p.). All sources do agree that Moncada, as a freedom fighter, used the Brujos de Limón for patriotic purposes. Some state that they have been told that Antonio Maceo knew where Moncada's troops were located by following the sound of the *cata* that they played as part of their Tumba music, while others state that the group, made up of '*negroes franceses*,' acted as a front for the *mambises*. During their carnival performances they could more easily smuggle supplies to the freedom fighters in the mountains, because there were so many people on the streets and the authorities were diverted. (This is the same reason that Fidel chose to attack the Moncada barracks during the carnival of 1953.)

The exact relationship of Brujos de Limón and the Tajona/Tumba Francesa from the barrio of Los Hoyos is less important than the interaction of and subsequent melding of cultural influences from French Haitian immigrants with Afro-Cuban culture in Santiago and Oriente and the subversive nature of this tradition. Many militant youths from the barrio of Los Hoyos joined the freedom fighters, and today a famous carnival song refers to this.

The Jamaican artist I. M. Belisario sketched these performers during a Christmas street festival in Kingston, Jamaica, in 1837. Known as the *French Set-Girls*, these same Afro-Haitian performers came to Cuba in the years following the Haitian Revolution. The style of drums on the right are still played by Tumba Francesa members in eastern Cuba. (Reproduction from the Institute of Jamaica).

This song was sung to me by Sebastían 'Chan' Herrera (born in 1920), who began playing with Los Hoyos in 1935 and has been a leader of the Los Hoyos carnival group since 1946.[8]

Mira con qué disimulo
Van los Brujos de Limón
Con su batuta en la mano
Para armar revolución estribillo
Choncholí se va para el monte
Cójelo que se va (que se te va)[9]

Roughly the song translates as follows:

Take up your instruments
Let us go play in the hills
Choncholí is going to the hills
Catch him because he is going

It was explained to me that 'Choncholí' is a very black bird, and the connotation of the song is 'the black one (man) is going to the hills; better grab him before he gets away.' Another related story states that the Tumba Francesa used to carry black birds with them during a parade, and they would release them at the soldiers to distract them from their diligent policing.

This reputation for political and cultural activism, combined with a prideful heritage, continues today. The remaining Tumba Francesa society in Santiago and its sister society La Tajona perform at all major cultural events and continue to educate the next generation of society members. In their 1989 Carnival performance La Tajona paraded with a complete entourage of young apprentices, and at their performance at the Foco El Tivolí during the Pan American games other young members also performed. The society is distinguished by its costume, which for the females is an imitation of nineteenth-century courtly dress. The men wear white pants and a long-sleeved white shirt. For Carnival, the king and queen might wear a crown and a wig, in reference to their royal nineteenth-century heritage. Sometimes the female members of the courtly entourage will wear a three-tiered skirt called *can-can* and a headtie called *madrás*. All costumes are sewn by the female members of the society.

Tumba Francesa and Tajona have specific music, instruments, and dances that are unique to these societies. The male solo dance is the *yubá* or the *frenté de yubá*.[10] This dance is performed to two different rhythms: one is the *yubá babul* (see below) and the other the *yubá cobrero*. In this athletic performance the dancer performs a dialogue with the drums as he ties scarves on his knees, arms, and around his chest. Often these scarves are red, especially in dances performed in honor of the spirit Ogún. Underscoring the Haitian heritage in Tumba and Tajona societies, it is important to note that in Vodún possession ceremonies in Haiti, a spirit can request that red scarves be tied above the elbows and across the chest as an emblem of possession by that spirit.[11]

The most popular couple dances are the Masón and the Babul (see below), while the boys and girls often perform the Maypole dance (El Tejido de las Cintas). The latter dance is said to have been introduced by the Haitian slaves and is performed in honor of the *mambises*. Colored ribbons representing the Cuban flag, in red, white, and blue, are always used. Other nationalistic elements include the use of a large barrel-shaped drum, strung and tuned on the peg system. This large drum traditionally is painted with Cuban or Haitian patriotic names, like the one on display at the Carnival Museum in Santiago, which is named La Escalera, in honor of the famous slave uprising, [12] and decorated with the Cuban national seal. It is said that this particular drum was played at the beginning of the Ten Years War, in 1868.

Another of the most important drums is the *bulá*, which is played while lying horizontally. The player sits astride it and applies pressure to the head with his feet, while playing with his hands. (This is the same as the drum used to accompany Kumina rituals in Jamaica.) This is accompanied by a second *bulá* and a *catá*. The *catá* is a hollow cylinder of wood suspended between two Y-shaped posts and played with two sticks.[13] Again, the connection to Haitian Vodún is clear. Vodún scholars Karen McCarthy Brown and Elizabeth McAlister write that the *bula* [sic] is the smallest in the drum battery for Rada rites, and that the rhythm played is Juba, used for the earth spirits and the *lwa* Azaca. The *kata* [sic] drum is the smallest used in Petro rites, but the name *kata* can also refer to 'a rhythm played with a single stick on *vaksins*, the bamboo instruments used in the Rará festival.'[14]

Another drum, the *requinto*, plays a special rhythm, the *masón*, which is also the name of the most famous couple dance. Accompanying these drums are *marugas*, which are said to have been introduced from Haiti. *Marugas* are also known as *chacha*, and are hollow cones, made from metal and covered with cloth or fiber, often decorated on the outside, with bells or ringers inside. They are played by shaking. The *masón*, which is probably a version of the contradance, is a slow, stately dance, said to be performed in imitation of the dances of the French plantocracy. In a performance I saw in 1991 three couples danced while the Duchess, a member of the Tumba, indicated when the couples should change partners by blowing a whistle. Another section of the dance is done in rows, called *champwell* in French.[15]

Although all written reports, and my own respondents, claim that the name *masón* is probably derived from the French *maison*, I doubt it and would like to propose another interpretation, first suggested to me by Karen McCarthy Brown. That the *masón* dance seems to be in 'imitation' of a European couple dance does not contradict other possible connotations. *Masón* is probably a Cuban Spanish version of the word 'mason,' as in the Masonic Order. There is documented evidence of Masonic lodges in Santiago as early as 1789, when La Perseverance and La Concorde were established under the direction of the Gran Logia de Francia (Guanche 1983:276). Masonic lodges in Oriente are still active. Pablo Milanés Fuentes, a *houngan* (leader) in the Vodún community in the Sierra Madre mountains of Oriente became a Mason in 1984. He is a member in the lodge of El Cobre under the jurisdiction of the Gran Logia de Cuba.[16] That rebellious and culturally resilient Haitian Cuban communities were involved with Masonic orders actually comes as no surprise. As early as 1811 José Antonio Aponte, a free black carpenter, organized an important uprising in Havana, and it is reported that Cuban Freemasons were solidly behind his strategies. In fact, the rebellion of 1868, better known as the Ten Years War, 'was planned in Masonic lodges in Puerto Príncipe, Santiago de Cuba, Bayamo, Holguín, Las Tunas, and Manzanillo' (Pérez, Jr. 1988:121). (This is the same conflict that the Tumba drum described above was played for.) This connection between Tumba societies and Masonic societies is underscored by Karen McCarthy Brown's research in Haiti, where Masons and Vodúnists share more than ritual formations, for in Haiti many Vodún priests are also Masons.

It is well known that Vodún is practiced in many Haitian Cuban communities in the mountains of Oriente. Although there does not seem to be much written evidence of the practice of Vodún in Santiago itself, there is a fascinating eyewitness account of a ceremony in 1876, written by a French visitor, Hippolyte Piron (1876:47–52), to Santiago. Piron, in discussing the French Creole presence in Santiago, noted that the belief and practice in 'Vodún remedies' had permeated their family life, especially because their children are raised by their slaves, who practiced Vodún. He also noted that many women who seemed quite '*comme il faut*' were members of Vodún temples. On befriending one such family, Piron was invited to a Vodún ceremony presided over by thirteen women, dressed in white (the *hounsis* [the initiates of a Vodún temple] chorus), who danced and sang while a young girl danced with a serpent[17] and eventually entered a trance.

It does seem extremely important to note that during Carnival in Santiago de Cuba or during the 'entertainment' that was supported by municipal government during the Pan American games in 1991 (Noches de Folklor, Magia y Música en el Santiago Panamericano), the performances of the Tumba Francesa and the Tajona were officially regarded as an homage to a 'quaint' and formerly important folkloric aspect of Santiago history. Yet the history of these Haitian Cuban societies alludes to cultural tenacity, political self determination, and solid hereditary lineage. 'Una tradición centenaria' (a century-long tradition) encompasses so much more than the label *folklórico* implies. As with many other tenacious and powerful Afro-Cuban traditions, the presence of the Tumbas and Tajonas in Santiago de Cuba today speaks to an ongoing system of survival and self-rule under the rubric of a national folklore agenda.

Notes

1. Cobre is a town outside of Santiago where the basilica of the Virgin of Cobre (Caridad del Cobre) is located, known to some as Ochún, an *oricha* of Santería.
2. Much of the information in this paragraph was also obtained during an interview with cultural worker Gladys Gonzalez Bueno on July 21, 1991.
3. Certainly the fact that in both the Tumba groups and the Carabalí societies the leadership is established through female descent merits considerably more attention than I have space for here.
4. This is parallel to the situation in Jamaica, where Jonkonnu troupes travelled from plantation to plantation 'entertaining' the plantocracy and other slaves.

5. At this moment, as I write, over 15,00 Haitians have fled Haiti by boat, attempting to reach the US naval base in Guantanamo, in eastern Cuba, attesting to the continued importance of this area for Haitians. Throughout this section of the text I make reference to *mambises,* the name given to the Afro-Cuban fighters of the Liberation Army. For additional information on the importance of eastern Cuba in the struggle for liberation and independence see Aline Helg, *Our Rightful Share: The Afro-Cuban Struggle for Equality* (Chapel Hill and London: University of North Carolina Press, 1995).
6. Interview July, 1991.
7. It is the famous Moncada barracks in Santiago that Fidel Castro chose to attack at the beginning of his revolution during Carnival 1953.
8. Interview, July 25, 1989. Chan was able to recite by heart the lineage of leaders and the themes of Los Hoyos since the turn of the century. I saw Chan during Carnaval 1998 when he was still leading Los Hoyos, but he died in 1999.
9. A version of this same song was recited to me by Gladys Gonzalez Bueno.
10. Although the most famous solo dance of the Tumbas is the Frenté, Gladys Gonzalez Bueno told me of another very special dance she had seen and done some research on. It was performed by a Tumba group that included Che Mojena, Maria Lungualon, and Mariano Duvalón. The principal dancer would wrap a drum, the one Ortiz calls the *mamamiero,* with a special kind of raffia rope (the *bejuco of the quaniquiqui*) and he would grab the drum by this rope with his teeth and carry it around. (This reminds me of another ritual performed by Haitian Cuban group; one where a table is lifted by the teeth biting a corner). Sometimes the first drummer of a Tumba group is called the *mamier.* Gonzalez Bueno also reports that this drum is usually adorned with vulture feathers, reminding me that in 'Congo' religions, like Palo, vulture feathers are very important. She even reports that there used to be a *cabildo* Congo in the barrio of Los Hoyos. Its name was changed to Club Juán de Góngora, for the recreation and assistance of the Congos. Interview, March 1990. I have recently completed two articles which discuss the importance of the Congo-based Palo Monte religion in Cuba. Palo Monte is very important in eastern Cuba, where it demonstrates strong parallels to Petwo, the aspect of Haitian Vodou which also derives from a Congo base. In fact, in eastern Cuba it is best to consider many religious practices Palo-Petwo, as the Haitian community is intertwined with the Cuban one. My articles are scheduled to be published by *The African Jamaican Institute of Jamaica* and *African Arts.*
11. Personal communication, Elizabeth McAlister, June 11, 1992.
12. In late 1843 a slave uprising, led by at least 200 individuals, began in Matanzas. The Spanish authorities found evidence of a 'far-flung' conspiracy and at least 4000 people were arrested by the authorities. The prisoners were tied to ladders for brutal floggings, thus the uprising was named La Escalera, the ladder.
13. According to Elizabeth McAlister, 'And Harold Courlander (1960:197) writes that in earlier times in Haiti, there was an instrument consisting of a length of bamboo lain across two Y-shaped sticks stuck into the ground, where the kata was beaten on the bamboo with two long sticks.' Personal communication, June 28, 1992.
14. McAlister, ibid.
15. Karen McCarthy Brown states that *champwell* is a Haitian secret society, most prevalent around Port-au-Prince and the Artebonite Valley.
16. This information as well as a photograph of the Masonic certificate was generously supplied by researcher Nancy Mikelsons, June 19, 1992. Since the early 1990s there has been increased interest in and scholarship on the Haitian communities of eastern Cuba and the practice of Vodú there. Researchers at Casa del Caribe in Santiago published a book-length study: Joel James, José Millet, Alexis Alarcón, *El Vodú en Cuba* (Santo Domingo: Republica Dominicana Ediciones CEDEE-Casa del Caribe, 1992 [republished in 1998 by Editorial Oriente, Santiago de Cuba]). Also, the important

houngan Pablo Milanes from eastern Cuba published an article in *Del Caribe*. 'Un saint qui ne sache faire que du bien n'est pas un vrai saint'. 1997 #26.

17. Karen McCarthy Brown reports that a serpent is no longer part of Vodún ceremonies that she has seen in Haiti, although she has heard stories about the former importance of the serpent. Personal communication, May 1992.

Flashback on Carnival: A Personal Memoir

Pedro Pérez Sarduy*

Before the days of aviation, travelers sailed into Havana from other ports. After a long sea crossing, they could form their first impressions while their boats slid gently through the narrow neck of Puerto Carenas, as Havana was then called.

One such traveler was the German Baron Alexander von Humboldt, who, in 1800, described the entrance to Havana port as one of the loveliest along the littoral north of Ecuador. It does not have the luxuriant vegetation of the Guayaquil shore, he wrote, nor the wild majesty of the Río de Janeiro coast, but the majestic vegetation of the torrid zone.

Like many of today's travelers, Humboldt ventured to explore the old 'walled' city, well fortified by the Spanish conquistadors to guard their coveted possession at the entrance to the Gulf of Mexico. Many of the old buildings, and part of the city wall itself, still stand today, to form an architectural colonial heritage that is among the best preserved of its kind; and Humboldt's name is still to be found on plaques marking monuments, streets and city parks.

When our aristocratic visitor became lost in the city hustle and bustle, he cursed the maze of streets, comparing Havana with European cities of old. He might have done so with London or Barcelona in mind. The latter, also a port city, has its Gothic District which is extraordinarily like Old Havana, such that the modern-day traveler would establish close similarities were it not for Havana's multitude of races and ethnicity.

Perhaps behind the supposedly poor street planning lay ingenious intent, driven by the tropical need to take refuge from the torrential, burning sun, again not unlike Barcelona's. Narrow streets and alleys mock the ground on which they are laid, snatching shade, fleeing the torrid sunset with a wise proliferation of corners:

> Barefoot, we counted the molten cobbles
> near Angel's Hill and the narrow street entry
> embracing the Franciscan monastery belfry
> calling for penitence.
> And yet, our presence was inopportune, unwanted,
> better still, mistimed.
>
> *Prey to a Summer's Fate*

The old city, or Old Havana, is in effect a city of shade: at daybreak, from the radiance rising over fortresses that could not hold back corsaires and pirates in their attack; alongside churches, Santa Clara Convent and the mansions of old, resplendent like gigantic medieval armor; disappearing at midday, when the sun knows no pity; then, at dusk, spreading out to the seafront, for nightfall to blend city columns with loving couples. Throughout the day, Old Havana is shade in contrast to all that came after in the 20th century, to the west of the city wall. New styles, some good, some bad, perhaps more bad than good, gave Havana, with its amalgam of people from all over the island, a peculiar symbiosis of styleless style. Havana became the baroque city, set apart in urbanistic terms from other cities of the continent.

> My clothes, always damp in months like this,
> traveled long solitary sensations with me,
> when suddenly an audience of false aberrations,
> reminiscent of more than one magnificent sunset,
> spreads over the colonial and republican districts
> of this walled inner part of Havana where we
> walked amidst night waste
> now and again coming across a contagious romp
> of vibrations not a bit conventional.
>
> *Prey to a Summer's Fate*

In past days and ages, on the streets of Havana, hawkers peddled their wares with bells or simply a capella, as in the world-famous 1920s song 'The Peanut Vendor' by Moisés Simons. There were the palm-covered fruit carts, as if out for Palm Sunday procession. Sellers of anything man and woman could find, in settings that engendered the perfect creole archetypes for popular farce, not least the black woman's wit, and the mulatto woman's baroque mentality and finery: a past often steeped in nostalgia and relived in contemporary Cuban film.

Streets the flavor of my streets of Havana;
tall old houses.
That transparent vision of vetiver
and twentieth-century marjoram
returning from the tropics.

Speculations in Paris

Such was the setting for the Havana carnival whose frenzied masquerades of blacks and mulattoes were nurtured on hunger and lust—those primordial ingredients of pleasure. Seemingly Christian in that it took place according to the Christian calendar—before Lent, on the Epiphany of Our Lord, or the 'Day of the Kings,' January 6—carnival might be thought to have come to America via Spain. But the masquerading or processional street dancing was undoubtedly of African origin. From 1886, when slavery was abolished, up until 1914, there were six major Havana masquerades: La Culebra (The Snake), El Pájaro Lindo (Pretty Bird), El Gavilán (Sparrowhawk), El Sapo (The Toad) and El Alacrán Chiquito (Little Scorpion). Researchers have linked the animal references with African ethnocultural elements, and the traditions are still with us today.

It was after the 1959 Revolution that the Cuban Government decided to move the Havana carnival to late July—and not without protest—for it to take place after the end of the sugar harvest. By then, it had become a parade and floats to be watched, rather than a street procession to join in.

Carnival in Santiago de Cuba, on the other hand, was famous for its *congas*. People were swept into the street dancing to strident music and rhythm. The Santiago carnival had a bad reputation in western and central Cuba, partly, no doubt, because it was associated with eastern Cuba's more predominantly black population, but also because of its rebellious history.

My first taste of Santiago Carnival was in 1971. My brother-in-law was then studying in Havana, but he had grown up in Chicharrones, one of Santiago's populous poorer neighborhoods, which had a famous masquerade. As we danced our way through the city, friends and family 'protected' those of us who were outsiders. Carnival has always been a time for settling debts and has taken its toll in lives, for it is relatively easy for anyone to slip away in the crowd. Just as this was a reason for the very start of the Revolution, with the attack on the Moncada Garrison in Santiago at the height of carnival, so also it was apparently one of the reasons for prohibiting the use of masks in carnival in the early years after the Revolution.

As we sweated and swayed to tireless musicians that still, damp night, with the temperature rising into the 100s, I sang along with songs improvised for us: 'Hey, compañero, take me with you to Havana. . . .' And I remembered the song made famous by the Aragón Band back in 1950, taken half in jest and half seriously by more educated blacks: 'No, black woman, don't dance *rumba* like that. . . . No, black woman, no, can't you see I'm society. . . .' Cos if they see me, dancing like Mangrove. . . . Gone will be my fine black veneer. . . .' In the colored societies of western Cuba, especially those catering to middle class black and mulatto families, the only acceptable collective form of public dancing was ballroom dancing, and carnival was proscribed.

In my home town of Santa Clara, in central Cuba, music and dance influences were more like those of the capital, Havana. But the surrounding province of Las Villas, with its thirty-two municipalities, was famous for its *parrandas*. In Camajuaní, Placetas, Remedios, Ranchuelo and Quemado de Guines, for the youth of the 1950s—myself included—these festivals would be the attraction of the year. With their fireworks, floats and masquerades, whole communities would be involved, and neighborhoods would compete for the carnival prize.

In good times and bad, dance has always been an excellent credential for Cubans. And what finer recognition for a poor black youth of 1950s Cuba than to be in one of the carnival masquerades? And so, despite the scolding of my grandmother, who from her matriarchal throne watched the every move of her fourteen children and thirty-five grandchildren, I joined my first and only masquerade, *Los Rumberos* of Villa Clara. It was very demanding: firstly, just keeping pace with the dance formation along the carnival route, round Vidal Park, past City Hall and the Institute of Higher Education where I had just started to study; past cinemas, theaters and hotels; past the most respectable cultural institutions to which the most distinguished families of Spanish descent belonged; and the creole copies of North American life—Santa Clara Tennis Club, Odd Fellows, Country Club, etc.—none of which boasted a Jim Crow-type sign but were nonetheless for whites only.

We rehearsed in Condado, one of the poorer neighborhoods on the other side of the insignificant River Bélico, which divided Santa Clara's opulent central district from its more marginal areas, infected with brothels, drugs and alcohol. Three times a week, after eight at night, one of the narrow streets would be closed to traffic, and the musicians would play their rough instruments, interrupted only by self-taught choreographers giving their instructions.

The most moving day for not only novices, but all masqueraders, was the evening before the parade, when our tailor-made costumes were given out; then you really knew you belonged. There were 48 couples in our group, all young blacks and mulattoes, of similar class background, though there were always some exceptions. I was one of a small group of high school students, and we were all called by our professional inclination or by some family name. 'Tell López's son to come over here a minute' . . . or . . . 'tell the Guamuta writer to mark the opening beat . . . ,' referring to a difficult step in which I had to join my partner on the other side of the street. Guamuta was the nickname used for several of the men in our numerous family. A cousin of mine, a car mechanic, had legendary fame across the city neighborhoods as a skater, dancer, and womanizer. His 'romantic' virtues helped no end in my getting selected, because, always buried in books, I was obviously no 'home boy'; but then, and now, I've always instinctively reacted against stereotypes.

The great moment came when I finally stood in front of the mirror and contemplated my street graduation. I was laughing inside as my aunts helped me do my sideburns, thin moustache and pointed beard. Our costume was a Panama-type hat, brown jacket almost down to the knees, long-sleeved pink shirt, and bow tie of the same material as the jacket, 19th-century style. The baggy white trousers were made out of flour sacking, and had a silver plated chain slung from a belt loop to one of the pockets. This crucial part of the dress served the double function of chaining the wallet and protecting it against any eventuality. The pointed shoes were shiny white, imitation patent leather. The girls were in yellow and white, with gold sequins, bare-shouldered and with a light red stole. Our whole outfits were a throw-back to that of the black dandies of Spanish colonial times.

That first evening we were met with great rounds of applause. 'Give it all you've got, kids!' were our words of advice from Don Macana, the old black founder of our masquerade. He was by then retired, but always went to give last-minute instructions to his boys, Candito and Berto, who were in charge of the group. The crowds loved our formation and the coquetry couples would at times improvise. My dance partner was great and our flirtation was part real, part dance. The choreography ended forming the eight letters of the word 'RUMBEROS.' The crowd could see this perfectly because we would go from the smallest, crouching down, to the tallest, on tip-toe, all in beat to the music, and singing 'Look us over and come on down, here the *Rumberos* are taking the town.' It was highly ingenious how Don Macana's boys achieved the effect. And this was shown by the applause.

Though we had some stiff competition the four Saturdays of carnival, three in January and the first in February, we took first prize on points in the various categories: choreography, costume and song. We had three short, simple, catchy numbers which were calculated to impress the judges.

Much later I discovered Don Macana had come up with an ingenious solution to a problem of sponsorship. Our tent was sponsored by the Hatuey beer company, which had started up a year earlier in the town of Manacas and provided jobs for almost 2,000 workers in the province. Hatuey, 'The

Great Cuban Beer,' had given us quite a lot of money for our masquerade, and we had to acknowlege this in one of our numbers. In Cuba, everyone knows that Hatuey was a famous Indian chief who in the early 16th century led a rebellion against the Spanish conquistadors, and was finally caught and burned at the stake. Chroniclers of the time tell the story that, moments before the flames consumed Hatuey's body, a Franciscan priest exhorted him to accept the Christian faith if he wished to go to heaven and achieve eternal happiness. In response, Hatuey asked if the Christians went to heaven, and when being told that they did, said he didn't want to go where there would be such cruel people. True or not, this is how the story has been taught in Cuban schools.

During this period, the president of Cuba was Fulgencio Batista y Zaldívar, who was not white but mulatto. Cuba had never had a non-white president. Perhaps because of his supporters and because of his straight hair, he was paid the compliment of being referred to as 'El Indio.' Since the indigenous peoples of Cuba had been all but exterminated by the conquistadors, to be 'Indian' was a rarity, and did not have the pejorative connotations it had in other Latin American countries. All the same, although he was president, the mulatto Batista was never allowed into exclusively white societies.

The problem for Don Macana was that the beer had a drawing of Hatuey on the label, and a cold Hatuey beer was popularly referred to as *un indio bien frío* (a cold Indian), in the same way that the Polar beer (another famous Cuban brand) had *un oso* (a bear). There was already growing opposition to Batista, and Don Macana was a *mayombero* (a practitioner of the religion Palo Mayombe or Palo Monte; *obeah* man) with a militant worker tradition, respected because 'he knew a lot about the spirits.' He didn't want a song praising Hatuey, not because he had anything against the Indian chief but because he didn't want it to be thought that his masquerade was singing to 'that son-of-a-bitch Indian assassin' (referring to Batista). Nobody in their right mind would want to get on the wrong side of Don Macana, but his boys convinced him there was a lot of money involved, and they came up with a song that had the rhythm of *guaguancó* (a type of *rumba*):

> If you say you didn't know me
> It's because you didn't want to
> Because I'm Hatuey, because I'm Hatuey
> Don't get it wrong
> Because I'm Hatuey, because I'm Hatuey
> The Great Cuban Beer.

The beer company was so pleased with the song that we had all the beer we could want during carnival, and even to take home with us, too. Don

Macana's song was bought by the company and used in their commercial on television, which was just coming into its own in Cuba in those years.

I was only in that one carnival, because the following year I was immersed in my studies and my interests lay elsewhere.

> I dance Havana rhythm
> my years masked with false attributes
> flagellating mercenary images
> emaciating the importance of night
> my ginger sweat
> like a rolling stone
> shouting splendid phrases in my Yoruba tongue
> trading my skeleton with dark glasses
> on the arm of Aeschylus down Prado
> beyond Hell
> sitting on the lap
> of an excommunicated god
> to tell my surprise
> while things like this happen
> I live the rhythm of the streets
> with carnival in July
> reinventing time passed
> and not finding it . . .
>
> *Like a Rolling Stone*

⋆ ⋆ ⋆ ⋆ ⋆

I arrived in Havana in July 1990, after being away for three years, right in the midst of carnival in one of the hottest months of the year. My six-week stay would also take me to Santa Clara and Santiago de Cuba, at carnival time. It was 19 years since my first Santiago carnival, and things had changed there, too: it was more like Havana.

Remembering that first visit in July 1971, carnival in Santiago de Cuba was then the height of genuine spontaneity. Over the years this had been gradually lost as local cultural institutions and government fell into the same trap as most of the western provinces. And, whereas the predominantly black neighborhoods had genuinely kept their own masquerades, floats had been taken over by social and cultural institutions, in much the same way as by commercial entities before the Revolution.

My last Havana carnival had been in 1986, because the following year I was enjoying a very different carnival in Notting Hill, London, organised by the city's Caribbean community for more than 25 years. The largest festival of its kind in Europe, it too has suffered from incomprehension and interference from state institutions. My return to Havana in 1990 was after a year in New York, where an even more colorful variant of the Notting Hill carnival is organized by the Caribbean community in Brooklyn.

In Havana, staying at the Presidente Hotel, I was close to the seafront section of carnival. This in itself was a relatively recent move. Up until the 1940s, the carnival procession route was Paseo del Prado up to the special seating beneath the Capitol Building—carbon copy of Washington—where each masquerade would perform its choreographed piece. The route cut through populous downtown Havana neighborhoods that have produced some of Cuba's great musicians: Atarés and Jesús María, bordering on the docks, Regla and Guanabacoa, along with Los Sitios and Cayo Hueso, famed for its cigar and cigarette factories, along with *conga* player Chano Pozo who in the 1940s revolutionized big band jazz with Cuban rhythms.

Around the mid-1970s, Havana carnival organizers decided to move carnival to the whiter, more middle class Vedado section of the city: the seafront, G Street and Paseo Avenue down to the Riviera Hotel, once the property of U.S. gangster Meyer Lansky. Taken out of its natural setting, carnival became a hybrid form. Its traditional followers were initially ill at ease following into alien territory, and when they did, it was to mill around the kiosks selling food and drink. Carnival became anything but its principal function: enjoyment. Only after lengthy discussions and changes introduced by the organizers in 1986, did Havana carnival start to regain some of its former glory.

In 1990, I found myself in a central seat on Seafront Drive alongside the National Hotel: in front of me, the amputated monument to the Maine Victims, minus the eagle that had been toppled soon after the Revolution; close by, the former Embassy, now Interests Section, of the United States. A pleasant breeze accompanied the parade. To my surprise, seated near me were two Havana carnival veterans, founders of one of Havana's most famous masquerades, the now 50–year-old *La Sultana* (The Sultana): retired printer Oscar Rivero and dockworker Antonio Echevarría.

Talking over a beer together, they told me how a group of neighbors in Havana's Colón and La Punta districts had started up The Sultana in 1939. Rivero and Echevarría had wanted something different and hit on an elaborate Far East choreography, based on the story of a eunuch falling in love with the Muslim sovereign's harem favorite, and making off with her.

As we went back to our seats, The Sultana was approaching, with its colorful costumes and choreography in the 's' form. The first curve of the 's' was the harem, and the second the Sultan's court. There were princes, princesses, odalisques, courtesans, lantern-bearers and ambassadors of far-off countries dancing *rumba* at the court in homage to the sultan. There are steps that are repeated year after year, but there are others that are new, plus the latest rhythms, and the favorite of the harem has to perform her exotic dance at some point.

Rivero and Echevarría told me there had been 192 dancers that first year in The Sultana: workers, students and housewives, all from Colón and La Punta. The costumes were as ostentatious as they could make them, raising the funds locally and each contributing what they could. Tailors and seamstresses in the area made their money, but all the turbans and head-dresses were done free of charge by a hatter. Today, masqueraders receive their costumes at no cost from the state.

They laughed remembering an incident in carnival in the 1940s, when they were arrested by the police after the parade because of The Sultana. There was a float in the masquerade with sultans and two palissades; in one there was the favorite of the harem and in the other a woman in white, enchained. As the story went, at one point in the dance, the sultan condemned to death the enchained beauty—who was of course white—while she was dancing for the court. A dancer came at her with a knife, and, with the help of bags of red-colored water, she fell to the ground 'bleeding.' People were said to have fainted with shock, and although the beautiful 'victim' was soon back dancing, the chief of police ordered the organizers' arrest. They were released the next day, and can laugh about it now, but can't have spent a particularly happy night!

Even so, my impression of Havana carnival wasn't changed by being in that privileged spot, alongside judges, journalists and VIPs, with a bird's eye view of the whole parade and the thousands in the crowd, seated or strolling in the gentle seafront breeze.

* * * * *

Memories again came crowding back, this time of my first carnival Saturday in 1964, when I was a student at Havana University and taking my first steps in journalism on the University paper Alma Mater. It was my first assignment. The university students had been rehearsing for weeks. There was a certain amount of skepticism but also curiosity about their participation. It was taken for granted that a masquerade was not the most fitting form of entertainment for a university student, yet at the same time new ideas were shaping the new society in hitherto unheard-of directions. Deep-seated change was a challenge to the imagination, bringing down barriers to social and ethnic integration.

Race had been a latent yet ever-present issue of my student days. When I entered the University of Havana School of Arts and Letters in 1963, I was one of a tiny group of non-white students which included the first African students, who came from wealthy backgrounds and, for political reasons, had been withdrawn from Paris and sent to revolutionary Cuba by the progressive government of the Republic of Guinea. The political effervescence of those early years helped offset prejudice. As students we were pleased to have among us both Africans and East Europeans, though their cultural differences were often cause for derision.

Covering student participation in carnival would be another test of how the new revolutionary ideology was trying to sweep aside race codes among the student body. Implicit in this was not drawing attention to the obvious, which was the ethnic composition of the masquerade. The following is taken from what I wrote at the time:

> It was the first Saturday of the Havana carnival, 1964. The University Student Federation (FEU) had been assigned the task of organizing a float, a masquerade and five kiosks [sidewalk stands] in the annual festivities of music, dance and entertainment. It was 10:00 at night. The University masquerade group was assembled in an alley between San Lazaro and the Seafront Drive, waiting for the University float which would be part of the FEU spectacle. The young students, in their well-designed costumes for a well-conceived choreography, were met with applause from the crowd. While all along the seafront, the contagious notes of carnival could be heard on the salt air; 50 student couples waited nervously for the whistle to start. Impatience mounted until at last . . . the students spotted the float coming from 23rd Street along Seafront Drive. I hadn't seen it and was expecting something very different. Certainly not carnival drummers surrounding women posed on a replica of the University's white Doric columns. Who had introduced this motif? Could the float take the musicians as well? In the end, some musicians did go up on the float, while others stayed down on the street.
>
> What was a great success was the dancing. That was also organised by the FEU, but, when it came down to it, was 95 per cent made up of junior and senior high school students. They were the ones who stole the show. Where were the University students? In effect, little had been done to attract them. When the papers came out on Monday, they carried the news that "the crowd had applauded the University Student Federation masquerade." But, in all truth, the junior and senior high students saved the day. . . .

My article was published, with a lot of editor's corrections, and even then it wasn't well-received. Though looking back it might seem the most naive piece of writing I've ever done, not so in those early years of Revolution. We wanted to take giant strides and sweep aside social barriers, but without any specific race program. In effect, the white women students had not wanted to be associated with black musicians and dancers. Dancers couldn't be recruited among the university students because there were few black students, and the white students either couldn't play and dance the *conga*, or did their best to avoid having to come forward. It was a total fiasco, but over the years many things have changed.

★ ★ ★ ★ ★

I didn't know at the time that the 1990 Havana carnival was supposedly an improvement on previous years, on the recommendations of journalists, writers, performers and others concerned with popular art forms. One contributor to the popular weekly magazine *Bohemia* had speculated on plane loads of people coming to Havana for carnival, as if to Trinidad or Río or New Orleans: a dream that could well be made reality, it was felt. According to the journalist, 'a level of organization had been achieved in the administrative, technical and artistic running of carnival that could cope with daily festivities, catering well to half a million people over several kilometers.'

The two main questions raised by the journalist were the same ones to have been raised piecemeal by carnival organizers over the last 30 years: how to organize the event so that it was true to 'the artistic aims and profile of carnival in its historical context' and 'the physical location and extension favoring its orderly enjoyment.' The problem is that no satisfactory solution has ever been found for either.

There have always been those who have suggested putting an end to these popular festivities—as in the case of Notting Hill, London, carnival. The argument is that there are fights where crowds gather, drinking without dancing it off. In Havana, shortages compounded the problem, and carnival was again becoming a moment to unleash inhibitions and repressed emotion—tension, due to the poverty of the big city populations, and anxiety, over not seeing immediate ways out. On the one hand, the crowds are more cohesive than ever and carnival is certainly no longer the domain of non-white, popular sectors; the festive climate, on the other, can have more violent and disturbing consequences. The end-result has been a police patrol on every block that almost turns carnival into a state of siege, with possible police reaction to the slightest provocation.

Press articles on the 1989–90 carnival were measured in their criticism. 'There has never been such a turnout for carnival as in these first two days . . . Saturday and Sunday were explosive . . . . Families and children turned out confidently to form a vast sea of people enjoying carnival . . . . Floats, costumes and choreography were colorful and in good taste . . . . In these first two days of popular festivities, the most common source of irritation was the lack of places to eat and drink: many were either closed or with such poor service that people were in for a long wait. All the same, it was an encouraging start.'

It was not so encouraging in summer 1991 when carnival was suspended because of the Pan American Games which were being held in Havana and Santiago de Cuba. The austerity the Cuban people are facing in these last years of the century makes the dreams expressed by the *Bohemia* journalist seem far remote. But more than things material, carnival needs a freer reign, allowing the creativity and spontaneity of people to come through. As Cuba and the people have changed, so carnival festivities are not the same. And yet, it should still be possible to recapture the catharsis of Carnival.

*All poems quoted in this chapter are by the author.

These Things Happen in My Country! Carnival in Havana during the *Período Especial*

Pedro Pérez Sarduy

The *Período Especial* is the name given to the current period of austerity.[1] Carnaval was canceled beginning in 1991 and did not reappear until 1996, with the first signs of economic recuperation, and even then obvious signs of hard times were evident. Nevertheless, it is precisely during this period of redoubled scarcity that Havana Carnaval begins again to try to revolutionize its *cubanía* with a more African image. I must ask to what degree has this effort succeeded if, at the same time, racial prejudices have increased in the last decade of the twentieth century? Ironically there has also been a frenzied renewal of interest in reevaluating our traditions of African origin, with implications for the Cuban (and Pan-American-Caribbean) conception of these celebrations.

Similar to what occurred during the three decades after 1912[2]—when the authorities suspended the popular *comparsas* composed mainly of blacks and mulattos—these celebrations increasingly lost their traditional elements in favor of creating an appealing tourist spectacle. It was not until 1937, because of the absence of foreign visitors (most of whom came from the U.S.), that the street festivals were again permitted. Although currently the presence of *norteños* is hardly significant, the rest of the world continues to be drawn to this large, magical island and its unbridled culture of rhythm. Truthfully, however, there is still a lot lacking before Havana Carnaval can compete in humor and collective entertainment with those in Río de Janeiro and Salvador de Bahía, in Brazil, or the 'bacanales' of Trinidad & Tobago, in the West Indies.

For the more than three hundred years that the slave trade lasted in Cuba, the only things the blacks could bring with them from Africa were the memory of their characteristic festivals, and their religious beliefs.

Venerated and respected by many, but equally profaned and prohibited by others, the drum has reigned ever since among musical instruments in Cuba, to the point where it has become almost impossible to imagine any type of Cuban music without the deliberate or impetuous beats resounding from its membranes.

The *conga* is, of all our musical genres, the one that best expresses the contagious joy shown by Cubans in dance. Some elderly individuals still remember old-time *comparsas* in Havana. These *comparsas* represented different neighborhoods that used the *conga* and rapid drumbeats to accompany infectious songs that have extended their influence into the present. Such is the case of the *comparsa* El Alacrán (the Scorpion), founded in 1938 by Santos Ramírez Arango in a working-class barrio of the district of El Cerro. This was the first year when *comparsas* reappeared after their official 1912 prohibition—an occurrence that provoked a huge polemic between their defenders and their detractors, who were scandalized by the reaffirmation of the 'Africanness' of the Carnaval's founders and participants.

> Oye colega, no te asustes cuando veas . . .
> al alacrán tumbando caña . . .
> son cosas de mi país, mi hermano . . .
>
> *Listen friend, don't be startled when you see . . .*
> *the scorpion cutting sugar cane . . .*
> *these things happen in my country, my brother . . .*

Besides this zoomorphic relationship linking the *comparsa* to African cultural and ethnic elements, El Alacrán, in their performances, represented other socioeconomic elements from the Cuban past, for example, slaves cutting the sugar cane and transporting it to the factory, and included as their main characters the overseer, the assistant, the master, the runaway slave, the lottery ticket seller, and others typical of the era.

The middle of the nineteenth century was marked by the arrival of North American minstrels: companies of white actors who performed the music and dance of blacks in the U.S., while wearing their characteristic clothing and blackface. By the turn of the century that type of entertainment had a profound impact on popular theatrical trends in Cuba and introduced elements which were codified in the *teatro bufo* on the island. Similarly, the rich white society from the colonial period began, among themselves, to imitate the minstrels, putting on blackface, dressing up in typical slaves' clothes, and staging *tango* dances during Carnaval.[3]

An interesting aspect of El Alacrán's history, and an indicator of the complicated social history of Havana's Carnaval, occurred in 1908 when El Alacrán was made up of whites who put on blackface and executed pirouettes to the subtle beat of *timbales* and clarinets. African-born Gerónimo, the father of Ramírez Arango, was *nganga* (a person of African Bantu origin)[4] and was the only black to participate in that festival, and he played the role of an African, being an African himself!

The late 1930s represented the height of segregated society (of blacks, whites and mulattos). Once the prohibition of Carnaval and festival public celebrations was lifted in 1937, Santos Ramírez introduced *conga* drums and trumpets into the instrumentation and began to compose for El Alacrán. In this way, new *comparsas* were created with fresh ancestral spirit. Two of these, the Marqueses de Atarés, from the seaport zone of Habana Vieja, and El Alacrán, from El Cerro, were among those most rooted in popular culture.[5]

The fact that El Alacrán arose in El Cerro is not fortuitous. A little bit of history reminds us that the first colonial towns outside the walls of Havana began to be built along the Calzada del Cerro. The first *casas-quintas*[6] were built along this long and sinuous route, the places of recreation for counts and marquis. Along with this architectural style arose the first industries of ice, beer, and malts, among others. With these, workers began to arrive to build their own houses, different and more modest, of course, from those of the aristocracy.

The diverse expressions of African culture, their gods, their costumes, their rhythms and their dances, that during the year often remain hidden in *casa-templos* (sanctuaries and even entire rooms within private houses), are brought out into the streets during Carnaval. Carnaval performances recreate mythology and blend the ritual with the profane. From the beginning, this tradition has been present in El Alacrán which, according to those who saw it in 1908, was associated with Yemayá, the *oricha* associated with the sea in the Afro-Cuban religion la Regla de Ocha, or Santería. For this reason, El Alacrán participants dress in blue, reflecting the sea.

'El Alacrán is a great comparsa, because it represents my country's sugar cane,' Mrs. Beneranda Betancourt proudly declares, going on to say: '. . . What is the sugar cane if not Cuban sugar? And we are the cane cutters!' In fact, it was black Africans who were first brought to Cuba to harvest the cane and make sugar the island's primary industry.

The above commentary by Mrs. Betancourt appears in an interview included in a short documentary by the Cuban filmmaker Gloria Rolando (who tirelessly works to recapture the lost memory of our culture).[7] Filmed in the same Havana barrio of El Cerro where El Alacrán was founded, Gloria Rolando's documentary pays tribute to the 60 years following Ramírez

Arango's formation of the group. Then in her youth, Mrs. Betancourt had been one of the first participants in El Alacrán, and she remained loyal to the rhythms for 40 years, as a dancer and as Tesorera (treasurer) of the *comparsa*.

The analogy derived from her words has multiple nuances. 'When sugar was king in Cuba' was incessantly repeated to us, as was 'without sugar there is no country.' Although today the tourist industry occupies the space left by low national sugar production and depreciated prices in the world market, even now sugar remains valuable to the complete economic recovery of this Caribbean island. It is also a staple ingredient in the Cuban diet. The members of El Alacrán, almost all of African descent, reclaim with dignity the contributions of our people, the treasures of our nation, in good times and in bad. In this short but valuable documentary, the current director of the *comparsa*, Santos Ramírez Ugarte, the son of Ramírez Arango and Beneranda Betancourt, appears and speaks about his *comparsa*.

In the same way that the sacred drums confirm the rebirth of those initiated into the religions of African origin in Cuba, El Alacrán also embraces the sign of the gods from the distant motherland, supported by profane drums.

In an attempt to recover tradition, the Havana Carnaval of 1999 which began on Friday, July 23, and lasted until Sunday, August 15—always on weekends—included at least twenty *comparsas* and paid homage to the *comparsa* Los Guaracheros de Regla on its fortieth anniversary. Los Guaracheros de Regla is another *comparsa* rooted in African tradition and located in the small seaport town of Regla, at one end of the wide, deep Bay of Havana.

In 1999 there were metal chairs in tiers and boxes along some two miles of the Malecón (Havana's famous seaside boulevard), in addition to folding stalls for the vendors of food, beer, and rum. For many of Havana's residents, the Carnaval had lost its splendor a long time ago. In the afternoon hours, men and women crowd around the tanks for drinks, seeking inebriation, now more than ever because the authorities have recently introduced a period of prohibition of the sale of alcoholic beverages between the hours of 6 in the morning and noon. Such restrictions, implemented in other parts of the world many years ago, are inconceivable in the Caribbean.

Many Cubans who remember former Havana Carnavals feel saddened by what was but no longer is. The Carnaval is happiness, they say—costumes, dances, the noise of the crowd, good *comparsas*, elegant floats. They consider the current festivals to be none of that, but rather a simple parade, officially organized and run, that demonstrates what is not, what *does not happen*.

Perhaps the same Cubans who complain about governmental regulations in Havana do not know that similar conditions exist everywhere, from the famous carnivals in Río, to those in Notting Hill, in London (celebrated for two days at the end of August), or to those in Brooklyn. These conditions

A performer with the *comparsa* El Alacrán during Havana Carnival July 1999. He is wearing a costume reminscent of the dancer called 'la Culona' by Fernando Ortiz. © David H. Brown.

exist also in Mardi Gras, in New Orleans, and in the MAScarades, in Trinidad & Tobago.

In these very different settings, the commodification of popular festivals comes from the same source as the demand for the globalization of the world's economy—tourist packages with 'everything included.' This commodification produces the arrangement of a form of entertainment that has more to do with the visitor 'from elsewhere' than with local initiatives.

In the case of Havana, for example, for the first time in the summer of 1999, the floats full of lights and beautiful women, especially blacks and mulattos, crossed the Malecón accompanied by public announcements, in other words, advertisements paid for by several of the more than 400 foreign companies investing in Cuba, none of these U.S., so far!

The Havana Carnaval, once recognized for the splendor of its spectacle and considered the second most famous of the continent after the one in Río, has undergone so many transformations in the last 40 years that it has been converted into a hybrid street festival. Perhaps, too, the original location of the Havana Carnaval, in the older, more black, and working-class section of the city, no longer responded to the island's need to push the festival as a commodity to the numerous tourists who travel regularly to Cuba.

Just as happened during the prohibition of Carnaval and festivals at the beginning of the twentieth century, when a group of progressive intellectuals lobbied for the lifting of that prohibition, in 1999 many prominent writers and artists publicly expressed their concern and suggested that Carnaval return to its previous date and locations—in February when the parade route was from the Capitolio along the entire length of the Paseo del Prado (newly refurbished in 1999).

Today the crowd extends along the entire Malecón, and spectators passively enjoy the spectacle from the gardens of the splendid five-star Hotel Nacional de Cuba, or the more modest art deco Hotel Deauville, at the other end of the Malecón. Throughout this zone there is an abundance of kiosks that do business in dollars, and perhaps a few others who negotiate in the national currency.

Meanwhile, in various locations in Havana, the foremost Cuban bands literally heat up the festive atmosphere and it is in these more out of the way locations where the national passion, dance, has few limits. Here in their own neighborhoods thousands of couples, the vast majority blacks and mulattos, move to the beat of the *timba*, the most current expression of Afro-Cuban music, which, little by little, has been replacing the overused and generic term *salsa* for this other, which is much more resounding and well-known in the popular Cuban slang at the end of the century.

'*This* is Carnaval!' says a young man, as he and his partner spin rapidly in one of the many free open-air dances, impulsively marking the rhythm of the percussion and brass. 'You can enjoy the same things, whether you've got dollars or not. Hey, you know brother, these things happen in my country!'

Notes

1. Erica Miller, a graduate student in the Spanish Department at Emory University, assisted with translating this essay from the Spanish original.
2. It is important to note that the 1912 Race War had many repercussions throughout Cuban society. See Aline Helg, *Our Rightful Share: The Afro-Cuban Struggle for Equality, 1886–1912* (Chapel Hill and London: University of North Carolina Press, 1995).
3. For a fascinating history of this aspect of Carnaval see Robin Moore, *Nationalizing Blackness: Afrocubanismo and Artistic Revolution in Havana, 1920-1940* (University of Pittsburgh Press, 1997), pp. 66–72.
4. Editor's note: Although Sarduy uses the word *nganga* to establish Gerónimo's heritage, the word itself is most often used to name the sacred receptacle of the Afro-Cuban religion Palo Monte. In central Africa a *nganga* is a powerful spiritual leader.

5. Editor's note: For an eyewitness account of Havana's Carnaval in c. 1949, and a lengthy description of El Alacrán's performance, see Patrick Leigh Fermor, *The Traveller's Tree: A Journey through the Caribbean Islands* (New York: Harper, 1950).
6. This is a type of country farmhouse built in the suburbs of Havana, outside the old city's walls.
7. *El Alacrán*, La Habana 1999, Directora Gloria Rolando. Producción Freddy Moros, Televison Latina, La Habana, Cuba.

Glossary of Popular Festivals

Rafael Brea and José Millet

Introduction

The authors of this annotated glossary are researchers at Casa del Caribe in Santiago de Cuba. Many contend that Casa is located in 'the most Caribbean city in Cuba,' while others claim that it is 'the capital of the Caribbean.' Both assertions are well founded. Let it suffice to remind North American readers that Santiago de Cuba was the first Cuban capital city during Colonial times. It was a privileged geographical site through which significant and diverse commercial and cultural products flowed from nearby islands in what is called the American Mediterranean. Due to the contact, relations and interchange maintained throughout the centuries, Santiago de Cuba became a pivotal center for its neighbors, especially the Dominican Republic, Puerto Rico, and Jamaica.

Casa del Caribe is one of the most unique research institutes in Cuba, not only because of the international range of its work, but also because it is located outside the capital, Havana, where most, if not all, research institutes of this type are located. It is unique too for combining research focused on the areas of Cuban and Caribbean culture – such as traditional popular culture, non-institutionalized religions, etc. – while at the same time promoting and diffusing Cuban culture within the Caribbean, and likewise disseminating the knowledge of the largeness of Cuban culture within Cuba itself. These efforts have brought Casa much deserved international recognition. Casa del Caribe also sponsors a Festival of Caribbean Culture which has been held for eleven consecutive years, and which constitutes one of the few arenas within which the rich facets of this culture can come together. The Festival also provides an arena for the meeting of specialists and intellectuals from all over the world, focusing on one central theme: Caribbean identity.

It is especially appropriate that Casa del Caribe sponsors this Festival in Santiago de Cuba. Historically, significant and widespread socioeconomic factors, such as slavery and the plantation system, as well as the previously outlined cultural factors, helped Santiago de Cuba achieve a position of central importance for over half of the island, as well as making it a leader in effecting profound cultural changes fundamental to the configuration of a national culture for all Cuban people. To underscore this point we mention two such supranational expressions: the celebration in Santiago de Cuba of the most traditional carnival in Cuba and the neighboring sanctuary of El Cobre, home to the cult of the Virgen de la Caridad, who is the patron saint of the Cuban people.

If, indeed, Havana and Matanzas are identified as points where the widespread religious phenomenon known as Santería crystalized, then Santiago de Cuba can be identified as the center of another important Cuban tradition, namely carnival, as well as of other folkloric expressions. As one of the primary points of immigration for the victorious Franco-Haitian slaves after the revolution in Saint Dominique – now the Republic of Haiti – Santiago de Cuba acquired a distinct character that sets it apart from other cities in Cuba. The influx of other significant migratory influences, from other Caribbean islands such as Jamaica, Guadalupe, Saint Kitts and Nevis, etc., continued, contributing to the uniqueness of Santiago de Cuba. The primary ingredients of these phenomena would be molded and transformed, giving rise to a cultural extreme that is, without exception, *sui generi,* the culture of Santiago today, unique in all of Cuba.

Our colleague, Joel James, director of Casa del Caribe, loves to say that as a city Santiago de Cuba is really a Caribbean Festival. And he doesn't lack arguments to support assertions like this. For, since the beginning, Santiago has been alive with the multiple poetry of its own history and its own culture. In 1981 a group of recent graduates from Oriente University helped to organize the first Festival of Caribbean Culture. A number of these graduates, including a team of eager students, had met in a cultural workshop – the only other local institution in the region alongside Casa del Caribe – whose goal was to analyze the puzzle which is Caribbean culture. These individuals were the ones who later became the founding members of Casa del Caribe in 1982.

Casa del Caribe, and its affiliated researchers, has had a significant impact on cultural life in Santiago. Two research groups were founded under the direction of specialists from Casa and research work was begun on festivals and popular religion in the area. Also, the Cabildo Teatral Santiago changed its direction and included more Santiago-based cultural expressions in its workshops and productions.

One of the most exciting non-institutional religious phenomenon that remained unresearched until recently is Vodún, as it is practiced in Oriente Province. A result of our work is the extensive study entitled *Vodún in Cuba,* soon to be published in the Dominican Republic (excerpts have appeared in the magazine *Del Caribe* published by Casa del Caribe). Another expression of religious faith that also has received attention is a very little studied phenomena, Espiritismo de Cordón. The study group responsible for this publication is headed by José Millet.

The staff at Casa del Caribe is responsible for conferences; papers presented in national and international events; radio and T.V. programs; scripts for theatrical spectacles like 'Ercilí,' which was choreographed by the famous Jorge Lefevre, director of the Royal Ballet of Walonie, Belgium; workshops in the comparative study of religions; and, of special note, advisory work on four important documentary films: 'Huellas' (Vodún), 'Ceremonia' (Congolese cults), 'Cordón' (Espiritismo) and 'Ocha' (Santería). Casa del Caribe also sponsors lecture courses offered in Cuba, Poland, the Museum of Man in the Dominican Republic, and at the University in Santo Domingo.

Contributing author Rafael Brea has focused all his efforts in the investigation of popular festivals. Together Brea and Millet have done fieldwork with the principal groups in Santiago carnival and the directors of *comparsas* and *paseos. Caperos, salidores, tocaderos, cornetistas, bailadores* and common people were interviewed in order to have a written record of all the main events that take place and with the intention of establishing an oral history archive so that information will not get lost as members of each group die. The fruit of this work, that began in 1985, is the book *Folk Groups of Santiago de Cuba,* published by Editorial Oriente in December 1990. We are currently working on the second edition.

In 1983 Rafael Brea became a member of the research staff at Casa del Caribe. It was then that the direction of his interests and research changed, as he was moved in a manner similar to Alejo Carpentier's description of the effect of his visit to Haiti in *El reino de este mundo.* Now Brea concentrates his research on those facets of culture embedded in festive environments of the Caribbean. No less extensive is Brea's work on the theme of popular festivals in Cuba and in the Caribbean. He has accomplished fieldwork in municipalities of Oriente Province, such as San Luis, Songo-La Maya, Palma Soriano, and Contramaestre, as well as in other provinces, such as Granma, Holguín, and Camagüey. It is in Camagüey that the popular Feast of San Juan is celebrated.

Casa del Caribe also sponsors projects involving exchanges between Cuba and foreign groups, and has sent delegations to Guyana, Santo Domingo, and Angola, locations where Casa researchers have done fieldwork. These projects have been in response to our desire to internationalize the carnival of Santiago de Cuba by introducing elements from these countries with rich festival traditions.

It is obvious that fieldwork done in eastern Cuba has enabled all scholars to accumulate extensive factual data with which to appreciate regional variations that, beyond their local significance, are of national pertinence. With this information researchers at Casa understand elements essential to a national Cuban culture that is only rarely acknowledged, validated or properly situated within the cultural arena. Consider, for example, the extensive semantic palette of idioms and speech gathered in this *Glossary* which point to the presence of French and Haitian culture within the eastern part of the island.

It is important to point out that in producing this *Glossary* we have not only worked with oral information but also with relevant written sources from local authors who have drawn deeply from both general and specific knowledge of the culture of Santiago. Thanks to the existence of the Center for Documentation at Casa del Caribe, which houses a valuable collection of completed research and documentation of work in progress by scholars from the provinces of Oriente and Camagüey, as well as by scholars at Casa del Caribe, we have been able to complete this *Glossary* according to the standards of quality and breadth we had hoped to achieve. To mention one example, *Oriente folklórico,* a work by the famous scholar of folklore Ramón Martínez Martínez, about whom the Cuban Fernando Ortiz speaks with high praise, is available at the Center for Documentation in manuscript form.

We hope that this introduction will serve to explain who we are, what Casa del Caribe is, and how our work came about and permitted us to compile this annotated *Glossary* which, in a certain way, complements and brings up to date the lexigraphic work done in Cuba or about Cuba by other well known authors, such as Fernando Ortiz.

Glossary of Popular Festivals

aguinaldo: A gift, most often monetary, given by the local authorities to the various music and dance groups, and masqueraders as they passed through the town hall during festivals in colonial times. The *aguinaldo* was originally given on the Día de Reyes ('Day of the Kings'), January 6, for the benefit of the Spanish soldiers and the so-called slaves of the king who came to pay their respects to the colonial authorities on that day.

ahijado: protegé. In carnival, a person who receives the sponsorship of someone with a better economic position. With this help, the cost of the *mamarrachos*, costumes and personal adornments needed for the festival *congas* and parades could be defrayed.

arrollar: Rhythmic movement of a carnival dance group with people joining in behind, winding their way though the streets. It becomes a form of collective dance, marking time with the instruments of the *congas* and parades with a variety of agile steps and body movements, in circle formation, jumping, crouching and whirling, and improvising biting and erotic chants, while constantly on the move. The group of persons is so tightly packed that they roll along like a car and everything within its radius is swept up and carried along with the crowd.

aura cerrajera: A body costume made of black muslin, used during the nineteenth-century War of Independence to hide and transport arms destined for the rebel camp.

ayaca: An expression referring to a highly nutritious and exquisitely flavored dish prepared from tender ground or grated corn with chorizo sausage, bacon, lard, salt, and lightly fried garlic, onions and herbs in tomato purse, wrapped in corn husk leaves and tied with strands of the same leaf, and boiled in a pot for about 30 minutes. It is a typical carnival dish. In the north of Oriente it is known as *tamal.* Used widely in the former province of Oriente, especially in Bayamo, Manzanillo and Santiago de Cuba.

baccine, baccín, baksín, or basín: *(vaccine* or *vaksins* in Haiti) Musical instrument used by the orchestra of the *bandé Rará.* It is made from a meter-long piece of hollowed-out bamboo, known in Oriente as *bambú* or *cañambú* and in the western part of the island as *caña brava.* A substitute piece of plastic tubing of approximate proportions can also be used. Currently it is used by the Haitians and their descendants who live mainly in the eastern provinces of Camagüey and Ciego de Avila.

bailador: Dancer; member of a dance group; person who moves rhythmically and keeps tempo with the carnival dance group.

bandé Rará: A Rará performance group (see Gagá). The name given by the Haitians to the dance groups and masqueraders who, singing and dancing, performed over long distances during Easter or Holy Week festivals. The principal settings for these festivities were the rural areas of the former provinces of Oriente and Camagüey. The groups were accomplished in their diverse performances en route, one of which was the machete dance.

banderola: A flag slightly smaller than the usual size, carried by someone participating in a carnival parade.

Barrio de los Hoyos: Neighborhood situated in the northern part of Santiago de Cuba and bordered by Paseo de Martí, San Fermín, Los Maceos and Calvario Streets. According to Santiago tradition, the name Los Hoyos [*hoyos* means 'holes'] derives from the period when the coastal strip of what are Gallo Aquilera and San Antonio Streets was being reclaimed and the excavations left holes and ditches. As early as the 19th century this neighborhood was a major center of Afro-Cuban culture. The heart of the neighborhood is La Plaza de la Yerba. During the pseudo-republic it was officially named Barrio Moncada, in honor of Guillermo Moncada, a general in the 19th-century War of Independence, who was born on San Salvador (now Moncada Street) between San Antonio and San Mateo. A *barrio* of strong carnival traditions, it is the home of the extraordinary and much-celebrated Conga Los Hoyos, heir of El Cocoyé.

bastón: Baton made from a tree branch with attached tips of ornate metal containers filled with pellets and bits of nail or seed to provide a rattle effect. In the *Gagá* dance groups, the drum majors use a simple polished guava branch.

bastonera: Drum majorette who directs certain dances and plays an important part in the various types of carnival dance groups, such as the Tajona and the Carabalí.

bastonero: Drum major, with great dancing ability, who carries in his hand a baton or ornamental scepter. He performs a similar function to that of the majorette. At 19th century Havana balls in private salons, this word was synonymous for the one who paired up male and female dancers. It appears that it was the girls who requested their pairs. An article published by Ventura Pascual Ferrer in *El Regañon* in December,1800, reads: "Throughout the minuets, the drum major who was called D. Liborio never stopped walking from one side of the room to the other. One girl would beckon him and whisper: 'I want you to take me to dance with the one in the blue ruffle.' Another would whisper: 'Find me a good partner for the contredanse'"; and she successively cites various similar situations.

The *bastonero* or musical director of La Tajona performing during Carnival 1989, Santiago de Cuba. © J.B

batá: 'Musically, they are the richest and most varied in sound of the Afrocuban drums....There are basically three types of these drums: the religious *okonkilo or orele, itotels* and the *iya.* They are used in ceremonies practiced in Cuba by the Lucumís and Yorubas and their descendants, Creoles....The *batá* form a full Yoruba orchestra' (Fernando Ortiz 1952).

bocú, bokú y bocúses: The drums used in Santiago de Cuba carnival music and dance groups. They come from the African *bocú,* which in the Kikongo language means drum. Its sound is sharp and high-pitched. In the *congas* of eastern Cuba, they use an indeterminate number of drums, anywhere from four to sixteen. Ortiz says that he has seen them used in ritual music of the *Orilé cruzao,* in Oriente province.

bomba: 'In the Ñáñigo vocabulary, drunkenness.' (Fernando G. Campoamor 1985.) Type of music and dance of the runaway slaves in Puerto Rico, and the equivalent there of our *conga.* The *bomba* is a whole institution in the festivities held for Santiago the Apostle in the city of Loíza, in Puerto Rico, where the influence of African culture is very notable.

bombo: 'Instrument of European origin, creolized in the Americas, characteristic of military bands. Consists of a box with two drumheads secured by two hoops. It is played with a mallet, a bobbin or by hand. In Cuba this instrument is used in the *congas.'* (Helio Orovio 1981:53)

bongó: 'Creole instrument. Consists of two small drums joined by a piece of wood. The two drums are almost identical, but one is the *macho* and is slightly smaller by about 20 centimeters....Its roots are definitely African. Originally in Oriente, it consisted of two small drums, similar to those used in the groups of Tahona (or Tajona), tied together by a leather strap that was supported on the knee. Sometimes only one small drum was used.' It reached its splendor when it arrived in Havana from eastern Cuba. According to Ortiz, 'The *bongo* is the most important synthesis in the evolution of the twin drums attained by Afro-Cuban music.' (Helio Orovio 1981:54-55)

bulá: Drum used in the Tumba Francesa. It is a little smaller than the former, sharp, high-pitched sounding one. It is used to maintain the main rhythm.

buylayer: m.s. The drummer of the *bulá* in the Tumba Francesa.

cabezones: Described by Ramón Martínez (1940:32) as a *comparsa* of *mamarrachos* who paraded in celebration on the feast days of Santa Cristina, Santiago and Santa Ana. The *cabezones* covered their heads with double masks that depicted the facial features of African slaves, imitating their facial expressions and language in songs such as this:

> That big headed black
> is thinking to himself
> that because he has fame
> I am whining
> lies, he has nothing
> lies, he has nothing
> lies, he has nothing
> may the lie curdle him

cabildo: Word coined during slavery in Cuba. Originally denoted a coalition of organizations of slaves grouped by the African nations from which they had come. Eventually, these organizations began to abandon traditional tribal and ethnic organizational structures and embraced the ethnically varied culture of Cuba. Originally linked by religious practices, they would later become centers for the preservation and transmission of an important aspect of our cultural traditions. During the carnival period it is a festive group. According to Ramón Martínez (1940:33), 'It was a *comparsa* of the ones who came out for the *mamarrachos* of Santa Christina, Santiago and Santa Ana, and were the pride of the town. Originally it was made up of French Blacks, then it was Cubanized and finally there was a mix of both Black and Whites.'

We disagree, however, with one aspect of Martínez's description and believe that it was not just 'French Blacks' who were members but instead, and more generically, all Afro-Cubans.

cabriola: A swift, agile jump resembling the caper of a goat. Typically, it is executed by persons in response to the exuberant and liberating atmosphere of carnival.

caíman: A humorous word that refers to an opportunistic, lazy or slow person.

caja de luces: A wooden structure covered with multicolored cloths on which masks are painted. They are illuminated by and hung from lampposts throughout the city. Their function is similar to that of the masks of carnival.

campana: A percussion instrument known as a 'brake drum' used in *conga* music. It is held at shoulder level and struck by a nail or a railroad spike or other pieces of metal.

campanero: Person who plays the *campana,* or 'brake drum,' for the *conga* group.

campanita: A bronze bell with interior clapper, used in the *comparsas* of the Cabildo Carabalí, as well as during worship ceremonies for the saints of Cuba. When the ceremony was held for Babalú Ayé (Saint Lazarus) the faithful rang the bell to announce the visitors to the saint.

cancancito: Franco-Haitian decorative adornment made of lace or cloth for a suit or dress used in the festivities.

canutillas/os: Small ornamental glass tubing sewn to braids, tassels and cords as adornments; often a component of the costumes of the *comparseros.*

capa: A skillfully crafted cape or cloak used as carnival apparel, notable for its color and ornamentation. It constitutes an important and identifying element of specific *congas* or *paseos,* and appears to be of medieval origin and representative of the wardrobe worn by medieval nobility. A particularly well-crafted *capa* is often regarded as an object of high artistic or monetary value.

capero: The individual who specializes in the yearly construction, decoration and display of a *capa,* used in the *comparsas* year after year, taking care of its coloring, design and beauty. The *caperos* form different groups in the *comparsas.* The *caperos* are awarded prizes based on the quality and message of the capes.

Carabalí (The people): A generic name for the slaves who were introduced to Cuba from southern Nigeria during the course of the slave trade (from the end of the eighteenth century until the 1840s), so named through metathesis of the Nigerian Calabar. The use of this name dismissed the complex ethnic and tribal makeup of these 'pieces of ebony' who had been brought from this region of Africa. The Carabalí, and later their descendants, were able to organize themselves into *cabildos* that paraded as *comparsas* in the festivities of the *mamarrachos.* Two *comparsas* Carabalí exist to this day in our city.

carabalí (The dance): The name given in the southern part of the ancient province of Oriente to slow paced, rhythmic dances, the performance of which includes songs patterned after African singing: a main singer leads the words of the song, and the chorus echoes them back. Its origin dates to the colonial period when free Blacks, descendants of slaves from Calabar, established *cabildos.* In practice, the *cabildos* functioned like a mutual aid society; evidently in these mutual aid societies, the beat and sound, songs and African dances were transculturized to give way to artistic forms of grand originality.

carabiné: 'This is a dance of *compas* in two by four time, consisting of two parts: the *paseo* (promenade, not used much anymore) and the refrain of a song. /... / It is generally played on the accordion, *balsie,* gourd, three-string guitar, guitar and tambourine, and in some parts is accompanied by (gut string) violins. These instruments are almost never played all together, but rather when there are string instruments there is no accordion and vice versa. Generally, the requested performances are done in patios.' (Fradique Lizardo Barinas 1961:3-8)

careta: Mask. Used extensively in carnivals to cover an individual identity. It is utilized as a disguise, to avoid social prejudices and to practice vengeances or other acts. It has little by little been discontinued in use in the popular dances, but has been maintained in the *comparsas.*

Carnival: Word of Latin origin. Used to indicate the time period and practice of public festivities observed from the 'Day of the Kings' through Ash Wednesday. It is also understood to mean the three festive days that precede Ash Wednesday. From earliest times, festivals, and in particular carnival, marked a period of private and collective freedom in Europe, from where the tradition was brought to the New World. In these territories it acquired specific modalities, in terms of both form and content, that were the result of the mixing of the cultural traditions of Europeans, native peoples, and African slaves. On the Iberian peninsula an extraordinary variety of festivals exist, many of which were brought to Cuba by the colonialists. All manner of positive occasions in the life of the colonists, or of significance in the motherland, were cause for these public festivals, from the birth of a prince, the wedding of a king, a saint's feast day, Christmas or Holy Week. A festive spirit existed within the social and cultural milieu. An extensive list of official and religious festivals existed in Santiago. However, for economic reasons linked to the seasonal end of sugar and coffee production, as well as to the city's maritime activities, public festivities reached a high level of social acceptance, especially those celebrated during the summer months. Among these are the celebration of the Feast Day of San Juan, Santa Cristina, Santiago Apostol, and Santa Ana. With the passage of time these festivals became established as traditional celebrations inspired by the symbols of Christianity.

Santiago Apostol was the recognized patron of Santiago de Cuba by all sectors of the society. Both free Blacks and slaves equated the representation of Santiago Matamoros, as he is traditionally depicted-on horseback with a raised sword—with Ogún Guerrero from the pantheon of Cuban Santeriá. Due to the power of this Christian Saint, July 25th became the most important of the festival days. However, from the start of the festive period, June 24th, Catholic processions were held that combined both religious and secular elements, such as *mamarrachos, titereteros, diablitos, trasvistes, borrachos, cabildos, Tajonas, comparsas and parranderos.* During the colonial period this festive and popular period was known as Fiesta de Máscaras as well as Mamarrachos. Beginning in the nineteenth century through to the present day it has been generically referred to as carnival in both Santiago and many other Cuban cities. On July 26, 1953, the feast day of Santa Ana, during the period of carnival, the Centennial Generation carried out the attack on the Moncada Barracks; since 1959 this date has been declared a national holiday.

carroza: A float attached to a vehicle with a small electric generator that produces the necessary current for illumination. The platform is made of wood and is covered with bright colors. On the float dancers execute their choreography accompanied by an orchestra or recorded music. The *carroza* originated in the North American carnivals (New Orleans and Miami); with the passage of time it has been converted into a traditional element of the Cuban carnival.

cascabel: A small hollowed metal ball with small copper bearings in its middle that produces a sound when shook. It is often attached to capes and other types of carnival dress.

catá: A tree trunk or piece of hollowed wood, opened at both ends, which rests upon a wooden base and is played with two sticks. The *cata* is used in small musical ensembles, and produces a strong penetrating sound.

cencerro: 'Creole imitation of *ekon ñáñigo.* A cowbell sold in livestock hardware stores. The clapper of the bell is removed. The bell is struck on the outside with a metal or very hard wooden stick. The bells give off two distinct sounds: one, a high sound at its narrow section close to the handle and two, a low sound on the wide perimeter of its opening.' (Helio Orovio, 1981:81)

cepillo (pasar el) ("passing the hat"): General practice among popular artists to collect money from the spectators at the end of every performance. This practice is slowly becoming extinct.

chacha: 'A type of metallic *maraca* which is used in the Tumba Francesa of Oriente province. It is a cylinder with flat ends at its extremities, with a handle inserted in the center. It is decorated with many multicolored ribbons and is shaken high in the air. This cylindrical type of *maruga* or *maraca* comes from Haiti.' (Helio Orovio 1981:111)

chancleta: A slipper without a heel, generally made of wood with rubber straps over the arch. Some participants of the *comparsas* and *paseos* use this type of shoe. It is also known as *cutara de palo.* In a dance called the *baile de la chancleta* the dancers move their feet rhythmically substituting their foot stomps for the drum beats. This musical expression originated in the eastern part of Cuba and then spread to the western part of Cuba. It is mainly danced during the period of carnival.

charanga: 'Type of musical group also named *francesa.* It began in the early years of the 20th century and was derived from a typical orchestra or wind orchestra.' (Helio Orovio 1981:114)

charangas (de Bejucal): This refers to a *comparsa* in Bejucal, a neighborhood of Havana. Often *charanga* and *comparsa* are used interchangably. The *charangas* of Bejucal are famous in Cuba because of their music, songs, dances, and traditions. During these festivals, celebrated annually from December 24 to January 1, the ceremony of the presenting of the flags takes place. These flags are known as *La ceiba de plate* and *La espina de oro,* whose distinctive colors are blue and red, respectively. Each group is accompanied by a *comparsa* or *charanga* and beautiful and colorful parading floats at the grand festivals celebrated on December 28, 29, and January 1 of each year. These festivities were first organized during the first half of the nineteenth century. Together with the carnivals of Santiago and the *parrandas* Remedios they represent the profound energy of celebration in Cuba.

chuparle el rabo a la jutía: 'Accustom oneself to hard liquor.' (Fernando G. Campoamor 1985:133) An expression that has emerged, in the context of the celebration of festivities, to refer to the Cuban who has immigrated to a more liberal surrounding but who has kept his old traditions.

Cocoyé (comparsa or conga): The popular name known throughout Cuba for the *conga* of Los Hoyos. To this day this *comparsa* sings the following refrain:

> Open, for here comes the Cocoyé!
> Careful, or I will move you!
> Open, here comes the Cocoyé!
> Careful, or I will move you!

cocoyé: A type of music of Dahomeyan origin introduced during the immigration of French-Haitians to eastern Cuba during the late eighteenth and early nineteenth centuries. In Cuba this style developed into music, songs and dances which were rapidly incorporated into the Santiago carnivals.

The Santiago folklorist Ramón Martínez (1940:47) wrote: 'First heard in Santiago was a type of music entitled *Cucuyé Haitiano* (Haitian Cocoye) which is found in the Museo Bacardí. Later there was a *cocoyé* arranged by a Catalonian named Casamitjana, a bandmaster of the Catalonian Regiment. It was originally a song composed from two *comparsas,* one by María la Luz González and the other by María de la O.'

The notes of the *cocoyé* song were transcribed by Mr. Casamitjana, as we noted before, upstairs from the café La Venus, which faced Plaza de Armas (today known as Cespedes Park) at 2:00 a.m. one day in August, 1836.

Eleven years later (1847), the musical folk composition by Lauro Fuentes Matons was played for the first time. Entitled *Potpourrí Cubano,* it was a collection of Cuban compositions with the theme from 'María de la O.' It was performed by the Cuban Philharmonic Society on September 3, 1847.

This potpourri, arranged for military band by Don Manuel Ubeda, a musician in the Union Regiment, with the addition of other refrains, was also given the name Cocoyé or Ajiaco Cubano. It was performed for the first time by the Regiment of Queen Isabel 11, and was directed by Don Julián Reinó (July, 1849). At its conclusion it was applauded like no composition had been previously applauded. Even today this type of Cuban music is the favorite of most Santiageros.

Today there are many types of *cocoyé,* such as the Cocoyé of Casamitjana, a happy and nostalgic African song; the Cuban Cocoyé of Lauro; the 'potpourri' of Santiago songs; and the Cocoyé by Ubeda, which is the Cocoyé of Lauro for military bands.

columbia (baile la): A dance. 'At the beginning of the *rumba,* a man moves in acrobatic gestures derived from the *íremes* or *diablitos* of the Abakuá society. The dancer moves in a gestural manner in front of a new recruit with whom there is a danced rhythmic exchange.' (Helio Orovio 1981: 369). Sources indicate that the name of this dance comes from the rural zone in the province of Matanzas named Columbia.

columbia (toque la): *El quinto.* A small five-chord guitar which produces a particular sound very popular with players of a *rumba* in the *comparsas* of Santiago. Its origin is attributed to Feliciano Mesa who belonged to a *comparsa* from the neighborhood of El Tivolí.

comidas (del carnival): Typical dishes prepared and sold during the carnival are: banana chips, barbecued pork, *chicharrones de chivo,* mixed rice and beans made from red, black and black-eyed peas, corn meal stew, casaba, 'ayacas,' fried cod fish, rutabaga, fruits like mango, guayaba, pineapple, melons and oranges, small half-moon shaped meat pies, enchiladas (spicy crab stew), yuca bread, etc.

comparsa: A group of carnival masqueraders wearing costumes. Also a name given to the gathering of masqueraders accompanied by a drum major and musicians playing *tumbas, bongó, tantán, maracas,* etc. These gatherings are held from June 24, St. John's Day through July 26, Santa Ana's Day. Among the most popular groups are: La Música de los Perros, Las Viudas, La de los Mamelucos, Los Hijos de Nené Los Cabezones, Las Banderolas, Los Curros de la Havana.

comparsero: A member of a *comparsa.*

Componedores (de Batea): A famous *comparsa* from the neighborhood of El Tivolí. Memorable to the people of Santiago for the time when the group formed a human representation of a boat in front of the carnival jury. The people of Santiago still remember the special song that accompanied this performance.

composé: In the Tumba Francesa society, he is the individual who sings, composes, organizes the chorus and signals the *catá* to begin the music.

conga (dancing-musical group): A type of musical group where the dominant instruments are percussive, drums and brake drums. It originated centuries ago in the festivities performed by the slaves. Today it is one type of carnival *comparsa.*

conga (instrument): Drum of African origin that is very popular in Cuba. It is approximately a meter in length and has a somewhat barrel-like shape. 'It used to be tuned by the flame of a candle, but today it is tuned with keys. It is played while sitting, standing or marching. It is the source for the music of the same name.' (Helio Orovio 1981:99)

conga (type of music): A musical style with strong singable and danceable qualities. The instruments are predominantly drums of various types: *conga, tumbadora, quinto, bombos, cencerros, sartenes,* and other percussion objects made of metal.

contradanza: "Its origin is in the European contradanse. This dance is believed to have been brought to Cuba by the French at the end of the eighteenth century, although some oral tradition insists it was introduced by the Spanish. The name is derived from the fusion of 'country-dance.' The dance steps are called *paseo, cadena, sostenido* and *cedazo.*" (Helio Orovio 1981:100). This dance was first practiced by the Blacks who met at the Tumba Francesa societies which were wide-spread in the eastern region of Cuba.

cordonero: Dancer who dances holding hands with other *cordonero* dancers and who together form a large oval of approximately 8 to 10 meters in length and move along the carnival route in this manner.

corneta china: A wind (reed) instrument of Asian origin incorporated into the *comparsas* and an essential element of the *congas.* The coronet was introduced by the Chinese who lived in their own neighborhood in Havana during colonial times. The coronet emits five high-pitched notes, penetrating nasal ringing sounds. Oral tradition documents the *corneta china* as having been introduced into Santiago carnival in 1915, and today it has become symbolic of Santiago *congas.*

cueros (calentar los): Tightening the drum heads using a small campfire. This is done to prevent deterioration or tearing of the skins; once they are flexible, they are tightened with keys, screws, or wedges. This process is done before playing in the *comparsa.*

cumbanchero: According to Fernando Ortiz (1974:182): 'It is the voice of African ancestry, derived from *cumbé,* the ancient dance of negros and sound to which they danced.' This musical style is rather new in Oriente province. It can also signify persons who produce a lot of noise while dancing. The *cumbé* was derived from *cumbancha,* which is synonymous with fiesta, from which came *cumbanchero.*

desfile (de carnival) (parade): A parade or procession that is secular in character. The *comparsas, paseos* and *carnivalescos* take part and present their dance and musical performances in front of a jury.

diablito (little devil): A person who disguises himself as a devil in the processions and masquerade parties. Mischievous rebel. The *diablitos* came out during Corpus Cristi or 'Day of the Kings,' January 6. According to Fernando Ortiz (1974:224), African masqueraders were thus called when disguised for their processions.

Día de Reyes ('Day of the Kings'): Festival of Catholic origin that was celebrated in Cuba on January 6, a day when the slaves were given permission to play their drums and make their own special food. The slaves of the rural areas had their dances at the plantations and in the atrium of the cathedrals of the city. These festivities were also known as Día de los Reyes Magos or Epiphany.

disfraz: To disguise by wearing a mask. An article to conceal the true identity of the individual. It is common to use a disguise in carnivals. The people dress up in clothing typical of other countries and/or use masks.

enramada: Lightweight roof-top made of palm leaves, installed in places where food and drink are sold. Presently, it is known by the name of *toldos* (awning), and is made of canvas.

esclavo de nación: Refers to the 'nation' of origin of slaves, often to their African ethnicity. This was the name given to the slaves in Africa. They organized themselves in *cabildos,* which reflected their African ethnicity.

estandarte: An insignia or flag. It was used by certain *comparsas* and *paseos* to distinguish themselves from the rest of the groups. A symbol of power often in imitation of the banner of the Spanish Army.

fantasía: Expression used to designate a style, generally of an exotic character, of certain carnival groups. The *paseo* of La Placita incorporated it as an distinctive element of the annual titles they used at carnival. In this way they have presented Brazilian, Russian, and Panamanian *fantasía* among others. This style, created for popular festivities, resonates in the way that Martin

Alonso (n.d.: 612) describes the term: 'imagination applied to reproduce by means of images the things past or distant.'

farolas: Originally an illuminated lantern that accompanied the *comparsas* at night. Originated from the *ciriales,* Easter candles, or *velones* (which is a brass lamp with a movable reservoir) of the Catholic processions. It is decorated with multi-colored whimsical and unpredictable figures. They are carried by the *faroleros,* who are particularly skillful at moving these lamps in time to the rhythm of the music. They appear at the beginning of the *comparsa,* and they separate from the dancers when the dance performance begins.

fiesta: The most general and accepted meaning is a solemn religious or civil affair with which an important event is commemorated. There exists a tendency in the character of the Cuban national to reject the solemnness. And in Cuba this is expressed in the festive behavior: the happiness, the merriment or entertainment.

fiestar: Going to festivities. In Mexico and Puerto Rico the term is *fiestear.* (Francisco Santana 1942: 639)

fiestero: A person who is very fond of and participates in these types of festivities; one who is happy, jovial and good natured, rejoicing, and noisy.

Focos Culturales (cultural centers): In Santiago de Cuba many distinct and diverse neighborhoods have specific cultural traditions. In addition to the older social groups, such as *cabildos* and *rumbas,* newer groups, such as *paseos* and *congas,* also exist. These are meeting centers for large portions of the population. In the late 1970s and 1980s local government helped to establish a permanent meeting place within certain neighborhoods for these groups. Such permanent centers are located in the neighborhoods of: Los Hoyos; El Tivolí; La Carabalí Isuama; Carabalí Olugo; Tumba Francesa; La Placita; Paso Franco; El Paseo del Comercio and the Comparsa de San Pedrito.

folklore: In a general sense, the union of customs, festivities, ceremonies, superstitions, ballads, proverbs, etc., that form part of what is popular. Science that studies these manifestations of the culture of a town transmitted by way of oral tradition as well as example. Term equivalent to traditional popular culture. The definition published by UNESCO (1985:27) is equally important: 'The folklore (in a large sense traditional and popular culture) is a creation that emanates from a group and is founded in tradition, expressed by a group or by individuals that gratefully respond to the expectations of the community when they express their cultural and social identity; the standards and values are communicated orally, by imitation or by other means. Its customs include among other things, the language, the literature, the music, the dance, the games, the mythology, the ritual, the customs, the artistry, the architecture and other manifestations.'

fondo: In Santiago de Cuba this term is used to describe a musical instrument called the *bocú* (a type of drum). It is part of the musical ensemble of the Santiago *congas.*

fotuto: Also called *guamo* or *lambí.* Whistle, trumpet, or horn, generally made of clay.

francé (bailar): To dance in tune to all types of music of Franco-Haitian origin. It was done wearing a dress coat made of wool, gloves made of chamois skin and a necktie for a high collar, according to the style of the European aristocrats (a cravat); an imitation thereof.

Franceses (Negros): Name given to the slaves brought by the Franco-Haitian plantation owner. Coming from Haiti, they settled in the eastern region of Cuba toward the end of the eighteenth century and the beginning of the nineteenth century. This name was also given to the rest of the slaves who assimilated the customs of the plantation owners. Many participated in the creation and continuation of the Tumba Francesa.

frenté: Dance of Franco-Haitian origin. In the dances of the Tumba Francesa the dancers keep rhythm to the beat of drums while marching softly and steadily. One dancer ties a handkerchief to the waist of another dancer, crossing it around the chest. This movement signifies a gesture of salute.

Gagá: Known as Rará in Haiti. Folkloric tradition which originated in Haiti and was introduced to Cuba (Oriente and Camagüey) during the expansion and construction of new coffee and sugar centers in these provinces (1913-1915). Originally these dancers came out during the religious Holy Week, pre-Easter celebrations. These performances included songs and drumming. Generally, the principal performers were the following: Lamé (guide), Mayor Drapé (standard-bearer), Guayá (king of the *cabildo*), Mayor Tablé (table bearer), Mayor Sambá (one who strikes the iron instrument), and Mayor Jonc (batonist). The use of 'Mayor' is given to a member of the *bandé* who holds a position of relative importance (see *bandé Rará).* In Haiti, a *Rará* band consists of the following named individual performers:

The flag-bearers; the master or chief and the avant-garde; two or more *major joncs,* who twirl a metal jonc or baton; the queen and her attendants; a musical ensemble; and the rearguard. The table-bearer [the performer who lifts a table off the floor by grasping the edge with his teeth] is no longer part of Haitian groups, losing popularity by the 1960s.

galleta: 'Type of drum similar to the *bombo* but flatter; it is used in the *congas* of the carnival of the eastern region.' (Helio Orovio 1981:159). It is also common to use the term *conga* to refer to the same instrument.

Galletas (Baile de las): Traditional dance which originated sometime in the early years of the twentieth century. Performed on July 6th, after the fiestas of San Juan held in the city of Trinidad, Sancti Spiritus. Because the dance is exclusively for married men, the women would call these '*galletas con gorgojos*' ['cracker with a dwarf']. The dance hall would be decorated with crackers of different sizes hanging from the ceiling, and the ladies would wear a necklace from which they would hang a cracker as if it were a medallion. This old and entertaining custom has been brought back in Trinidad by the *Club de Jubilados* [Retired Person's Club].

gallo tapao: 'Frequently, in Cuban dialect, used to indicate something concealed until the opportune time, or a prepared surprise. In the carnivals, each *comparsa* carries a hidden surprise, concealed in an unimaginable place. At the appropriate moment the surprise is revealed with deliberate intention to win some of the prizes that are awarded in the parade. This surprise is a small representation of the *comparsa.*' (Fernando Ortiz 1974:266)

guamo: Also called *lambí* or *fotuto.* Whistle, trumpet, horn. A sea shell used as a horn by Haitian descendants. It served to announce to the neighbors that the festivities were about to start.

guaracha: A Cuban song and dance. It is based on social commentary about popular subjects or humorous events. The result: festivity, *cumbancha.*

guarachero: Comes from *guaracha,* in other words, a festivity, *a fiestero* or *parrandero.*

hierro, muela o melé: In Santiago de Cuba this is the name for the *guataca* (spade) or *azada* (hoe) used as a musical instrument, one of the typical sounds in the *comparsas carabalí* and in the *bandé Rará.* Generic reference for all metallic instruments.

itótele (tambor): 'It is the medium sized drum of the *batá* drums. It produces three sounds. To learn to play this drum takes a long time. It is the second of the *batá* drums that a person learns to play.' (Fernando Ortiz 1981: 43)

iyá (tambor): "It is a major drum of the batá ensemble, also called *chaworo.* It has a grave and serious sound. Some extra leather straps are put in each one of the ends in which are inserted rattles, cowbells and jingle bells made of bronze. 'Iya' in Yoruba means 'mother.' It is the last drum that one learns to play." (Helio Orovio 1981: 43)

jazz band cubana (orquesta): 'A type of gathering demonstrating North American influence in Cuba during the third decade of this century. Vehicle used to interpret almost all of the styles of our music and much music worldwide. It is composed of the following instruments: piano, contrabass, drums, four or five saxophones (two altos, two tenors, and two baritones), three or four trumpets, also bow, Cuban percussion (*tumbadora, bongó, paila criolla*) *maracas, guiro* and a singer. It was most popular during the decade of the 40s. The typical Cuban styles acquired a new form of expression in the incorporation of the new sonorities' (Helio Orovio (1981: 216). These musical gatherings were first introduced in the eastern section of the country and later extended to the whole island. During carnival they are used by *paseos* and also are popular during *verbenas* (block parties).

lambí: Of Indo-Cuban origin, also called *guamo* or *fotuto.* An instrument used by the Haitians to communicate by emitting harmonic sounds in the orchestra of the *bandé Rará or Gagá.* It is a simple marine shell or *cobo.* It was utilized by the aborigines in their gatherings.

leguedé: Musical instrument. Unimembranous drum used by descendants of Haitians who live in the provinces of Oriente and Camagüey. It is used widely in both secular and sacred festivities.

lentejuelas: Vibrant colored round sequins made of metal or crystal which are used on a dress to make it sparkle. Characteristic of the dress of the *comparsero/a.*

limbo: Afro-Antillian dance. A rod is balanced upon two poles while the dancer, supported only by his or her legs, must bend backwards while passing under, without unbalancing, the rod, or causing it to fall. Every time the dancer passes, the rod is lowered until the dancer is crossing almost horizontally underneath.

Loma del Intendente: formerly called La Colorada, later referred to as Loma Hueca, and is now called Loma del Intendente. A hill situated on General Rabí Street, in a district of very strong cultural traditions. One of the oldest neighborhoods of Santiago de Cuba, called El Tivolí.

Luceros (del Carnival): Formerly, young women selected for the beauty contest that was held in the days preceding carnival. The female chaperones for the winner or queen of the festivity. During the 1940s and 1950s this contest was accompanied by a grand campaign of commercial publicity for industrial companies. It is no longer part of carnival.

madrina (de la comparsa) (Godmother): Person who contributes economically to the *comparseros* of the *comparsas* or *paseos.* During the 1940s or 1950s some commercial firms and industries, such as the distillery of Bacardí Rum and Edén cigars, took on the role of the *madrinas* during carnival.

mamamier: First drummer of the Tumba Francesa.

mamarrachos (Fiesta de Mamarrachos o de Masearas): Historically, a group of masked or costumed persons who danced rhythmically in the streets following the *parrandas* or *comparsas* during the major festivals in July. These characters originally gained such importance in the Santiago carnival that carnival itself became identified as the *Fiesta de mamarrachos,* and was thus called until the present century.

mambú (instruments): A type of grass or stalk: *caña brava,* a kind of bamboo. It is commonly known as *mambú or cañambú* and has varied uses as a musical instrument. From this stalk is made the *baccine* of the *comparsas, bandé Rará or Gagá.* Also, on occasion, an instrument used by the *catá* that is mounted on stakes and is struck by two sticks made of this bamboo. It is used in folkloric gatherings. The musical group, Cañambú, from San Luis, in Santiago province, uses various instruments made from the trunks of the *caña brava.*

marcha (toque de): It is one of the basic unique marching rhythms that gives the impression of alternating rhythms just by the rapidity with which it is played. It is original to the Tajonas, which are of Franco-Haitian origin, and is also used in the Cabildos Carabalí. Generally used to designate all rhythms used for street dances.

maruga (maraca): 'Formed from two hollow tin or metal cones, soldered or welded at their base. The outer part of the cone is perforated with designs.

The extremities are truncated and a handle, also made of tin or metal, is attached on one end. In Santiago de Cuba, they hang multicolored streamers from them.' (Helio Orovio 1981:241). Used in the French Tumbas and in the Comparsas Cabildos; it is also known as *chacha.*

mascaras a pie: Individuals who march in the streets in disguise to entertain. One favorite is *la muerte en cuero,* a skeleton, painted on simulated naked bodies, representing death. Vultures, grotesque dolls, the pirate, the Mexican bandit and the little horse are some of the most famous. Each year new masks and disguises of grand originality are created that promote adult laughter and at times terror for the children.

mascarones: These are grotesque multicolored, grimacing masks about one meter high, made of *papier maché.* They represent traditional types such as the drunkards, the clowns, and all that the imagination of the designer can create. They are found fastened on street lamp posts in the plazas, etc. They are one of the most common expressive adornments during carnival in urban areas and contribute in creating a festive environment.

masón (baile de): Couple dance performed by the Tumba Francesa, developed by the slaves imitating the dance of their masters. The *composé* begins to sing the praise of the *masón,* with a women's chorus repeating the refrain. [Although popularly said to derive from the French '*maison,*' perhaps its derivation is 'Masons,' as in Masonic influence in Haiti and Vodún.] (See 'Tumba Francesa' and 'Tajona, Tahona o Taono')

masón (toque o golpe de): A specific beat of Franco-Haitian origin, used enthusiastically in the French Tumba dances. This beat was incorporated into the repertoire of the Santiago *congas* with great results.

mesitas (las): small wooden tables set in neighborhood streets. First placed under trees and then under canopies, with food for sale displayed on them.

minué (minuet): A nineteenth-century dance of French origin. In Cuba it is almost always danced by Blacks in the homes of high standing. It is the assimilation of the bourgeois salon music adopted by the common people. Generally, it was danced by a single couple in the middle of the salon.

montompolo: The final *comparsa* performed at the end of all the festivities of the month of July. It was the 'grand finale' uniting all the *congas* of the city.

muerte en cueros: A type of *mamarracho*, dressed in mesh or body stocking which has a human skeleton painted on it. On occasion the masquerader holds a scythe and lantern in his hands. This masquerader travels the streets and festivals entertaining the adults and scaring the young, even though it also forms part of the *comparsa*. Some of these marked participants are dressed in short pants and a cape, and on their bodies, using white paint, they design the form of a human skeleton.

obia (toque de): In the *comparsa* Carabalí a slow beat creating a true polyrhythm. It is performed as an acknowledgment to the judges.

okónkolo or kónkolo (tambor): 'It is the smallest drum of the *batá* drums, and is also known as *Omelé*. Its sound is sharp and piercing. To learn to play this drum can take anywhere from three months to a year.' (Fernando Ortiz 1952: 279).

órgano oriental (player organ): A multi-instrumental musical aparatus, modeled from a similar device developed in Manzanillo. According to investigator Wilfredo Naranjo, the introduction of this instrument to eastern Cuba started at the end of the nineteenth century. The first to be introduced was the cylindrical model from Cienfuegos and then from Europe, a type made from pieces of cardboard. Widely used in this part of the island in various types of festivals, especially during carnival. The popularity of the sound produced by this instrument is in decline, and it is mostly played in revival orchestras.

padrino (de la comparsa) (Godfather): Male equivalent to *madrina*.

pañuelo (handkerchief): Piece of cloth of diverse colors used by the dancers of Yuba. It is used frequently in the folkloric dances of the *comparsas* and *rumba*. Often associated with dances from the countryside.

parrandas criollas: *Joigorio, juerga, jarana*. Group of persons who come out to the street playing musical instruments and singing to entertain themselves during the week of carnival. Many *comparsas* and *paseos* are organized from neighborhood *parranditas*. The *parrandas* are a type of carnival gathering that has almost been forgotten in Santiago de Cuba. The most famous are the Parrandas de Remedios.

parrandona: A larger *parranda*. In earlier times, carnival had small *parrandas* made up of families and friends who went around several blocks behind the *parranda major*.

paseo: A step or formation that is part of the contradanse. It is done by taking your partner by the waist and escorting her through the center of two rows of dancers until reaching the last couple. (Helio Orovio 1981:294)

paseo (comparsa): 'Type of *comparsa* but instead of Tajona, the accompaniment was orchestra music, *pasodobles* and light marches' (Ramón Martínez 1940:107). The *paseos* used Jazz Band orchestras, even though they have more drums and interpret popular current musical pieces.

pendón: A rectangular banner or flag. It is used by Santiago *comparsas.* At times, they are shaped like a double triangle, with two points, and are very colorful. Attached to a wooden pole, the banner moves continuously in the hands of a *comparsero* during the parade. It appears to be reminiscent of the *estandartes* of the Catholic processions of the colonial period.

pendonero: The person who holds the *pendones* or banners, which can be painted with a variety of themes and with predominantly primary colors. These *compaseros* are characterized by their rapid movements and by the way they make the banner dance gracefully in their hands.

pilón: The name given to the two headed drum whose dimensions are larger in terms of both the size of the heads and the distance between them. It is also known as *conga, tambora*, or *tambor mayor.* It is used by the musical ensembles of the *congas* and *cabildos.* [Also a pounding mortar.]

poo-labí: See **lambí**.

prémier: (principal *tumba*). A large drum of Franco-Haitian origin with a deep sound. It is usually refered to as *cortador*, and frequently used by the Tumba Francesa.

propina (bailes de): Type of popular dance gathering in which couples were charged for each dance. These gatherings were organized by bands, most of which originally played only instrumental music, such as Furquet's organ, from Manzanillo. More recently these groups have played player pianos or several orchestral instruments, and have been hired to perform at specific dances. In other parts of Cuba it became common to charge only an entrance fee to the party. These were generally evening dances that often lasted until dawn. The promoters were often obliged to pay a monetary tribute to the local authorities. In Manzanillo, said Wilfredo Naranjo, the *organo oriental* was the obligatory instrument that was used in this type of dance. In some cases, the dance was held in improvised spaces with floors of pressed dirt, in which they installed kiosks to sell roast pork, fried cod fish, *empanadillas*, and cold beer or rum.

pru: "It is a sweet and strong drink that has been a tradition since time immemorial in Santiago de Cuba. /. . ./ Its principal ingredients include: the *raiz de china*, '*jaboncillo*' or '*palo del Brazil*,' leaf of pepper, leaf of cinnamon and pine nuts brought from the woodlands. It is a delicate process of cooking and fermentation." (Margarita Pécora 1985:6). During carnival, in the more traditional neighbourhoods of Santiago de Cuba—such as those of El Tivolí, El Guayabito, etc.—this drink was sold, and it is still consumed in other eastern areas of Cuba.

quimono (kimono): Dress of Asian origin made with rich luxurious cloths, used by Santiago *comparseros* who acquired great fame. This costume gave its name to one of the most famous *paseos* of Santiago de Cuba: La Quimona.

quinto (or requinto): 'Cuban instrument of African origin that emits a ringing sound and is used by popular music ensembles. It is smaller than the *tumbadora* or *conga* and is used in *rumba* and *conga* groups. It has a shrill loud sound. In the past it was tuned by heating the drumhead; now it is tuned with keys. When marching, the player carries it as his side, hanging by a strap that passes across his shoulder.' (Helio Orovio 1981: 318). In the case of the Santiago *congas*, the *fondo* and the *bocú* are smaller in size than the rest, and are also known as *quintos*, while the *requinto* is yet a smaller drum.

redoblante: Rapid and lively drum beat occasionally used by musicians during carnival.

redoblante (instrument): Drum of European origin with a long sound box and two heads. It is used in the instrumental groups of Santiago *comparsas.*

reflectores: Small decorative elements made of mirrors in the shape of suns, moons and stars, which provide a great deal of vivacity to the *comparsa.* Introduced by the *comparsa* 'Los Imperiales Modernistas,' which originated with Los Hoyos.

reina o estrella (del carnival): A young girl who presides during the Carnival parades due to her charm and beauty. However, exterior factors intervened and competed with the aesthetic and created a commercial event with too much publicity, so in Cuba today carnival groups no longer elect a queen.

Relaciones (Teatro de): From 'relate; to tell,' as in the representation of a thing, especially in terms of the theatrical nature of carnival. It becomes the theatrical opportunity to express the imagination, as well as that which is droll and amusing in any situation. On occasion, dramatic elements were introduced. Among those personages that are legendary bufoons of Cuban burlesque and have their origins in this type of production are the Gallician, the blackman and the *mulata.*

remachadores: It is a reference to the official of the Remachadores de Batea, the title of a famous *comparsa* from El Tivolí from which originated folkloric songs that are remembered in the towns. (See *componedores*)

repique: A type of drum that plays with the *comparsa* Tahonas or Tajonas. It also is a way of playing the drums.

requintos: A two-headed instrument used in the *conga* orchestras, similar to the small drums of the rhythmic bands.

resistencia (baile de) (marathon dances)**:** Organized by private parties, these dances had the deliberate intent to produce a spectacle in order to attract the affluent public. Generally, they were performed in large theaters. They were competitive events. The participants could compete alone or with a partner. The music opened the event and played night and day as long as there was a dancer willing to dance. The competitors were subjected to strong psychological pressure from the judges and the public. They had brief recesses for their necessary biological functions. The couples announced what they ate and what brand of products made them strong. For the small towns and cities, these events derived from popular festivities. Some of these dancers transcended their local reputations to the point of obtaining titles of national champions, and they established a record among themselves. Now, due to a lack of the money which maintained them in the past, this type of dance is extinct.

rigodón: A dance of French origin. All the couples did the same steps. This dance was part of the Tumbas Francesas and was popular in the dance salons of the colonial period.

rumba de cajón: An older type of *rumba* that was played on empty wooden boxes. They used two or three boxes, actually made of cedar or other wood. Many folkloric groups frequently interpret this rhythm. A very popular musical style in many Santiago neighborhoods.

salidor: A name for the person who initiates the percussion section of the Tumba Francesas. Also, the name given to the persons who sign up in the *comparsas* and *paseos* to participate in them as *comparseros.* Also the name of the musical instrument that begins the performance.

sambá: A simple hoe (in the western part of Cuba it is known as *guataca*) used in the *bandé Rará* or *Gagá* as a percussion instrument. It is also used in place of the ancient cow bell. The instrumentalist that plays it is called the Mayor Sambá. It is struck with any object of metal.

Santiago Apostol: Saint James the Great. The patron saint of the city of Santiago de Cuba. Carnival was celebrated precisely on his day, July 25, so that the Carnival festivities and religious processions would coincide. In Santiago de Cuba, this saint is associated with Ogún, a Yoruba-derived diety. He was a fisherman and Saint John's brother. He traveled to Spain as a missionary. After he was beheaded in 43 A.D., his body was carried to Spain, and his remains were eventually buried at Compostela. The military order of Santiago was instituted by Ferdinand II in 1175.

sartén: 'Instrument composed of two small skillets, attached to a wood armature that serves as a support. It is hung in such a way that it will fall over the abdomen. It produces distinctive tones. It is struck with two metal sticks. Created by the popular imagination, it is a noisy and rhythmic element in the *congas.*' (Helio Orovio 1981:381) Today in most Santiago *congas* this instrument has been replaced by the Tumbas Francesa, who employ the brake drums, known ordinarily as *campanas* by virtue of their musical function.

second, segon, segond: Small drum used in the Tumba Francesa. It has a sharper tone than the *secondier,* and echoes the beat of the *bulá.* It is similar to the *Sakai madulé.* Its dimensions are: 22cm diameter at the top, 17cm diameter at the bottom, and 59.5cm in length; the thickness of the wood is 2cm; it has four circumferences and five keys. It is played in the vertical position over and between the legs of seated players.

secondier: One who plays the second drum in the Tumbas Francesas.

sonaja: Cymbals. A pair of metal plates attached with a wire, which are attached to some musical instruments. The term also can refer to a hoop with a handle with rattles. Used in the Tumba Francesa and by other folkloric groups and professionals.

Tajona, Tahona o Taona (*comparsa*): Fernando Ortiz (1974:457) describes this as a noisy revelry *orgia ruidosa.* A folkloric tradition practiced in Santiago de Cuba and its neighboring areas, it was introduced by the slaves who immigrated with their masters from Haiti after the Haitian Revolution. It is a parade organized similarly to the Tumba Francesa, incorporating songs of *pulla,* or songs of satirical character. It uses fundamental beats that are danced to: one slowly *de camino,* and the other rapid *de Tajona.* These types of festive gatherings grew in popularity under the influence of French-Haitians in the nineteenth century in the eastern part of Cuba. *La Tajona* includes a king, queen, servants, and batonists with costumes and representative attitudes. Its members carry special emblems, banners, and flags, and dance along the roads and rural villages and towns during the celebrations of San Juan, San Pedro, Santiago, Santa Ana and San Joaquin. *Pulla* songs were improvisational. Musically, the rythm of *Tajona* is related to the *rumba* and the Tumbas Francesas. Presently, this type of dance is in the process of extinction. (See chapter 'Tumba Francesa and Tajona of Santiago de Cuba.')

tambora: A large drum used in a band. A generic name for all drums.

tambora Rará: A group of drums used to play Rará music by the Haitians during Holy Week and other festivities.

tambor mayor o quitapesare: 'The largest of the drums used by the Comparsa Carabalí Isuama. Permanently displayed in the *cabildo* and only brought out when serious matters were at stake or when this *comparsa* met another one that was equally strong, or when the situation of the *comparsa* was critical. According to *cabildo* members, this drum is very powerful.' (Nancy Pérez, et al. 1982: 22).

tamboriles: Archaic name used by some Santiago informants to signify certain types of drums.

tarasca, tarascon o **serpiente tarasca:** *Mascara a pie* or individual masquerade of grand proportions, with the reproduction of a serpent and tail of cloth carried by various men. Originally appeared in the processions of Corpus Christi. A special pantomime was acted out by this group, as the serpent ate cherries that were fed to it. From this action developed the saying '*eso es como tirarle guindas a la tarasca.*' Presently this *mascara a pie* has been revitalized by the *comparsa* of San Pedrito of Santiago de Cuba.

tarima: A wooden platform or low bench. Usually built at the rehearsal sites of folkloric groups and in the areas of the city where the people dance popular dances. Sometimes the percussionists and the horn players of the *comparsa* play on this platform.

Teatro de Relaciones: Traditional comedic satirical theater. Derived from 'to relate': to tell, to represent a thing. It is an opportunity to guarantee the ingenious. Refers to those characters that have become legendary in Cuban comedy: the Gallego, the little negro, the *mulata* and has its origin in these stories. This theater style has been resurrected professionally by the Cabildo Teatral Santiago. It is a type of theater essential to the Santiago carnival context. (See Relaciones)

timbal: According to Helio Orovio (1981: n.p.) 'It is an instrument composed of two drums whose heads are attached to a metal structure over a tripod. In the past, they would tune them over a fire; now they use keys. This developed as transformation of the *timpani,* used by the *charangas* who interpreted the Cuban *danzón* at the beginning of the century.'

tocador: The one who plays a musical percussion instrument. It is popularly used synonymously with 'drummer' or 'percussionist.'

toque: Name given to a determined structured rhythm, a special beat, or it can be used in reference to a particular instrument (example: *toque columbia, masón, etc.*).

totem: A decorative element introduced in the Santiago carnivals in the 1960s. It is utilized in open spaces such as parks and avenues to decorate and give ambiance to these festivities. Totems are usually figures, more than 10 meters high, designed with great imagination and constructed of wood, metal and paper. They are decorated with designs, primary colors and lights of red, blue, yellow, white. They contain emblems that announce the logo of the carnival and other things.

tragalenguas: The major or primary drum, employed by the Comparsa Carabalí Olugo. It emits a deep, grave sound.

trisagios: A special *mascara a pie* acted by three men disguised as old religious devotees who appear to be praying the rosary, but they are actually gossiping about other people. In this masquerade the attitude of certain people who hide behind a religious appearance to cover up their defects was criticized. The appearance or renaissance of this mask on the part of the comparsa of San Pedrito caused sensations during the parades of the Santiago carnival of 1984.

Above left, the *bandera* or *estandarte* used by Comparsa El Guayabito during Carnival 1989. This cartoon-like characterization is frequently seen in Carnival representations. In the background are two *farolas*. © J.B.
Above right, a *bandera* or *estandarte* designed for the Comparsa Paso Franco for Carnival 1989, Santiago de Cuba. In 1989 Paso Franco used various Africanized motifs to illustrate their theme of Latin American and Caribbean Unity. © J.B.

These *banderas* are being paraded during the performance of Paseo La Placita during Santiago Carnival 1998. © J.B.

A dancer performing with Comparsa La Kimona during Carnival 1987, Santiago de Cuba. Each year La Kimona invents a theme that requires an 'Oriental' costume style. © J.B.

Tumba Francesa: A social club and mutual aid society founded by the Blacks and French-Haitian mestizos, self-named 'franceses,' that entered Cuba towards the end of the eighteenth century and the beginning of the nineteenth century. Its music and its dances are marked with the distinctive seal of the French-Haitian culture, as many of its songs are sung in creole. The most important instruments that are used are named *prémier* or *redublé second, bulá, catá, tambora, timbal* and *maruga.* The dances are named *babú grasiná, yubá* and *masón.* Its festivities were under the protection of virgins and saints whose images are hung on the walls, next to photographs of Cuban patriots, some of whom participated in these festivities before going to the War of Independence. The Tumba Francesa is not only a musical phenomena, but is also social. During the colonial period Tumba groups helped to conspire against Spain. Now, there are Tumba Francesas in Santiago de Cuba, Guantanamo and Sagua de Tánamo.

tumbas: Name given to some drums in the eastern part of Cuba. It is also a name for the group of percussion instruments and drums of the Santiago *congas.*

tumberos: The name for the men who play the instruments of the French *tumbas* in the eastern section of Cuba.

vasallo: A second level member of the Comparsa Carabalí and Tajona. A name used in the majority of carnival gatherings to designate a type of *comparsero,* or member of a *comparsa.*

verbenas: A synonym for popular day and night fairs, or popular festivals. Can also refer to streets adorned with bunches of palm or coconut leaves, and with small pieces of colored paper in the form of small flags or red bulbs. Kiosks are installed in these special streets for the sale of drinks and typical foods, as well as *traganíquel* [slot-machines] and handstands for musical groups.

verbenas benéficas: Night festivities characterized by enthusiastic popular participation. They were organized by an *ad hoc* commission that was in charge of collecting financial contributions from local families, commerce and industry. Generally, the funds were donated to public institutions such as rest homes for the elderly, sports groups, Red Cross and fire departments to fight the meager amount that former governments gave for subsistence. These festivities were usually limited to a sealed-off area—generally a street without much traffic, located in a central area. An entrance fee was required to dance to the local orchestra. After the 1959 revolution this activity disappeared, due to the new regulations in Cuba.

Vodún, Vodú, o Jodún: Popular religion of the Haitian people, and the fusion of the practices and beliefs of African religion and Catholicism. It is a cult of an agrarian society, and has an extensive social base in this Caribbean island. It constitutes one of the most important factors of its culture. Containing a rich mythology, this religious practice lends itself to both singing and dancing; it has generated a type of dance known as *vodú* or *jodú* among Haitians and their descendants in the old Cuban provinces of Camagüey and Oriente.

yambú: 'This is the oldest dance of the *rumba.* A very slow dance. It is a style of *rumba* which is slower than the *guaguanco.*' (Olavo Allén Rodriguez 1977:87)

yubá: Dance of Franco-Haitian origin, older than the *masón;* in it couples dance in the middle, while others form a circle around them, accompanied by singing and dancing. Then a solo dancer gets in the center doing special movements, improvising with the music, creating a competition with the principal or premier *tumba* or drum.

zanco: The poles of the stilt dancer who appeared in the carnival; can still be seen today in some folkloric contexts and recently again in carnival.

Notes on the Contributors

Judith Bettelheim received her Ph.D. in Art History from Yale University in 1979 and has been a Professor of Art at San Francisco State University since 1983. Bettelheim has been doing fieldwork in the Caribbean consistently since 1975, focusing on Afro-Caribbean culture and festivals. Her doctoral work was on the Afro-Jamaican Jonkonnu festival. In 1988 she co-curated and co-authored *Caribbean Festival Arts* (University of Washington Press) with John Nunley of the Saint Louis Art Museum. Bettelheim has done fieldwork in six different Caribbean countries and since 1985 she has been doing fieldwork in Cuba, with support from an American Council of Learned Societies fellowship in 1989–90 and a National Endowment for the Humanities Fellowship in summer 1998. Recent publications include 'José Bedia Reflects on the Song of the Immigrant,' in *Crónicas Americanas, Obras de José Bedia* (Museo de Arte Contemporáneo de Monterrey, Mexico, 1997). Her articles have appeared in the *African Caribbean Institute of Jamaica Journal,* the *Journal of Ethnic Studies, Caribbean Quarterly,* the *Art Journal*, and *African Arts,* among others.

Rafael Brea is a researcher at Casa del Caribe and an adjunct University professor. He directs research at Casa on the theme of Cuban festivals and similar events in the Caribbean. Brea is co-author of *Folk Groups of Santiago de Cuba* (1990) and *Barrio, Comparsa y Carnaval Santiaguero* with José Millet and Manuel Ruiz Vila (Santiago de Cuba: Ediciones Casa del Caribe, 1997). Brea has done fieldwork in Cuba, Guyana, and the Dominican Repuplic, as well as having participated in international events held in Mexico and Spain.

David H. Brown received his Ph.D. in American Studies from Yale University in 1989. He was Assistant Professor of Art History at Emory University from 1990 to 1997 and Senior Lecturer at the University of Texas at Austin during 1998–99. Supported by a number of grants and fellowships, such as the Wenner-Gren Foundation for Anthropological Research, the Center for Folklife Studies at the Smithsonian, the American Council of Learned Societies, and a Senior Research Fellowship for the 'Black Atlantic Project' at the Rutgers Center for Historical Analysis, he has researched and written about Afro-Cuban religious and artistic practices for more than 15 years. His first book, *Thrones of the Orichas: Innovation and Change in the Afro-Cuban Religion Santería/Ifá,* is forthcoming in 2001.

José Millet is a researcher at Casa del Caribe and an adjunct University professor. At Casa he heads the research team that studies popular religions in Cuba and similar manifestations throughout the Caribbean. Millet has published in Cuban journals as well as abroad. He is co-author of *Folk Groups of Santiago de Cuba* (1990) and *Barrio, Comparsa y Carnaval Santiaguero* with Rafael Brea and Manuel Ruiz Vila (Santiago de Cuba: Ediciones Casa del Caribe, 1997). He also published *El Vodú en Cuba* with Joel James and Alexis Alarcón (Santo Domingo: Republica Dominicana Ediciones CEDEE-Casa del Caribe, 1992, republished in 1998 by Editorial Oriente, Santiago de Cuba). Millet has done fieldwork in Cuba, Angola, the Dominican Republic, Barbados, and Haiti. Millet is a member of the Regional Studies Group of the European Congress for Latin American Studies.

Pedro Pérez Sarduy is an Afro-Cuban poet, writer, journalist and broadcaster resident in London. He has worked in Cuba for national radio (1965–79) and for the Latin American Section of the BBC World Service (1981–94). He is the author of *Surrealidad* and *Cumbite and Other Poems* (New York: Center for Cuban Studies, 1990); co-editor of *AfroCuba: An Anthology of Cuban Writing on Race, Politics and Culture*, and co-author of the introduction to *No Longer Invisible: Afro-Latin Americans Today*. He co-authored *Afro-Cuban Voices: On Race and Identity in Contemporary Cuba*, a book based on interviews with Afro-Cubans currently living and working on the island and discusing race issues (University Press of Florida, 2000). The recipient of several literary awards, he was (Ford Foundation) Writer in Residence at Columbia University, New York (1989); a participant in CUNY Caribbean Exchange Program, Hunter College (1990); Rockefeller Visiting Scholar at the University of Florida, Gainesville (1993); and a participant in the Rockefeller Fellowship Caribbean 2000 Program, University of Puerto Rico, Rio Piedras (1997).

Jean Stubbs is a British social historian who specializes in Cuban history and culture. She is currently Professor of Caribbean Studies, University of North London, United Kingdom. Stubbs is co-editor with Pedro Pérez Sarduy of *Afro-Cuban Voices: On Race and Identity in Contemporary Cuba* (Gainesville: University Press of Florida, 2000) and *AfroCuba: An Anthology of Cuban Writing on Race, Politics and Culture* (Melbourne, New York and London: Ocean Press, Center for Cuban Studies & Latin America Bureau, 1993). She is co-editor with Leila Haines and Meic Haines of *Cuba: An Annotated Bibliography* (Oxford: Clio Press, 1996). Stubbs authored both *Cuba: The Test of Time* (London: Latin America Bureau, 1989) and *Tobacco on the Periphery: A Case Study in Cuban Labour History, 1860–1958* (Cambridge: University of Cambridge Press, 1985).

Selected Bibliographies

Annotated Glossary to Fernando Ortiz's 'Day of the Kings'

Abraham, R. C. 1946. *Dictionary of modern Yoruba*. London, Sydney, Auckland, Toronto: Hodder and Stoughton.

Abrahams, Roger. 1983. *The man-of-words in the West Indies: Performance and the emergence of creole culture*. Johns Hopkins Studies in Atlantic History and Culture. Baltimore and London: Johns Hopkins University Press.

Abrahams, Roger D. 1968. 'Pull out your purse and pay': A St. George Mumming from the British West Indies. *Folklore* 79 (Autumn):176–201.

Alonso, Ana Maria. 1990. Men in 'Rags' and the Devil on the Throne: A Study of Protest and Inversion in the Carnival of Post-Emancipation Trinidad. *Plantation Society in the Americas* 3(1):73–120.

Angarica, Nicolás. N.d. [1955]. *Manual del Orihaté*. Havana: N.p.

Apostolos-Cappadona, Diane. 1994. *Dictionary of Christian art*. New York: Continuum.

Bakhtin, M. M. 1984. *Rabelais and his world*. Trans. H. Iswolsky. Bloomington, Ind.: Indiana University Press.

Bascom, William. 1951. The Yoruba in Cuba. *Nigeria* 37:14–20.

———. 1952. Two forms of Afro-Cuban divination. In *Acculturation in the Americas*, gen. ed. Sol Tax. 3 vols. Proceedings and Selected Papers of the XXIX International Congress of Americanists, vol. 2. Chicago: University of Chicago Press.

———. 1969. *Ifa divination: Communication between gods and men in West Africa*. Bloomington, Ind.: Indiana University Press.

———. 1973. *African art in cultural perspective*. New York: W.W. Norton and Company.

Bastide, Roger. 1972. *African civilizations in the new world*. Trans. Peter Green. Foreword by Geoffrey Parrinder. New York: Harper and Row, Harper Torchbooks.

———. 1978. *The African religions of Brazil: Toward a sociology of the interpenetration of civilizations*. Trans. Helen Sebba. Johns Hopkins Studies in Atlantic History and Culture. Baltimore: Johns Hopkins University Press.

Beckwith, Martha Warren. 1929. *Black roadways: A study of Jamaican folk-life*. Chapel Hill: University of North Carolina Press.

Bettelheim, Judith. 1988a. Festivals in Cuba, Haiti, and New Orleans (ch. 5) and 1988b. Jonkonnu and other Christmas masquerades (ch. 2). In *Caribbean festival arts: Each and every bit of difference*. Exhibition catalogue. Contributors Rex Nettleford, Barbara Bridges, Robert Farris Thompson, and Dolores Yonker. St. Louis and Seattle: St. Louis Art Museum and University of Washington Press.

Blanc, Julio, et al. 1992. *Wifredo Lam and his contemporaries*. New York: Studio Museum in Harlem.

Blier, Suzanne. 1995. *African Vodun: Art, psychology, and power*. Chicago and London: University of Chicago Press.

Brandon, George. 1993. *Santería from Africa to the New World: The dead sell memories*. Bloomington: Indiana University Press.

Bremer, Fredrika. 1853. *The Homes of the New World: Impressions of America*. 2 vols. Trans. Mary Howitt. New York: Harper Brothers.

Brown, David. 1989. *Garden in the machine: Afro-Cuban sacred art and performance in urban New Jersey and New York*. Ph.D. Dissertation, Yale University. University Microfilms International 1990.

———. 1999. Altared spaces: Afro-Cuban religions and the urban landscape. In *The gods of the city: religion and the contemporary American urban landscape*, ed. Robert A. Orsi, 155–230. Bloomington: Indiana University Press.

Brown, Karen McCarthy. 1989. *Mama Lola: A Vodou priestess in Brooklyn*. Berkeley: University of California Press.

Cabrera, Lydia. 1970. *La Sociedad Secreta Abakua: Narrada Por Viejos Adeptos*. Miami: Ediciones C.R.

———. 1975. *Anaforuana: Ritual y símbolos de la iniciación en la sociedad secreta Abakuá*. Madrid: Ediciones R.

———. 1980. *Yemayá y Ochún*. New York: C.R. Publishers.

———. 1983b [1954]. *El monte: Igbo-finda, ewe orisha-vititi nfinda; notas sobre las religiones, la magia, las superstitiones, y el folklore de los Negros criollos y el pueblo de Cuba*. Miami: Colección del Chicherekú en el Exilo.

———. 1984. *Vocabulario Congo (el Bantu que se habla en Cuba)*. Miami: Ediciones C.R., Colección del Chicherekú en el Éxilo.

———. 1986a. *Anagó: Vocabulario Lucumí (el Yoruba que se habla en Cuba.)* Miami: Ediciones Universal.

———. 1986b. *Reglas de Congo, Palo Monte, Mayombe*. Miami: Colección del Chicherikú.

———. 1988. *Lengua sagrada de los Ñáñigos*. Miami: Colección del Chicherekú en el Éxilo.

———. 1994 [1954. *Orígenes*, year 11 (26):8–20]. El sincretismo religioso de Cuba. In *Páginas sueltas*, 363–82. Ed. Isabel Castellanos. Miami: Ediciones Universal.

Campoamor, Fernando G. 1985. *El hijo alegre de la caña de azúcar: Biografía del ron Cubano*. Havana: Editorial Cientifico-Técnica.

Castellanos, Isabel. 1996. From Ulkumí to Lucumí: A historical overview of religious acculturaltion in Cuba. In *Santería aesthetics in contemporary Latin American art*. Washington, D.C.: Smithsonian Institution Press.

Castellanos, Israel. 1916. *La brujería y el ñáñiguismo en Cuba desde el punto de vista médico-legal*. Havana: Lloredo y Compania.

———. 1928. El 'diablito' Ñáñigo. *Archivos del Folklore Cubano* 3 (October-December):27–37.

Castellanos, Jorge, and Isabel Castellanos. 1992. *Cultura Afrocubana 3: Las religiones y las lenguas*. Miami: Ediciones Universal.

Courlander, Harold. 1960. *The drum and the hoe: Life and lore of the Haitian people*. Berkeley: University of California Press.

Crowley, Daniel J. 1956a. The midnight robbers and 1956b. The traditional masques of carnival. *Caribbean Quarterly* 4 (March/June):194–223.

———. 1984. *African myth and Black reality in Bahian Carnival*. Museum of Cultural History Monograph Series no. 25. Los Angeles: University of California Museum of Cultural History.

Daniel, Yvonne. 1995. *Rumba: Dance and social change in contemporary Cuba*. Bloomington: Indiana University Press.

Deschamps Chapeaux, Pedro. 1964. Margarito Blanco: Ocongo de Ultán. *Boletín del instituto de historia del archivo nacional* 65 (July–December):97–109.

———. 1968. Cabildos: Solo para esclavos. *Cuba: revista mensual* (January):50–51.

dos Santos, Juana Elbein, and Descoredes M. dos Santos. 1968. Ancestor worship in Bahia: The Egun cult. *Journal de la Société des Americanists* 58:79–108.

Drewal, Henry, et al. 1989. *Yoruba: nine centuries of African art and thought.* New York: Center for African Art, in association with Harry N. Abrams, Inc., Publishers.

Fernández Carillo, Enrique. 1881. El Ñáñigo: Carta cerrada y abierta. In *Típos y costumbres de la isla de Cuba.* Artist, Victor Patrício de Landaluze, intro. by Antonio Bachiller y Morales. Havana: Miguel de Villa.

Helg, Aline. 1995. *Our rightful share: The Afro-Cuban struggle for equality, 1886–1912.* Chapel Hill: University of North Carolina Press.

Herskovits, Melville J. 1958 [1941]. Herskovits, Melville J. *The Myth of the Negro Past.* New York: Beacon Press.

Howard, Philip A. 1998. *Changing history: Afro-Cuban cabildos and societies of color in the Nineteenth-Century.* Baton Rouge: Louisiana State University Press.

InterAmericas—Society of Arts and Letters in the Americas. 1998. *Miscelanea II of studies dedicated to Fernando Ortiz.* New York.

Kinser, Samuel. 1990 *Carnival American style: Mardi Gras at New Orleans and Mobile.* Chicago and London: University of Chicago Press.

Kutzinski, Vera M. 1993. *Sugar's secrets: Race and the erotics of Caribbean nationalism.* Charlottesville: University of Virginia Press.

Lachatañeré, Romulo. 1961. Nota Historica Sobre Los Lucumi. *Actas del folklore* 1 (February):3–12.

Landaluze, Victor Patricio de. 1881. *Tipos y costumbres de la isla de Cuba.* Intro. by Antonio Bachiller y Morales. Havana: Miguel de Villa.

Leib, Elliot, and Renee Romano. 1984. Reign of the leopard: Ngbe ritual. *African Arts* 18(1):48–56, 95, 96.

León, Argeliers. 1984a. *Del canto y el tiempo.* Havana: Editorial Letras Cubanas.

León, René, and Emilio J. León. 1986. *Fernando Ortiz: Bibliografía sobre el tema negro.* n.p.

López Valdés, Rafael L. 1985. La sociedad secreta Abakuá en un grupo de trabajadores portuarios. In *Componentes Africanos en el etnos Cubano,* 151–185. Havana: Editorial de Ciencias Sociales.

MacGaffey, Wyatt. 1986. *Religion and society in Central Africa: The Bakongo of Lower Zaire.* Chicago: University of Chicago Press.

———. 1988. Complexity, astonishment, and power: The visual vocabulary of Kongo minkisi. *Journal of Southern African Studies* (London) 14 (2):188–203.

———. 1991. *Art and healing of the Bakongo: Commented by themselves: minkisi from the Laman Collection.* Stockholm: Folkens Museum Etnografiska.

MacGaffey, Wyatt, and Michael Harris. 1993. *Astonishment and power.* Washington: D.C.: National Museum of African Art.

Mason, John. 1996. *Olóòkun: Owner of rivers and seas.* Brooklyn: Yoruba Theological Archministry.

Martinez-Alier, Verena. 1974. *Marriage, class and colour in nineteenth-century Cuba: A study of racial attitudes and sexual values in a slave society.* Ann Arbor: University of Michigan Press.

Martínez Furé, Rogelio. 1979. *Diálogos imaginarios.* Havana, Cuba: Editorial Arte y Literatura.

Martínez, Juan. 1994. *Cuban art and national identity: The Vanguardia painters, 1927–1950.* Gainesville: University Press of Florida.

McAlister, Elizabeth A. 1995. *'Men moun yo;' 'Here are the people': Rara festivals and transnational popular culture in Haiti and New York City.* Ph.D. Dissertation, Yale University.

Metraux, Alfred. 1972 [1959]. *Voodoo in Haiti.* Trans. Hugo Charteris. New York: Schocken Books.

Mauss, Marcel. 1967. *The gift: forms and functions of exchange in archaic societies.* Trans. Ian Cunnison. New York: W.W. Norton and Company.

Mintz, Sidney W., and Richard Price. 1992 [1976]. *The birth of African-American culture: an anthropological perspective.* Boston: Beacon Press.

Murphy, Joseph. 1988. *Santería: An African religious system in America.* Boston: Beacon Press.

Nunley, John, and Judith Bettelheim. 1988. *Caribbean festival arts: Each and every bit of difference.* Exhibition catalogue. Contributors Rex Nettleford, Barbara Bridges, Robert Farris Thompson, and Dolores Yonker. St. Louis and Seattle: St. Louis Art Museum and University of Washington Press.

Ortiz, Fernando. 1921. Los Cabildos Afrocubanos. *Revista Bimestre Cubana* 16 (January–February):5–39.

———. 1922. Los afronegrismos de nuestro lenguaje. *Revista Bimestre Cubana* 17 (6):321–36.

———. 1923. *Un catauro de Cubanismos; apuntes lexicográficos.* (Collección Cubana de Libros y Documentos Inéditos o Raros, no. 4.) Havana: n.p. Reprint of installments published in *Revista Bimestre Cubana* 16, nos. 1-6 (1921) and 17, nos. 1-5 (1922).

———. 1924. *Glosario de Afronegrismos.* Havana: Imprenta 'El Siglo XX.'

———. 1929. Los afrocubanos dientimellados. *Archivos folklore cubano* 4(2):16–29.

———. 1939. Brujos o santeros. *Estudios afrocubanos* 3(1–4):85–90.

———. 1950. *La africanía de la música folklórica de Cuba.* Havana: Ministerio de Educación, Dirección de Cultura.

———. 1951. *Los bailes y el teatro de los Negros en el folklore de Cuba.* Havana: Ediciones Cardenas y Cia.

———. 1952. *Los instrumentos de la música Afrocubana,* vols. 1,2,3. Havana: Publicaciones de la Dirección de la Cultura del Ministerio de Educación.

———. 1953. 'Los diablitos' de Landaluze. *Bohemia* 45(44):36–38,99–101.

———. 1954. *Los instrumentos de la música Afrocubana,* vol. 4. Havana: Publicaciones de la Dirección de la Cultura del Ministerio de Educación.

———. 1955. *Los instrumentos de la música Afrocubana,* vol. 5. Havana: Publicaciones de la Dirección de la Cultura del Ministerio de Educación.

———. 1960 [1920]. *La antigua fiesta afrocubana del "Día de Reyes."* Havana: Ministerio de Relaciones Exteriores, Departamento de Asuntos Culturales, Division de Publicaciones.

———. 1973a [1960]. *Historia de una pelea cubana contra los demonios: Relato documentado y glosa folklorista y casi teológica de la terrible contienda que, a fines del siglo XVII y junto a una boca de los infiernos, fue librada en la villa de San Juan de los Remedios por un inquisidor codicioso, una negra esclava, un rey embrujado y gran copia de piratas, contrabandistas, mercaderes, hateros, alcaldes, capitanes, clérigos, energúmenos y miles de diablos al mando de Lucifer.* Madrid: Ediciones Erre [R].

———. 1973b [1906]. *Los negros brujos: Apuntes para un estudio de etnologia criminal.* Miami: Ediciones Universal.

———. 1983a [1940]. *Contrapunteo Cubano del tabaco y el azúcar.* Havana: Editorial de Ciencias Sociales.

———. 1983b. *El nuevo catauro de Cubanismos.* Glossary. Havana: Editorial de Ciéncias Sociales.

———. 1985 [Habana: Ediciones Cardenas y Cia, 1951]. *Los bailes y el teatro de los Negros en el folklore de Cuba.* Havana: Editorial Letras Cubanas.

———. 1986 [1927]. *Los negros curros.* Havana, Cuba: Editorial de Ciencias Sociales (serialized in *Archivos del Folklore Cubano* 2, nos. 3 and 4; 3, nos. 1, 2, 3, and 4).

———. 1987 [1916]. *Los negros esclavos.* Havana: Editorial de Ciencias Sociales.

———. 1993. Ethnogenetic processes and cultural transfer in Afro-American slave populations. In *Slavery in the Americas,* ed. Wolfgang Binder, 337–363. Wurtzburg: Konigshausen un Neumann.

Real Academia Española. 1984. *Diccionario de la lengua española*. Madrid: Real Academia Española.

Roche y Monteagudo, Rafael. 1925. *La policía y sus mistérios*. Havana: Imprenta 'La Prueba.'

Rodríguez Herrera, Esteban. 1959. *Léxico mayor de Cuba*. 2 vols. Havana: Editorial Lex.

Scott, Rebecca Jarvis. 1985. *Slave emancipation in Cuba: The transition to free labor, 1860–1899*. Princeton, N.J.: Princeton University Press.

Sosa Rodríguez, Enrique. 1982. *Los Ñáñigos*. Havana: Ediciones Casa de Las Americas.

Thompson, Robert Farris. 1974. *African art in motion: Icon and act*. Exhibition catalogue, National Gallery of Art, Washington, D.C. Los Angeles: University of California Press.

———. 1983. *Flash of the spirit: African and Afro-American art and philosophy*. New York: Random House.

Turner, Victor. 1983. Carnival in Rio: Dionysian drama in an industrializing *cultural performance*, ed. Frank E. Manning, 103–24. Bowling Green, Ohio: Bowling Green University Popular Press.

Urrutía y Blanco, Carlos. 1882. *Los criminales de Cuba y el inspector Trujillo: Narración de los servicios, prestadados en el cuerpo de policía de La Habana*. Barcelona: F. Giró.

Urfé, Odilio. 1984. Music and dance in Cuba. In *Africa in Latin America: Essays in history, culture, and socialization*, ed. Manuel Moreno Fraginals, 170–88. New York: Holmes and Meier.

Verger, Pierre. 1954. *Notes sur le culte des orisa et vodun à Baie de tous les Saints, au Brésil et à l'ancienne Côte des Esclaves en Afrique*. Memoires de L'Institut Français D'Afrique Noire, no. 51. Dakar: Ifan Dakar.

———. 1993. *Orixás: Deuses Iorubás na Africa e no Novo Mundo*. São Paulo: Corrupio Edições Ltda.

Vinueza, María Elena. 1986. *Presencia Arará en la música folklórica de Matanzas*. Havana: Casa de las Américas.

Carnival in Santiago de Cuba

Administración del Alcade Dr. Antonio Beruff Mendieta.1937 *Las Comparsas del Carnival habanero, cuestión resulta*. La Habana: Molina y Cia.

Bakhtin, Mikhail. 1984. *Rabelais and His World*. Bloomington: Indiana University Press.

Birmingham, David. 1988. Carnival at Luanda. *The Journal of African History*, #29.

Brea, Rafael and José Millet. April 1991. Acerca de la presencia africana en los carnivales de Santiago de Cuba. *Revista de la Biblioteca Nacional José Martí*, #3.

Bremer, Fredrika. 1853. *The Homes of the New World: Impressions of America*. London: Arthur Hall, Virtue & Co.

Brown, David H. 1989. *Garden in the Machine: Afro-Cuban Sacred Art and Performance in Urban New Jersey and New York*. Ph.D. dissertation, Yale University.

Brown, Karen McCarthy. 1989. Systematic Remembering, Systematic Forgetting: Ogou in Haiti. In *Africa's Ogun: Old World and New*, ed. Sandra T. Barnes. Bloomington: Indiana University Press.

Cabrera, Lydia. 1975. *Anaforuana: ritual y simbolos de la iniciación en la sociedad secreta abakuá*. Madrid: Ediciones C.R.

Feliú, Virtudes. Septiembre 1985. La Fiesta Cubana. *Revolución y Cultura*, #9.

Forte, Jeanie. 1990. Women's Performance Art: Feminism and Postmodernism. In *Performing Feminisms: Feminist Critical Theory and Theatre*, ed. Sue-Ellen Case. Baltimore & London: Johns Hopkins University Press.

Glaze, Anita J. 1981. *Art and Death in a Senufo Village*. Bloomington: Indiana University Press.

Goodman, Walter. 1873. *The Pearl of the Antilles or An Artist in Cuba*. London: Henry S. King & Co.

Hall, Stuart. 1990. Cultural Identity and Diaspora. In *Identity: Community, Cultural, Difference*, ed. Jonathan Rutherford. London: Lawrence and Wishart.

Moliner Castañeda, Israel. May-June 1987a. *Matanzas en el VII Festival de la Cultura Caribena*. Santiago de Cuba: Casa del Caribe.

Nettleford, Rex. 1988. Implications for Caribbean Development. In *Caribbean Festival Arts*. John Nunley and Judith Bettelheim. Seattle: University of Washington Press.

Nunley, John W. and Judith Bettelheim. 1988. *Caribbean Festival Arts*. Seattle: University of Washington Press.

Ortiz, Fernando. Enero 1921. Los Cabildos Afro-Cubanos. *Revista Bimestre Cubana*, XVl (1).

———. 1925. La fiesta afrocubana del 'Dia de Reyes'. *Archivos del Folklore Cubano*, 1.

———. 1985 [1923]. *Nuevo Catauro de Cubanismos*. La Habana: Editorial de Ciencias Sociales.

Pérez, Nancy, et al. 1982. *El Cabildo Carabalí Isuama*. Santiago de Cuba: Editorial Oriente.

Roche-Monteagudo, Rafael.1925. *La Policia y sus Misterios*. Habana: La Moderna Poesia.

Villarreal, Juan Jerez. 1960. *Oriente: biografia de una provincia*. La Habana: Editorial Siglo XX.

Carnival in Santiago de Cuba at the End of the Millenium

Basso, Hamilton. 1952, December. 'Havana,' *Holiday* 12, no. 6.

Benítez-Rojo, Antonio. 1992. *The Repeating Island*. Durham and London: Duke University Press.

Bettelheim, Judith. 1998. 'Women in Masquerade and Performance,' *African Arts* 31, no. 2 (Spring).

Bettelheim, Judith. 1994. 'Ethnicity, Gender and Power in Carnaval in Santiago de Cuba,' in *Negotiating Performance in Latin/o America*, ed. Diana Taylor & Juan Villegas. Durham and London: Duke University Press.

Bettelheim, Judith. 1991. 'Negotiations of Power in Carnaval Culture: Santiago de Cuba,' *African Arts* 24, no. 20 (April).

Davies, Carole Boyce. 1998. 'Carnivalised Caribbean Female Bodies: Taking Space/Making Space,' *Thamyris* 5, no. 2.

Kutzinski, Vera. 1993. *Sugar's Secrets: Race and the Erotics of Cuban Nationalism*. Charlottesville and London: University Press of Virginia

Moore, Robin D. 1997. *Nationalizing Blackness: Afrocubanismo and Artistic Revolution in Havana, 1920–1940*. Pittsburgh, Pa.: University of Pittsburgh Press.

Ruf, Elizabeth. 1997. 'Issues of Gender, Color, and Nationalism in Cuba's Tropicana Nightclub Performance,' *The Drama Review* 41, no. 1.

Schwartz, Rosalie. 1997. *Pleasure Island: Tourism and Temptation in Cuba*. Lincoln and London: University of Nebraska Press.

The Tumba Francesa and Tajona

Berenguer, Carlos Jorge. 1977. La inmigración Francesa en la Juridicción de Cuba. Santiago: Revista de la Universidad de Oriente. Junio-Septiembre (26–27).

Courlander, Harold. 1960. The Drum and the Hoe. Berkeley: The University of California Press.

Duharte Jimenez, Rafael. 1988. El Negro en la Sociedad Colonial. Santiago de Cuba: Editorial Oriente.

———. 1988. La Huella Francesa en Santiago de Cuba 1800–1868. Paris: Editions L'Harmattan.

Guanche, Jesus. 1983. Procesos Etnoculturales de Cuba. La Habana: Editorial Letras Cubanas.

Pérez A. Jr., Louis. 1988. Cuba Between Reform and Revolution. New York: Oxford University Press.

Pérez de la Riva, J. 1975. El Barracon y otros Ensayos. Habana: Editorial de Ciencias Sociales.

Piron, Hippolyte. 1876. L'Ile de Cuba. Paris: E. Plon & Cie.

Glossary of Popular Festivals

Alonso, Martín. [n.d.]. *Diccionario del español moderno.* Madrid: Editorial Aguilar.

Allén, Rodríguez, Olavo. 1977. La Habana. *Géneros de la música cubana. 1ª* parte. Editorial Pueblo y Educacíon.

———. Las sociedades de Tumba Francesa en Cuba. *Santiago* 25 (marzo): pp.193-209.

Bacardí Moreau, Emilio. 1961 [1925]. *Crónicas de Santiago de Cuba. v.* 1-10. Santiago de Cuba: Tipografía Arroyo y Hermanos.

Barinas Fradique, Lizardo. 1961. El Carabiné. *Actas del Folklore* 7 (julio): pp. 3-8.

Barnet, Miguel. 1983. *La fuente viva.* La Habana: Editorial Letras Cubanas.

Berenguer Cala, Jorge. 1979. *La emigracíon fancesa en la jurisdicción de Cuba.* Santiago de Cuba: Editorial Oriente.

Brea López, Rafael. 1984. Un día de San Juan en Los Hoyos. *Del Caribe 5* (julio/septiembre): pp. 64-67.

Campoamor, Fernando. 1985. *El Hijo alegre de la caña de azúcar.* La Habana: Editorial. Científico-Técnica.

Conjunto Folklórico de Oriente. 1982. *Revolución y Cultura* 115 (marzo): pp. 47-48.

Duharte Jiménez, Rafael. 1983. Carnival y plantación. *Del Caribe* (octubre/diciembre): pp. 38-48.

Franco, José Luciano. 1966. *Historia de la revolución en Haiti.* La Habana: Academia de Ciencias.

Hernández Balaguer, Pablo. 1964. *Breve historia de la musica cubana.* Santiago de Cuba: Universidad de Oriente.

Lara, Francisco. 1971. Los carnivales de Santiago de Cuba, su origen y evolución. *Boletín de la Biblioleca Provincial Elvira Cape* (4): pp. 3-16.

León, Argeliers. 1981. *Del canto y el tiempo.* La Habana: Editorial Pueblo y Educación.

———. 1964. *Música folklórica cubana.* La Habana: Departamento de Música de la Biblioteca Nacional José Marti.

———. 1963. Música popular de origen africano en Cuba. *Etnología y Folklore.* 8 (julio/diciembre): pp. 33-65.

Linares, María Teresa. 1970. *Introducciónes a Cuba: la música popular.* La Habana: Instituto del Libro.

Orovio, Helio. 1981. *Diccionario de la música cubana.* La Habana: Biográfico y técnico. Editorial Letras Cubanas.

Ortiz, Fernando. 1965. *La Africanía de la música folklórica cubana.* La Habana: Editorial Universitaria.

———. 1984. *Ensayos Etnográficos.* La Habana: Editorial Ciencias Sociales.

———. 1981. *Los bailes y el teatro de los negros en el folkore cubano.* La Habana: Editorial Letras Cubanas.

———. 1952. *Los instrumentos de la música afrocubana.* La Habana: Dirección de Cultura, Ministerio de Educación.

———. 1974. *Nuevo catauro de cubanismos.* La Habana: Editorial Ciencias Sociales.

Pécora, Margarita. 1985. Pru Santiaguero. *Juventud Rebelde* 4 (Avril).

Pérez, Nancy, et al. 1982. *El Cabildo Carabalí Izuama.* Santiago de Cuba: Editorial Oriente.

Pérez de la Riva, Francisco. 1944. *El café: historia de su cultivo y explotación en Cuba.* La Habana: Jesús Montero Editor.

Pichardo, Esteban. 1985. *Diccionario provincial casi razonado de voces y frases cubanas.* La Habana: Editorial Ciencias Sociales.

Rodríquez, Joan Enrique. 1975. Apuntes sobre grupo de danzas haitianas en la provincia de Camagüey. *Signos* 17 (mayo/septiembre): pp. 51-58.

Santana, Francisco J. 1942. *Diccionario general de americanismos.* v.3. Mexico: Editorial Pedro Robredo.

La UNESCO y la protección del folklore. 1985. *El Correo de la UNESCO (avril).*

Index